Perspectives on Stephen King

ALSO BY ANDREW J. RAUSCH

*Fifty Filmmakers: Conversations with Directors
from Roger Avary to Steven Zaillian*
(McFarland, 2008)

Perspectives on Stephen King
Conversations with Authors, Experts and Collaborators

Andrew J. Rausch

McFarland & Company, Inc., Publishers
Jefferson, North Carolina

LIBRARY OF CONGRESS CATALOGUING-IN-PUBLICATION DATA

Names: Rausch, Andrew J., author.
Title: Perspectives on Stephen King : conversations with authors, experts and collaborators / Andrew J. Rausch.
Description: Jefferson, North Carolina : McFarland & Company, Inc., Publishers, 2019 | Includes index.
Identifiers: LCCN 2018046583 | ISBN 9781476674179 (softcover : acid free paper) ∞
Subjects: LCSH: King, Stephen, 1947– —Criticism and interpretation. | Authors—Interviews.
Classification: LCC PS3561.I483 Z79 2019 | DDC 813/.54—dc23
LC record available at https://lccn.loc.gov/2018046583

BRITISH LIBRARY CATALOGUING DATA ARE AVAILABLE

ISBN (print) 978-1-4766-7417-9
ISBN (ebook) 978-1-4766-3446-3

© 2019 Andrew J. Rausch. All rights reserved

No part of this book may be reproduced or transmitted in any form or by any means, electronic or mechanical, including photocopying or recording, or by any information storage and retrieval system, without permission in writing from the publisher.

Front cover images by RapidEye/Romolo Tavani (iStock)

Printed in the United States of America

McFarland & Company, Inc., Publishers
Box 611, Jefferson, North Carolina 28640
www.mcfarlandpub.com

To R.D. Riley, Constant Reader
(1969–2018)

TABLE OF CONTENTS

Introduction   1
Published Works of Stephen King   5

Interviews

Scott Alexander and Larry Karaszewski	9
Charles Ardai	22
Tyson Blue	33
Richard Chizmar	46
Robin Furth	56
Lee Gambin	65
Zak Hilditch	74
C. Courtney Joyner	82
Joe R. Lansdale	90
Richard Christian Matheson	102
Patrick McAleer	111
Stewart O'Nan	124
Kevin Quigley	133
Stephen J. Spignesi	145
Paul Tremblay	158
Bev Vincent	166
Stanley Wiater	181

Index   193

"A lot of people coming along now can't remember or understand the impact that Stephen King had on not only popular fiction, but on fiction itself. He actually changed the way books were published after that, both negatively and positively. He doesn't need to take blame for the negative aspects, but he can certainly take joy from the more positive ones. All of a sudden every publisher wanted to have their own Stephen King. People now wanted bestsellers or near-bestsellers and that's all they wanted. Every publishing house had its own horror writer who specialized in that. Most of them did not have King's staying power or his ability. It's been many years since he first impacted the publishing industry and he's still going strong. And that voice is what carried him through."—Joe R. Lansdale

"How can someone write so well and so much so steadily? That's why he's a very unique artistic voice, and we're all blessed to be living through his creative period. Imagine being alive when Picasso was painting, and there was media coverage of his latest work. Or being alive when Dickens was writing, and there was a timely same-day review of Tale of Two Cities in The New York Times. We take it for granted."—Stephen J. Spignesi

"I don't think it happens so much anymore with him getting awards and getting a medal from Obama and so forth, but he used to be dismissed as a horror writer. I don't think that's ever been the primary reason people read his stuff. He's a good writer, he's a good storyteller. He creates characters that you care about and are interested in. The rest of the gruesome stuff is just icing on the cake."—Tyson Blue

Introduction

Stephen King is likely the most written-about author of all time (books about him being a subgenre unto itself) and he's sold more than 350 million books worldwide. The man has the Midas touch. Everything he writes becomes a huge success, and just about everything he's penned has been adapted to film or television, often in multiple incarnations. Stephen King has not only single-handedly changed the way society views horror, which was once seen as a ghetto genre, but he has also defined American literature for the past five decades.

I arrived late to the party, but it couldn't be helped. Stephen King had already been a published author for a decade when I first discovered him in 1984. I was an eleven-year-old boy growing up amongst the wheat fields of rural Kansas, immersed in popular culture like Michael Jackson and Hulk Hogan. Literature to me, at the time, consisted of Louis L'amour westerns, Jules Verne, James Bond, and Remo Williams. I had only recently discovered Rod Serling's *The Twilight Zone*, which was my first introduction to horror, so I was primed for Stephen King. One day as I was looking at books in my middle school library, I came across a paperback copy of King's *Carrie* (1974). I didn't know anything about the book, but I recognized the author's name. In 1984, the name Stephen King was everywhere. It was a brand name of its own, and it was impossible to interact with popular culture without encountering it.

I dove into that short 199-page novel and devoured it in a day. Even though I was a boy who possessed neither telekinesis nor a crazy whackadoodle Christian extremist mother, I recognized many of the characters from the world in which I lived. I found King's colorful vernacular—the blue collar poetry of the everyman—to be something I was also familiar with. For all I knew, Carrie White was attending classes across town at the

Introduction

local high school. These were real, living, breathing characters King was painting, and they jumped off the page. I immediately recognized there was something unique about King, and even at that age, I knew he was special. With King-mania already in full swing, this was a glorious time to discover the author's work because it seemed as if there was an endless supply of King media to consume.

Being a kid at that time, I had no understanding that the public's treatment of King was different from that of those who preceded him. I wasn't aware that an author flooding the market the way King did at the time—making cameos in movies, appearing in American Express ads, and producing multiple bestselling novels in the same year—was something beyond the norm. For all I knew, this was the way it had always been. I thought it was normal because that was the only world I had ever known.

But the fact of the matter is it wasn't normal. It was rather extraordinary. King hadn't reinvented the wheel, but he'd updated it in such a way that he'd captured the public's attention in a manner that no writer since Shakespeare had. The life of an author is generally a solitary (and often thankless) occupation that consists of sitting in front of a typewriter or word processor for hours on end each day. It's not glamorous work. But that was not the case for King, who somehow became as recognizable a celebrity as Sylvester Stallone or Madonna were at the time.

Perhaps the most amazing thing is that King's work never seemed to falter through any of it. Sure, there was *The Tommyknockers* (1987), but every writer is entitled to a misstep or two. (And in truth, *Tommyknockers* is far better than a lot of novels published by lesser writers.) King famously battled both alcohol and drug addiction, was run down by a speeding van, and was, for many years, Public Enemy Number One for literary critics, suspicious of the unprecedented success he enjoyed. After all, they reasoned, books couldn't possibly be good if they were as popular as his were. (This wrong-headed perception has, for the most part, fallen to the wayside as King has now been celebrated and awarded just about every literary honor possible.) None of those things stopped him. He didn't just continue to churn out book after book, but he continued to produce *quality* literature.

For many of us, Stephen King has been one of the few constants throughout our lives. Popular athletes and U.S. Presidents have come and gone like the flavor of the month, and yet King has stood the test of time, releasing serial novels, e-books, and even Kindle and audiobook exclusives.

Introduction

Maybe he isn't saturating the market in quite the same way he did in the mid–1980s, but Stephen King's influence on literature and American society is visible all around us. Through his *Entertainment Weekly* columns and tweets, King has become something akin to a pop culture pundit.

Meanwhile he continues to write the books that brought us all here in the first place. At the time of this writing, there has been a King Renaissance of sorts. There have been no less than four King film adaptations released in the past year, he's freshly co-written a new novel (*Sleeping Beauties*, 2017) and novella (*Gwendy's Button Box*, also 2017), co-edited a new anthology (*Flight or Fright*, 2018), has a new Hulu television series (*Castle Rock*, 2018), and a forthcoming novel and novella have been announced. It would appear at this point that only death can stop King, and considering the gruesome accident he survived in 1999, it's questionable even that is a factor.

As Stephen J. Spignesi points out in his interview within this volume, we as readers are blessed to be living through King's creative period. "We take it for granted," explains Spignesi. "When (artists) are gone, we suddenly realize we are now going to miss their creative output. John Lennon died when he was only forty-years-old. A lot of people took him for granted whenever he would release something new, and now we fantasize about what his later work might have looked like."

As stated previously, there are many books about King, his work, and his legacy on the market today. This is, in fact, my third book on King. The two previous books were *The Wit and Wisdom of Stephen King* (2011) and *The Stephen King Movie Quiz Book* (2011), which I co-wrote with the late R.D. Riley. With this third project I wanted to explore and celebrate King's work in a different manner. Having previously worked as a celebrity interviewer for numerous publications, I set out to talk to noted King experts, collaborators, and well-known fans, asking them to weigh in and share their thoughts and insights on the man and his work. Each interview subject brings his or her own unique point-of-view, and sometimes their assessments are at odds with one another. There is, however, one consistent thread that runs through each of these interviews—a love and admiration of Stephen King's work.

It is my sincere hope these conversations entertain, educate, and spur further discussions on King, his work in all mediums, and his legacy as it stands now and moving forward.

PUBLISHED WORKS OF STEPHEN KING

Novels

1. *Carrie* (1974)
2. *'Salem's Lot* (1975
3. *The Shining* (1977)
4. *Rage* (1977) as Richard Bachman
5. *The Stand* (1978)
6. *The Long Walk* (1979) as Richard Bachman
7. *The Dead Zone* (1979)
8. *Firestarter* (1980)
9. *Roadwork* (1981) as Richard Bachman
10. *Cujo* (1981)
11. *The Running Man* (1982) as Richard Bachman
12. *The Dark Tower: The Gunslinger* (1982)
13. *Christine* (1983)
14. *Pet Sematary* (1983)
15. *The Talisman* (1984) co-written with Peter Straub
16. *Thinner* (1984) as Richard Bachman
17. *It* (1986)
18. *The Eyes of the Dragon* (1987)
19. *The Dark Tower II: Drawing of the Three* (1987)
20. *Misery* (1987)
21. *The Tommyknockers* (1987)
22. *The Dark Half* (1989)
23. *The Dark Tower III: The Wastelands* (1991)
24. *Needful Things* (1991)

25. *Gerald's Game* (1992)
26. *Dolores Claiborne* (1992)
27. *Insomnia* (1994)
28. *Rose Madder* (1995)
29. *The Green Mile* (1996)
30. *Desperation* (1996)
31. *The Regulators* (1996) as Richard Bachman
32. *The Dark Tower IV: Wizard and Glass* (1997)
33. *Bag of Bones* (1998)
34. *The Girl Who Loved Tom Gordon* (1999)
35. *The Plant* (2000) unfinished, partially published
36. *Dreamcatcher* (2001)
37. *Black House* (2001) co-written with Peter Straub
38. *From a Buick 8* (2002)
39. *The Dark Tower V: Wolves of the Calla* (2003)
40. *The Dark Tower VI: Song of Susannah* (2004)
41. *The Dark Tower VII: The Dark Tower* (2004)
42. *Cell* (2006)
43. *Lisey's Story* (2006)
44. *Blaze* (2007) as Richard Bachman
45. *Duma Key* (2008)
46. *Under the Dome* (2009)
47. *11/22/63* (2011)
48. *Joyland* (2013)
49. *Doctor Sleep* (2013)
50. *Mr. Mercedes* (2014)
51. *Revival* (2014)
52. *Finders Keepers* (2015)
53. *End of Watch* (2016)
54. *Sleeping Beauties* (2017) co-written with Owen King
55. *The Outsider* (2018)

Novellas

1. *The Mist* (1980)
2. *Cycle of the Werewolf* (1983)

3. *The Little Sisters of Eluria* (1998)
4. *Riding the Bullet* (2000)
5. *The Colorado Kid* (2005)
6. *Ur* (2009)
7. *Throttle* (2009) co-written with Joe Hill
8. *Blockade Billy* (2010)
9. *The Dark Tower: The Wind Through the Keyhole* (2012)
10. *A Face in the Crowd (2012)* co-written with Stewart O'Nan
11. *Gwendy's Button Box* (2017) co-written with Richard Chizmar
12. *Elevation* (2018)

Novella Collections

1. *Different Seasons* (1982)
2. *Four Past Midnight* (1990)
3. *Hearts in Atlantis* (1999)
4. *Full Dark, No Stars* (2010)

Short Story Collections

1. *Night Shift* (1978)
2. *Skeleton Crew* (1985)
3. *Nightmares & Dreamscapes* (1993)
4. *Everything's Eventual* (1982)
5. *Six Stories* (1997)
6. *Blood and Smoke* (1999) audiobook only
7. *Just After Sunset* (2008)
8. *Stephen King Goes to the Movies* (2009)
9. *The Bazaar of Bad Dreams* (2015)

Nonfiction

1. *Danse Macabre* (1981)
2. *Nightmares in the Sky* (1988)
3. *On Writing: A Memoir of the Craft* (2000)

4. *Secret Windows: Essays and Fiction on the Craft of Writing* (2000)
5. *Faithful* (2005) co-written with Stewart O'Nan

Children's Books

Charlie the Choo-Choo (2016) as Beryl Evans

As Editor

Flight or Fright (2018) co-edited with Bev Vincent

Original Graphic Novels

1. *Creepshow* (1982)
2. *American Vampire* (2010)

Screenplays

1. *Creepshow* (1982)
2. *Cat's Eye* (1985)
3. *Silver Bullet* (1985)
4. *Pet Sematary* (1989)
5. *Golden Years* (1991) [miniseries] co-written with Josef Anderson
6. *Sleepwalkers* (1992)
7. *The Stand* (1994) [miniseries]
8. *Michael Jackson's Ghosts* (1996) [short film] co-written with Stan Winston
9. *The Shining* (1997) [miniseries]
10. *Storm of the Century* (1999) [miniseries]
11. *Rose Red* (2002) [miniseries]
12. *Desperation* (2006)
13. *A Good Marriage* (2014)
14. *Cell* (2016) co-written with Adam Alleca

The Interviews

SCOTT ALEXANDER
AND LARRY KARASZEWSKI

Screenwriting team Scott Alexander and Larry Karaszewski first met at the University of Southern California School of Cinematic Arts in 1985, where they were roommates. In the late 1980s they sold a black comedy script about a terrible child who makes life hell for his father. The screenplay then evolved under the studio's supervision, ultimately becoming the broad comedy *Problem Child* (1990). The film was savaged critically, but proved to be a box-office success, ultimately spawning two sequels. While the film wasn't the type of project Alexander and Karaszewski were interested in making, it established them in the industry and paved the way for bigger and brighter things to come.

They later approached director Tim Burton and convinced him to make a biopic about offbeat Z-grade filmmaker Edward D. Wood, Jr. Alexander and Karaszewski then went to work on a screenplay, producing the shooting draft in a mere six weeks. The film, *Ed Wood* (1994), would be met with critical acclaim and received many accolades, including a Writers Guild nomination for Best Original Screenplay. The film would also win two Academy Awards for Best Supporting Actor (Martin Landau) and Best Makeup. After the success of *Ed Wood*, Alexander and Karaszewski's careers took off.

The duo would become known for writing quirky biopics such as *The People vs. Larry Flynt* (1996), *Man on the Moon* (1999), and *Big Eyes* (2014). They also wrote the biographical television series *The People v. O.J. Simpson: An American Crime Story* (2016). They have performed uncredited rewrites for a number of films, including *Mars Attacks!* (1996). They made their directorial debut with the comedy *Screwed* (2000), which starred

Perspectives on Stephen King

Norm Macdonald, Dave Chappelle, and Danny DeVito. Their screenplays have received many awards and nominations, and the duo has received two Writers Guild Awards for their work on their Larry Flynt and O.J. Simpson biographies.

While Alexander and Karaszewski are primarily known for biopics, they have also written several mainstream films including *Agent Cody Banks* (2003) and *Goosebumps* (2015). One of their most significant non-biographical projects was the Mikael Hafstrom–helmed Stephen King adaptation *1408* (2007). The screenwriters initially took the assignment, thinking it would be a project they would work on for a short period of time. They wound up spending a year and a half on the film, which would ultimately become regarded as one of the finest King horror adaptations to date.

Were you guys fans of Stephen King's work prior to working on the screenplay for 1408*?*

Larry Karaszewski: We both grew up in the 1970s, so that first giant wave of Stephen King books was very important for us. Particularly *The Stand* (1978), which was a book that meant a lot to both of us. We were teenagers when *Carrie* (1974) came out, so we experienced Stephen King mania as it happened. We were guys who went to the sneak previews of *The Shining* (1980), with that initial disappointment everyone felt about Kubrick not doing Stephen King's book justice. And then, obviously, *The Shining* has become recognized as one of the greatest films of all time. So King was obviously someone who was on our radar.

I don't know if we were necessarily giant consumers of his work. Stephen King was one of those guys who has just written so many books. I've probably read most things up until the *Christine* (1983) period. After that I sort of paid attention to what he was doing, but—

Scott Alexander: So you're saying you were caught up until thirty-five years ago? [Laughs.]

LK: Exactly.

SA: He actually wrote so many books that he came up with another name, Richard Bachman, so he could put out even more books!

LK: The guy was doing a lot of writing.

Scott Alexander and Larry Karaszewski

Had you guys worked on any other horror projects prior to 1408*? There aren't any on your filmography, but I wondered if maybe you'd had unproduced projects or had done any rewrites on horror films.*

SA: I had history with horror as a crew member. When I was in college, during the summers, I used to work as a production assistant or in other small positions on low-budget horror movies. This was during the early-eighties' slasher era. I'd been a boom operator on a few movies where there's a girl in a dark house and she's backing into a hallway and you can see a guy hiding behind her with a knife. That kind of stuff. I was familiar with the genre. I had been on the set of these movies, been in the cutting room, and I had worked as a music editor for a few years with Christopher Young, who had scored a lot of horror films. I had been there for the process when the filmmakers are trying to figure out how to make it scarier; how to do the jump-scares and how to build the tension. They were looking to the composer to amplify those moments. It's actually a very interesting and analytical process.

I've never really thought about this until you asked that question, but that was probably useful.

LK: I never thought about that either, but that was totally helpful because you were able to think about set pieces and scares, having worked on those films in the post-production of it all. I think you definitely brought that knowledge to the screenwriting process.

SA: In terms of the original question, I don't think we ever worked as writers on any actual horror films.

LK: That was the first time we ever worked on a horror film, and I think that's actually why we said yes.

SA: No, we said yes because we'd never worked with the Weinsteins.

LK: But also horror because we had this attitude that we had written different types of films, and one of the things we always liked about comedy writing was set pieces. Like in *Problem Child* where Junior was going off to play baseball. There were a lot of scenes with these big comic set pieces. We kind of thought, what if you brought that to the horror genre? Comedy is sort of similar to horror, but instead of a punchline it's a shock. So we were looking at it analytically like that.

SA: It was one of my favorite showbiz experiences. We had backed into the job for totally mercenary reasons, and then it ended up being a total blast. When we were doing all of our biopics in the nineties, Harvey

Weinstein was still sort of king of the world. We would have these celebrated biopics that would go into awards season, and then they'd end up getting crushed by whatever Harvey had out that week. And we had never actually worked for the Weinsteins. It seemed to be a gaping hole in our career, because they liked to make off-the-wall movies, and that's what we did. It's a total con job to try to make an off-the-wall movie at one of the major studios.

So our agent called us and said, "There's a rewrite of this Stephen King story with a guy trapped in a hotel room." We said, "Pass." And he said, "Well, it's with the Weinsteins and I think it would be really good for your career, just to establish a working relationship with them." So we said, "How long?" And he said, "It'll just be three weeks." So we said fine.

We were initially just doing it as some kind of career management, and then we ended up having so much fun with Bob Weinstein who ran the project, with Lorenzo di Bonaventura, the producer, and Mikael Håfström, who was the director. The five of us were swinging for the fences. Larry and I were brought in to do a rewrite on Matt Greenberg's script, which laid out the story well as a horror piece. But Bob was saying, "Look guys, let's shoot for greatness." We went in for the first meeting and he said, "Let's talk about Polanski. Let's talk about Bergman. It should be like *Wild Strawberries* (1957), with the old man looking out of the train." And suddenly there was this idea that we were going to try to elevate this and make one of the greatest horror movies of all time. So instead of leaving after three weeks, we wound up working on that project for a year-and-a-half, which was insanity because at a certain point the money ran out. But we were having so much fun that we just kept hanging around. We kept trying to do new stuff and Bob would say, "This is great. But it's only an A. I want you guys to give me a fuckin' A-plus!"

LK: The movies we talked about all the time were Polanski's *The Tenant* (1976), Bergman's *Hour of the Wolf* (1968), and *Repulsion* (1965). Lorenzo di Bonaventura would come out of these meetings and say, "What are you guys talking about?" [Laughs.] He didn't understand why we were spending all of this time talking about Ingmar Bergman movies, but we felt there was a way to do those things within the horror genre.

At a certain point you go into that project saying, "Our hands are tied behind our backs here, because it's one guy in a room." That's not a lot to work with. And the Stephen King story is barely even a story because he hadn't even intended for it to be a complete work. It was originally going to be a writing exercise in his book *On Writing* (2000), so it wasn't really a complete short story with a beginning, middle, and an ending. And even within that very short short story, half of it is just Mike Enslin sitting in the office with Mr. Olin.

SA: There's very little about what's inside the room, so the challenge became: how do you turn this into a movie? The game became trying to figure out how to make tension and how you then build it with psychological terror, and then how do you get out of that goddamn room? And you have to be crazy and clever and weird about it. We weren't taking any psychedelic drugs, but our attitude about the project was that we would keep going back to our office and saying, "Let's think as far outside the box as we can. How cuckoo can we go here?" And then we came back with all these weird fantasies within dreams within imaginary events kinds of stuff going on. And Bob would always joke, "I don't know what you guys are smoking." Lorenzo would say, "I've worked on 150 movies and this is the first one with no rules." And he said that with a big smile on his face.

So we just tried to push things as crazy as we could. One example would be our *Duck Soup* (1933) homage, where we managed to create the character of a guy across the street who's doing the mirror routine with Cusack, which has nothing to do with anything! [Laughs.] That was just us trying to see how crazy we could go. It was also, "Hey, we can go across the street!" Anything to try to get imagery that was outside that room.

LK: So for us, it really was about writing a script with your hands tied behind your back, in the sense of writing a script that takes place entirely inside one room. That became the fun of it. Where most people would say, "You can't make a movie like that," we looked at it from the other side. So we just went through everything we could think of.... What are the things inside a hotel room? There's the chocolate on the pillow. There's the folded toilet paper. There's the mini-bar. There are the people downstairs calling. There's the list of cable movies you could rent. So we went through literally everything a person would do that was banal, asking how we could make that banality evil. How can you make that stuff scary?

I remember being at one of the first test screenings. We take a long time to introduce the scares in that movie, but when that chocolate mint is missing.... The audience just freaked out. I remember Lorenzo said, "Holy shit, they jump at the mint!"

SA: When the mint reappears on the pillow, and then the toilet paper refolds itself.

LK: The audience screamed at the toilet paper. We got them. Another thing I want to say is there was a long build there. That was one of the things we brought to the piece. When it came to us initially, it had a bunch of fake-out jump scares in the first ten minutes of the movie. So we said, "Let's make a deal with the audience. We're not going to jerk them off. We're not going to have something scary happen, and then it turns out it was nothing."

SA: Bob was great about that. Bob said, "How long are you guys gonna go?" And we said, "We're thinking the entire first act. We want to go twenty or thirty minutes without a scare." So it's making that pact with the audience: "No bullshit here. We're going to be straight up with you."

LK: That was our conception, that yes, he is searching for haunted houses and that's his job, but those kind of houses aren't really haunted. Bad things happen, and he's got this emotional past where you know there's something funky going on, but it really is this dark sadness that's haunting this guy, not any sense of "it's the boogie man" or anything.

SA: Also, Larry and I brought a lot of our patented snarky cynicism to the first act in that he schleps out to this inn in the rain in the middle of nowhere, and nothing happens because there's nothing there. Because there's no such thing as ghosts. And then he schleps his way to a book signing, and it's not the movie version of a book signing with a crowd lined up outside the book store. He's not Stephen King. He's not a celebrity author.

I've had that book signing. I know what that's like.

SA: We did it because we had a friend who had just published his first book, and he'd gotten that cross-country tour from the publisher where he's staying in $68 motels, and then he's driving himself to the closest Barnes & Noble, and there are three people there and lots of empty folding chairs. And he sells one book, and then he drives to the next town.

LK: We were sort of putting this layer of sadness and loss of faith in Mike Enslin in his own sense of purpose. It's like his entire life is just a big jerk off. There's no point to anything. And that's the first act. There's just a lot of dark comedy and bleakness and he's by himself. But we thought this was the pact for the audience in that there's no bullshit here. We're just showing you his life and we're showing you why he doesn't believe in anything. Of course he doesn't believe in anything, because there's nothing to believe in.

I think you guys did a great job making something that elevates the material. There are some great King films, but when it comes to the horror stuff, a lot of it is not, let's say, Bergmanesque.

LK: [Laughs.] I'll give lots of props to Mikael Hafstrom and to John Cusack, who both understood the game we were trying to play. The mix of drama and comedy. It's not even really heightened, it's just a little sarcastic. Mikael was able to move so effortlessly between spookiness and sadness and jokes. So you never feel like you're just being jerked around in a jump-scare horror movie.

The observation that Mike Enslin makes about hotel rooms being creepy places comes almost verbatim from King's introduction to the short story.

LK: We tried to mine as much of Stephen King's observations about the story as we could and actually put them into the story itself. I'm happy that you caught the fact that we were using the intro to the story as much as we were using the story itself.

SA: There was so little to work with.

LK: By making Mike Enslin a writer, he becomes a guy who can actually talk flowery. When he presses that little record button, he can actually comment on the situation he's in. That's something that's rare for a character in a movie, because you don't want to have them saying what's going on or just coming out and saying their thoughts. But he could actually frame what we were watching, which I think made it kind of interesting. It made him seem intelligent, and it put things into context, because a lot of what King was talking about in that intro was the things that are actually kind of creepy and yucky about hotel rooms. You walk in there and you're like, "Who's been here before? Who's had a horrible night? What's happened on those sheets?" All that kind of stuff you prefer not to think about when you're actually in a hotel room because everything's all nice and perfect. But crazy shit has gone down there at some point. So we used the intro to set it all up.

SA: That's funny. I totally forgot we grabbed stuff from that intro. We were so happy when we realized we could use that.

LK: The amazing thing about King's story is that, for the most part, it's simply the Mr. Olin scene. It's literally mostly that sequence we made in the film with Sam Jackson. We decided to really just run with that scene. In a normal script, a scene is like two pages. But we decided to almost play that scene in Sam Jackson's office as a mini one-act play. Just these guys going back and forth with one another. We're very proud of that scene. Both guys are great, and the dialogue is snappy, and you actually feel them playing chess with each other over this hotel room.

SA: We were so happy with that sequence that we then felt compelled to try to keep Olin in the movie, which led to us being completely cuckoo for Cocoa Puffs and doing stuff like putting him inside the refrigerator. [Laughs.] "Hey, there he is again!"

Since you're on the subject of the refrigerator, I was wondering who stocked it. Since the hotel help don't want to come into the room and they don't rent this room out, how is the refrigerator stocked?

LK: No, they actually say maids come in and change the sheets, but they do it in pairs and they never close the door.

Okay, I stand corrected.

LK: That was one of those little funny things where the refrigerator scene really excited the director because he could do all those crazy perspective shots and things like that. But what's amazing and probably the most horrifying scene in the movie, is when it just cuts to Cusack yelling at the refrigerator. There's nothing in there, but he's just standing there yelling at it. You're just like, "Holy shit. Wow. He is gone."

SA: The section of the movie I'm the proudest of is when John Cusack leaves the room. He thinks he's escaped and gone back to his old life. And we decided to really go for it. And again, Lorenzo and Bob were giving us a full leash to run. We might have gone fifteen pages in the script. I mean, the movie started over. It really was him moving back to Redondo Beach and then Mary McCormack shows up. He just starts living his life again. We wanted people to believe it was actually part of the movie—that the third act of the movie was about this guy who learned a lesson about life in a hotel room, and then he gets his life in order.

And there's the whole conceit of the dream-within-a-dream, you know? The *Nightmare on Elm Street* movies always did this really well. You get faked out in those, but you get faked out for like a minute-and-a-half and then the movie goes "gotcha," and you find that it was actually a dream. Again, *1408* was the movie with no rules, so it was like this was the third act. And that just goes and goes and goes. We shot all this stuff, and we were all just giggling. "Oh my God, this movie is out of its mind!"

The movie had a lot of test screenings, which were really useful. What we started learning in the test screenings was that there was a certain point where the fake-out would alienate the audience. We didn't want to do that. If it went on for too long, it would turn into an exercise where the giggling filmmakers were pulling the strings and saying, "Can you believe we got away with this crazy shit?" But yeah, if John Cusack is in Redondo Beach for twenty-five minutes, of course you got away with it. But when you would go "gotcha, he's actually still in the room," the audience would get really angry because we had overstayed our welcome in California. So then it became this whittling down, where we started pulling parts out of that section. We wanted to go as long as possible, because that was the fun of it; the fun was seeing how long you could stay out of the room without the audience becoming angry and saying, "Fuck you, *1408*! You broke the pact!" We were always trying to be honest with the audience, so that section probably got cut in half in the final cut.

There's a section in that sequence where he actually went and visited his father, and he sort of comes to terms with his father, paying off all the father relationship stuff. It was this really heartfelt scene. We're led through it, and he's finally making things right. But we threw that on the cutting room floor because we were breaking our bond with the audience. We were taking too much glee in watching them see this stuff that didn't really happen.

The first time I saw the scene in the version that was released in theaters, I remember feeling so winded when he ends up back in that room. It was just so brilliantly done. It's commendable.

LK: It's really cool when Cusack goes back into the room. He's sitting there and the room is now totally bombed out. That next five or ten minutes is just hell on earth for him. He's in such an existential hell.

Sometimes when I go to a high school and talk to them about screenwriting I say, "The first act is you get a man in a tree. The second act is you throw rocks at him. And the third act is you figure out a way to get him down from the tree." So what I do sometimes is run *1408* at a higher speed so it goes by really quickly. Then I say, "See? We're getting him up the tree. Now we throw rocks at him." Watching the movie at that speed, it's literally throwing rocks at this guy. There's a flood; there's a wall; there's his dead daughter. It's just all these horrible things happening to this guy, and then the movie resolves. It's really a funny screenwriting lesson in five minutes.

Did you get any feedback from Stephen King himself?
   SA: We heard that he liked it. I don't know if he read the script, but he really liked the movie. My memory of it is that part of the deal was that you couldn't put Stephen King's name on a movie poster without his permission at that time, because he'd been ripped off so many times by all the *Children of the Corn*–type movies. When he saw the movie he gave the Weinstein Company permission to use his name in advertising.
   LK: I think Mikael drove a copy of the movie up to Stephen King's house and screened it for him. Stephen King said, "This is great. You can use my name." At the time we were told it had been twenty years since he'd let his name appear on a poster, which was a big deal. We were all really happy about that.

How would you assess the final film once everything was said and done?
   SA: We actually had the rare opportunity to see the movie again recently, with an audience. The Cinematheque here in Los Angeles did a month-long tribute to Stephen King. I found the film very satisfying. Like my favorite movies that Larry and I have done, it has a mix of tone. I'll credit Mikael for having the ability to sustain that even keel for two hours. I just love the mix of reality and scares and sadness with a lot of jokes. And Cusack gives one of his all-time most incredible performances. He just holds that tone.
   LK: Cusack is phenomenal in the film, and it's such an intense character study. What he goes through and all the emotions he experiences… . My reaction to the film is I'm just very happy with what we did with the character. We start tracking this character from the bookstore signing and then tell the story of the daughter, and you really become simpatico with the story of Mike Enslin. And Cusack just knocks it out of the park.
   SA: It's hard to remember specifics ten years later, but Larry and I have always taken a certain glee in being secretly autobiographical in our screenplays. That script is just packed with things he and I were going through during those eighteen months. There are just so many references

within the movie to our own lives that nobody but us knows about. That brings me a certain morbid pleasure.

LK: It's funny, with a movie like that you think you're not really inserting your personal lives into it, but we did. For instance, my grandmother was in a nursing home at the time. I remember walking into the nursing home and hearing an old woman shouting, "I wish I was dead! I wish I was dead!" And I was thinking, *This is Crazyville.* Then I walked around the corner and it was my grandmother. That was just bone-chilling. And that's what we had Enlsin's father say when he sees him.

SA: For the fans, we should probably discuss the wackadoodle various endings to the movie. There are so many versions in circulation.

All four versions of the ending still exist and either air somewhere or appear on a different version of the DVD. The endings are like the ghosts in this movie—they refuse to die.

SA: You can be a fan of the movie and say, "I'm gonna watch *1408* again," and you never know if John's going to live or die this time! [Laughs.] When the movie first came out the Weinsteins had some exclusive deal with Blockbuster. So the movie that screened in theaters, John lived in that. Then in the Blockbuster Blu-ray version John dies. And this information had not been imparted to anybody. Nobody passed this along! Just to entertain ourselves, Larry and I used to go to the IMDb message board. And people would get in fights on there because they would talk about him living, and then someone else would say, "You idiot, he doesn't live at the end. He dies!" They'd talk about the funeral, and someone else would say, "What funeral? There's no funeral!" They didn't realize they were seeing different movies. I mean, why would there be multiple versions? [Laughs again.]

In the short story he dies. He burns up to a crisp. Again, because we had such freedom on the project, we all had lots of conversations and the movie had a million revision pages. We were doing endless color revisions all through shooting. And one of the big conversations was, does he live or die? There wasn't a right answer. You could make an artistic case for both versions. We ultimately decided as commercial filmmakers, and because we had John Cusack whom we knew was a great actor who drew a lot of empathy, for all the guy's going to go through, why don't we just let the fucking guy live? He's gone to hell and back. Let's let him live at the end, for God's sake. It really was that simple. There wasn't a strong counterargument saying "No, he needs to die." No one had a strong opinion.

We just wanted the audience to walk out of the theater saying, "Wow, that's a great movie!" So we kind of said, "Fine. He's going to live." And then Larry and I messed around with all these different versions of "how freaky an ending with him living can we have?" We had all these A, B, C, D, E, and F versions of him with Mary at the end, in terms of, is he sane? Is he crazy? Do we want to put a weird final spin on things? So we ended up with the version that was basically the theatrical version, which is him back with Mary and then he finds the tape. He listens to it and they hear his daughter's voice, then they look at each other with a frightened expression, and the movie's over.

In the cutting room, Mikael and Peter (Boyle), the editor, were incredibly creative and they came up with a totally nutty version. I don't think this one ever made it into any of the versions in circulation. Maybe it did, maybe it didn't. In that version, they cut out the reaction shot of Mary. So they came up with a version of the closing scene where John finds the tape and Mary's across the room. He puts the tape in the player and the daughter's voice comes out, and John gets the frightened expression. And then you cut to Mary and she's just opening mail in the background. They just grabbed a shot of her from a different part of the scene. So in that edited version, it's all in John's mind. Just by flipping the shot of Mary, it completely reinterpreted the scene. It was really interesting and we were like, "Wow, that's kind of cool and crazy." And Mikael said, "Do you think it's better?" We weren't sure if it was better or worse, but it was really fascinating. I think it's the cleverest thing I've ever seen an editor do, in terms of reinterpreting a scene just by changing a single shot.

LK: All these endings are pretty good. I'm not sure we ever knocked the ending out of the park. Bob was like, "How can we make the ending better?" He was so proud of the movie, he really wanted the ending to have a little bit more, like a possible jump scare. We had a very extensive reshoot, which took place at Cusack's funeral.

SA: So we were like, he's gonna die now. So then we were asking ourselves what was the meaning of it all? And that was Cusack died to free the room. So we put those words in Mr. Olin's mouth when he comes to visit at the funeral. "Your husband died for a cause." And then we had him go back to his car and there's a dead Cusack in the backseat and it's a big jump scare. It got a huge reaction in the test screenings. But I think we all felt at the end of the day that the scene of Cusack and his wife alone listening to the tape had a general creepiness that the other stuff didn't have.

LK: I've always been kind of upset with the whole ending business because I actually think the theatrical version ends well. I think that original ending with Cusack and his wife was the definitive ending.

CHARLES ARDAI

Born in New York City the son of two Holocaust survivors, Charles Ardai grew up hearing the "grim and frightening" stories of his parents' struggles. These hardscrabble tales would perhaps play some role in Ardai's eventual fascination with the hardboiled crime stories published in the lurid paperbacks of yesteryear. He would later apply such elements to his own fiction, which would appear in such publications as *Ellery Queen's Mystery Magazine* and *Alfred Hitchcock's Mystery Magazine*, as well as numerous anthologies. Ardai also made a name for himself in 1996 as one of the founders of the Internet service provider Juno.

In 2004, Ardai, along with partner-in-crime Max Phillips, established Hard Case Crime, a publishing imprint created to recreate the sorts of crime novels the author had always enjoyed, complete with suggestive painted covers. Under the Hard Case Crime banner Ardai published his own debut novel, *Little Girl Lost* (2004), which he penned under the pseudonym Richard Aleas. That breakthrough novel was later nominated for both the Edgar Allan Poe Award and the Shamus Award. With Hard Case Crime, Ardai and Phillips would ultimately publish both new crime fiction and reprints of more obscure novels by the likes of Lawrence Block, Donald Westlake, and Harlan Ellison.

The following year Ardai inked Stephen King to a publishing deal for the novella *The Colorado Kid* (2005), which quickly became Hard Case Crime's biggest seller. King would later write a second work for Ardai, the novel *Joyland* (2014). In addition to editing and publishing these King books, Ardai also served as a writer and producer for the SyFy television series *Haven*, based on *The Colorado Kid*.

Hard Case Crime has now published nearly 100 novels (to date) and Ardai himself has penned the novels *Songs of Innocence* (2007), *Fifty-to-*

Charles Ardai

One (2008), and *Hunt Through the Cradle of Fear* (2009), as well as a novelization of the Shane Black motion picture *The Nice Guys* (2016).

I get the feeling you mostly read crime novels. How familiar with Stephen King's work were you prior to working with him on The Colorado Kid?

I was quite familiar even though I'm not a huge horror reader. I was just telling Steve a few days ago when *It* came out and became a huge box-office success, that *It* was the first book of his that I ever read. The reason I read it is because I was working as an unpaid intern at *Isaac Asimov's Science Fiction Magazine*. This was in 1986, I believe, and I was sixteen-years-old. They had a cardboard box they used for incoming review copies, and this enormous book called *It* (1986) showed up. It was the shortest title for the longest book! I was curious, so I took it home. Of course what I did by doing that was to deprive Stephen King of a review in the magazine, so I shouldn't have done it. But I fell in love with that novel. I read that book, and I thought he was an amazing storyteller.

I then went on to read as many of his books as I could find. I didn't read all of them, because you didn't have Amazon, where you could just push a button and get all of them. I tried reading other horror writers, but I didn't enjoy them quite as much. What really stood out to me was that Stephen King was a phenomenally-gifted storyteller who had interesting characters who engaged your affection, typically before you got to the end of the first page. It's one of those magic things he does, and I can't put my finger on how he does it. His son, Joe Hill, has exactly the same ability. You're only two or three paragraphs into a story, and already you care about the character. You want to know what happens to that character, and you don't want them hurt. How do you do that in two paragraphs? Some people write 300 pages and don't accomplish that. So I realized that I loved Stephen King, even though I didn't especially love horror.

As a fan of crime fiction, I wondered if you had read Stephen King's novel Blaze *(2007)? I think that's an exceptional crime novel.*

Blaze originally was going to be a Hard Case Crime novel. We did *The Colorado Kid* in 2005, and it was a terrific success. And then, at one point after that, Steve got in touch and said he'd written a new Richard Bachman novel called *Blaze*, and asked if I would enjoy reading it. Well, who says no to that? I read it and it was great, very much in the mode of Hard Case Crime. I think his original plan was for it to be a Hard Case Crime book. I don't remember exactly how he said it, or whether he said that expressly, but I certainly got that sense. And then I think Scribner put its foot down. They have a contract with him—they've been his home for well over a decade now. When he went to them with *The Colorado Kid* in 2004 he said, "Listen, you're my primary relationship, but there's this small outfit that I'd really like to help. I'd like to give them this novella I've written. Do you mind if I give this to them? I know Scribner would love to publish it, but I really hope you'll let me do this." They said yes, but when he went back to them three years later and tried it again, I think they told him no.

You'll see if you pick up the hardcover of *Blaze*, in the upper right-hand corner, Scribner published it with an orange two-tailed ribbon hanging down, very reminiscent of the gold two-tailed ribbon hanging down on the left side of every one of the covers of the Hard Case Crime books. Scribner had never done that before. And if you look in the foreword that Stephen King wrote, he talks about both Hard Case Crime and myself.

He showed me an early draft, I loved it, and I would have been thrilled to publish it, but it didn't turn out to be. The possible second child in our union went to another hussy instead, but he eventually came back to us in 2013 with *Joyland*.

I understand your publishing The Colorado Kid *came as a result of your seeking a blurb from King. I was wondering if you'd like to talk a little bit about that.*

Max Phillips and I came up with the idea for Hard Case Crime in the winter of 2001. We had worked together on an Internet company called Juno, and it had just sold that fall. So we were talking about what we wanted to do, and we had this idea for publishing a new line of books that looked and felt like the old paperbacks. I probably would have just dropped the whole thing at that point, but Max came back about two weeks later and said, "Do you remember that idea we discussed? I came up with some covers, and this is what it could look like." And when I saw those I said, "I can't just drop the idea. This is gorgeous work. I've got to get this out there." So I started talking to publishers, and it was very hard to get a publisher to put up the money to do this. Many of them said they loved what we wanted to do, but they said it was a niche property and they wouldn't be able to sell enough copies of any one book to get it off the ground. Finally we found a small publisher—one of the last two remaining independent paperback houses—called Dorchester. They said, "We'll try it. We'll try six books—half originals, and half reprints of old stuff. And if they do okay, we'll do another six."

So once we had that contract, I was trying to think how we could sell some books. I didn't want to get rich doing this, but I wanted to do more than six books. We had this notion that if we put out books by one-time popular writers like Day Keene or Earl Stanley Gardner, nobody today would know what these names meant. So I had this notion that it would be helpful if we found an author with a name that people did know, who could go out on the cover of our books and say something that would catch book-buyers' eyes. I thought, if you had a book by Day Keene, nobody would pick it up. But if you had a book by Day Keene, and on the cover there was a blurb by Stephen King saying, "These guys know pulp," it would do better. I thought one line like that might be enough to catch a reader's eye and engage their brain and ask themselves, "I wonder if this Day Keene guy might be good?"

I knew that Steve had grown up reading books like this, because he's written about them in essays and novels. I knew he loved guys like Donald Westlake, Lawrence Block, and Ed McBain. I had no idea how to reach him. I'd never met him. I didn't even know where to start. But I looked online and read a lot of articles about people he worked with. I found the name of his accountant, and the guy had an office on Park Avenue in New York City. So I thought, why not? Nothing ventured, nothing gained. So I put together a package of the dummied-up covers, and a letter explaining what the idea was. So I took a cab down to this guy Arthur Green's office. God knows why they even let me in there. This was before security had become super tight. I knocked on the door and said, "You have no reason to do this, but would you help me out? Could you get this package to Stephen King? He'll probably never respond, but maybe..." A month or two passed and I hadn't heard back.

Finally I got a call from Chuck Verill, Stephen King's agent. He said, "Steve wanted me to give you a call. He wanted me to let you know he does not want to write you a blurb." And then he paused. I said, "I can certainly understand that." Chuck continued, "Because he'd like to write you a book instead." And my heart either went through the roof of my chest cavity or down to wherever hearts go when they flop around. [Laughs.] I immediately realized how big a deal this was. He had received the package, had become excited about it, and wanted to be part of the fun.

Two months later I received the manuscript for *The Colorado Kid*. It was different in many ways from our other books. There was a dead man on a beach, that part was the same.... And in this book there isn't a solution—the mystery never gets solved. That makes it very different from the rest of our books. Very few authors can publish a crime story without having a solution. Stephen King is one of the only writers who can get away with that. I thought, this is great! So we enhanced that by putting the tagline on the cover: "Would she learn the dead man's secret?" Of course the answer is no. It's like "Buy this book and read it to the end and you won't find out either!" [Laughs again.] I think a lot of writers wouldn't have dared to write the story the way Steve did, and they wouldn't get away with it or publish it if they did. So I was very excited to be able to publish this.

And that is the history behind *The Colorado Kid*.

Could you talk about editing that book? How different was it editing King from editing a less-experienced author?

It's very different, because it doesn't need much editing. That's not always the case. A lot of our experienced authors need quite a bit of editing, for whatever reason. And sometimes they don't get it, so you see authors who have been working for decades and maybe their current editor doesn't put a lot of suggestions in there. Maybe he's too terrified to suggest edits. So you see some writers at the tail end of their career who could use the hand of an editor and aren't getting it. But that is not the case with Stephen King. His manuscripts are extremely clean. There is very little that needs to be done. With *The Colorado Kid*, there was literally nothing except some occasional anachronisms. I mean, there might have been a typo or two, but those are really small things.

Later, in editing *Joyland*, there was something slightly bigger because there were elements that were important to the climax that I thought hadn't been introduced early enough in the book to properly pay off. I told him he probably wanted to introduce that a little bit earlier and talked to him about where he might do that. But that was one thing out of a

70,000 word manuscript. Not surprisingly, his work does not require a lot of editing. Although I have no way of knowing how much editing he did before he sent it to me. That's another story. But my experience was that there was no need for a heavy hand.

With new authors it's sometimes a very different story. Sometimes I look at a book and see that it has a lot of merit, but every sentence has to be altered. Every single sentence. There are word choices that are awkward and things that are clichéd or don't make sense. I have to go in and put red ink on every single sentence, and that is clearly not the case with Stephen King.

As you mentioned, The Colorado Kid *is different than most of the other Hard Case Crime books. Would you have still published it if it had been written by an unknown author?*

We might not have, but only because of the length. Believe it or not, that's the only reason. In principle, length shouldn't be an issue. James M. Cain wrote *The Postman Always Rings Twice* (1934), which is a classic, and it's only about 25,000 words long. If you're a vintage publisher and you're reprinting that novel, you can make it the skinniest thing in the bookstore, with a spine so thin you can't even see the title on it, and it'll still sell enough copies to justify it. People will go out of their way to find that; they're looking for it. But if you're a no-name author, and your book is literally the skinniest on the shelf, it will likely go unnoticed in the literal sense. But apart from that, some book-buyers seem to buy books by the pound. I don't know if they do that consciously, but they do it. With the prices of books on the rise, money is tight and oftentimes people want to get value for their money. Of course a skinny book that's wonderful is clearly a better buy than a big thick book that's boring, but when you're standing there in the bookstore you don't know which one it's going to be. So a lot of people just don't buy skinny books.

I like short books. But the reality of the market now might mean that a short book is 60,000 words as opposed to the 100,000-word books we see frequently today. *The Colorado Kid* was about 35,000 words. My guess is that we probably couldn't publish a 35,000-word novella by an unknown author, because no one would pick it up. It would just be a money-losing endeavor and would serve nobody's interests. So for that reason we may not have published *The Colorado Kid*. But if you can imagine that same book at 60,000 words, then sure, I would have been extremely happy to publish it no matter who the author was. But I think readers might have given it less benefit of the doubt than they did because this was coming from an author they knew and loved. If you're going to do something provocative or unusual—something that challenges expectations—people will give you a little more rope if you've already earned their trust than if you haven't. If we had published it by an author that no one had heard of, readers may not have reacted as patiently to the material. But I would have still been delighted to publish it.

How important would you say Stephen King's contributions have been to the ongoing success of Hard Case Crime?

It certainly helped put us on the map. We got a lot of media attention and people learned that we existed largely because of Steve. We put out our first books in 2004 and *The Colorado Kid* came in 2005, so it was very close to when we started. It was our 13th title. It was the very first one we did after that initial contract that started with six and had an option for another six. I think if it weren't for the King title, we may very well have stopped at 12. We did what we planned, and we had a nice little shelf of books, and Max and I would have moved on to other things. So I think the fact that Hard Case Crime continued after the first 12 at all is largely because of *The Colorado Kid* and the attention and demand that brought us. People said, "These are good books. I'd like to see more." So we did more.

We don't release exact figures as that's private information, but it outsold any of our other books by a factor of maybe one hundred. It made a huge difference. One book that generates a decent profit can make up for several dozen books that only break even. We had plenty of books that only broke even or maybe only made a profit to the tune of $200. And you can't keep the lights on for very long with those kinds of profits. There's no real staff, so that keeps the costs down, but having a book that sells like an airport bestseller as opposed to a book that sells to a couple of thousand fans makes a huge difference.

Then *Joyland* did the same thing again. By then we had done something like 75 books, and again, that could have been enough. That could have been a good place to stop. But then along came this new book with a fresh injection of excitement and attention again. It was a bestseller and it was a really terrific book. Not everyone loved *The Colorado Kid* because of its unresolved ending, but pretty much everyone universally loved *Joyland*. And suddenly we were on the front page of everything all over again! It gave us a fresh lease on life and a fresh set of sales to support other writers who couldn't generate that kind of revenue on their own. It was great.

You worked as a consulting producer on Haven *(2010). What did that job entail, and what was that experience like?*

It was great fun; probably everything you've heard and then some. It pays better than book publishing, by far, and is also more annoying than book publishing, by far. [Laughs.] But it was fun. I had never worked on a TV series before, and I'm very glad to have done it. I wrote two episodes for the show and wrote a story for a third. I went through all of the scripts with a fine-toothed comb, trying to make them stronger. That's not to say that every suggestion I ever made was adopted, sometimes because of time constraints or budget limitations. It's all well and good to say, "I think this monster would be more exciting if he was 18-feet tall, but good luck filming that." Sometimes my ideas may not have been the right ones.

Basically the role was three-fold. First, I met with the producers who ended up doing the show, and together we cooked up the idea for doing it in the first place. We pitched it to ABC, who bought it and sat on it, didn't develop it, and then gave it back to us. So then we sold it to SyFy and put the show on. Then, once the show actually got sold and we had to produce 13 episodes for the first season, we sat in the writer's room breaking up the episodes and shooting down some really terrible ideas. I came up with a few terrible ideas of my own. And then actually going through all of the scripts one by one as drafts came in. Reading through treatments and finished scripts and then marking them up, saying things like, "I don't think these characters would do this. Here's why this isn't great."

The show turned out to be a lot of fun. Of course it had fairly little in common with the book that inspired it. There are brothers who run the local newspaper. The attractive female intern who appears on the front cover of the book is not a character on the show. She was in the early versions of the plot we cooked up, but it became obvious that we would be able to better sell the show with a female cop in the lead instead of a female newspaper intern. When it then turned out that that character was not in fact a cop at all, but a supernatural creature, it really didn't end up mattering whether she was a fictitious cop or a fictitious newspaper intern. And of course the town wasn't even called Haven in the novella. It was an island in Maine in the book. So there were a million things that were different, but we tried to make sure the spirit of it was true to Steve's work. We also tried to work in sly references to other King works just because it was fun to do that. We had a bad guy get off a bus in Haven, and over his shoulder you saw a rucksack with stenciled letters on it that said "Shawshank Penitentiary." The rucksack had to say something, and that's more fun than if it said something else.

We had a lot of fun with it, and the people who worked on the show were true fans of Steve's work, and they had a lot passion for creating a show that fans of Steve's work would enjoy. It was at a time when there wasn't as much of Steve's work on television or at the movies as there is now. It waxes and wanes. Sometimes you have a rich cornucopia of offerings, but at the time *The Dead Zone* (2002), which was produced by the same company, had been off the air for a while. We just wanted there to be some King representation on the air, and we were very happy to get to do that.

I understand that King played a role in convincing Michael Crichton to publish with Hard Case Crime. Could you talk a little bit about that?

I don't know how active a role he played. He certainly encouraged me to do it. I told him that I remembered reading and enjoying the eight books that Michael had written under the pseudonym John Lange, when he was in medical school. The story goes, although Michael never actually confirmed this to me, is that he was worried that if Harvard Medical School found out that he was writing sexy potboilers on the side, they would kick him out of school. And he was doing it mostly for the money. So he wrote them under a pseudonym and never really acknowledged it. Many years later when Harvard could no longer kick him out, he still didn't go back and allow these books to be reprinted. I mentioned them to Steve. I said, "Those were good. They were really fun thrillers. They would be terrific to reprint in Hard Case Crime. Maybe they're not based on his big ideas like *Jurassic Park* (1990) or some of his later books, but they're just terrific fun." I said, "Do you think he might be open to allowing us to reprint those?" And Steve said, "You should certainly try, and tell him that Steve said he should do it."

I don't know that Steve ever reached out to Michael himself or asked him to, but I said to Michael, "We're working with Stephen King. We would love to work with you." Now that I think about it, I think what Steve actually said was, "Tell him he should write a new John Lange book for you." So I suggested that to Michael. "I doubt you'd do that for us, but you have eight of them that you have never allowed anyone to reprint." And Michael said, "I love your covers so much that if you agree to give me a cover that looks like that, I will let you reprint one of them. And if it goes well, then I'll let you do another. And so on." But he said, "You can't reveal who I am. You've got to keep it secret." And I said, "Sure. Why not? I love the books whether your name is on them or not. Obviously we will sell far fewer copies. We would sell half-a-million with your name, and 5,000 without your name, but that's okay. What the hell?" And we stuck to it. We never mentioned his name. Not once, to anyone. Not to the sales force; not to the bookstores; not to anyone. The book covers said John Lange. That's all it said anywhere.

We did one called *Grave Descend*, which had been nominated for an Edgar back in the day, and it's probably my favorite of the eight. And we had a great cover by Greg Manches, and Michael loved it. And a year later we said, "What should we do next?" We did a second one called *Zero Cool* (1969), which had another great Greg Manches cover; this time of a beautiful woman lying on a beach with a man's shadow looming over her, and just for fun the book lying next to her is a miniature copy of *Grave Descend* (1970). So we had fun with that. And we were all set to do a third one. I was e-mailing with Michael, and he was kind of interested in doing *Drug of Choice* (1970), which is more of a science fiction one. It was a little bit *Westworld* and a little bit *Jurassic Park*. If I'm being honest it's one of my least favorite John Lange novels. It was very much a late sixties, early seventies druggie novel. But I thought, if Michael wants to do that one next, then okay. And then I got a phone call before we hammered out the contract. It was a guy from *Wall Street Journal* asking me to make a comment on Michael Crichton's death. I said, "What are you talking about?" He had just died. He was only in his fifties or sixties, but he had cancer. He had never mentioned that to me. I guess he had never mentioned it to most people in his life. And he was gone.

His estate was a mess. There were kids and widows and lawyers and doctors. It was all just a mess, so I just held off on publishing the other six. Then I got a call from his widow saying, "It's been five years. Let's publish these for the fifth anniversary of his death. Let's bring out all eight and this time we'll put his name on them." It's different now. When he was alive he had wanted his new books to be distinguished from the older stuff. He didn't want someone thinking, "Hey, this is the new Michael Crichton book," and then it turns out being something he wrote as a medical student. So we did. We put out all eight of the Lange books, reissuing the first two with his name on them. They're all out now and anyone who wants to read them can, and I'm very happy we did it.

We might have done it anyway even without Steve saying it was okay to use his name when we approached Michael. I probably would have approached him, but it certainly didn't hurt and I'm extremely grateful to Steve for being supportive.

How did Joyland come about?

I didn't do anything to make it come about. I got a call from Chuck Verrill. This was seven years after we'd published *The Colorado Kid.* Chuck said, "Steve has written something new. Would you like to take a look at it? He thinks it might be suitable for Hard Case Crime." I said, "Yes, please!" It was set in a carnival. Carnie noir is one of the classic staples of the old paperbacks. It's a whole sub-category. I can go to my shelf right now and pull off half a dozen books that were set in the world of traveling carnivals and circuses. So I waited, and the manuscript came. I read it and it just broke my heart. It made me blubber, despite my technically being an editor of Hard Case Crime. I was just bawling when I got to the last page. I said, "This is great. Of course I want to publish this." And then we did.

It was as pure an act of generosity on the part of any human being as you can imagine because I hadn't even asked for this. Steve had already done one book with us, so whatever impulse he had to be supportive.... I think anyone would have said he'd already gone above and beyond the call of duty. But here he was volunteering to do it again with a book that was even longer and arguably even stronger. He persuaded the folks at Scribner to allow that, and I'm forever grateful. I was already grateful for the first time, but this second time just floored me. Obviously I would love to do it a third time, but I'm not holding out hope for that. But I wouldn't have held out hope for the second time either.

TYSON BLUE

Tyson Blue attended college at Syracuse University, where he studied psychology and journalism. He wrote for the school newspaper, *The Daily Orange*, and also operated an underground radio station until it was shut down by the FCC. After college, he began writing media reviews for the *Courier-Herald* in Dublin, Georgia, where he wrote his first King-related article—a scathing review of the film adaptation of *The Shining* (1980). He later wrote a behind-the-scenes piece on the filming of *Maximum Overdrive* (1986) for *Twilight Zone* magazine, which included an on-set interview with King himself. Blue would continue to write about the author, penning "at least a hundred" articles for the now-defunct official King newsletter *Castle Rock: The Official Stephen King Newsletter*. He has also written about King in such publications as *Midnight Graffiti*, *Cemetery Dance*, and *Footsteps*, as well as Canadian, French, Italian, and German fanzines devoted to the author. Blue then wrote the highly regarded book *The Unseen King* (1989) for Starmont House. As a critic for the *Macon Telegraph*, his review was quoted on the original paperback version of *The Stand* (1978).

Blue's second Stephen King-related book was the now legendary *Observations from the Terminator: Thoughts on Stephen King and Other Modern Masters of Horror Fiction*, which, as Blue says, "has managed to put two small presses out of business without quite being published." The book contained reviews and essays on the horror genre, as well as interviews with luminaries like King and Harlan Ellison. The book also featured original artwork by noted artist Steve Bissette. But for reasons explained in the following interview, the book was never published. Interestingly enough, the book is listed beside Blue's name at the Library of Congress, despite its never being released to the public.

Perspectives on Stephen King

Continuing this unfortunate trend of completing good books that would end up unpublished, Blue was hand-picked by writer/director Frank Darabont to write *Walking the Mile: The Making of The Green Mile* in 1998. Blue spent time on the set of the film, and even ended up making a cameo in the funeral scene of the movie. But there would end up being complications, and the book would never see print.

Stephen J. Spignesi has called him the writer who has "written more about King and his work than anyone else on the planet," and Blue has contributed to almost every King-related book Spignesi has written or edited.

Blue's short fiction has also appeared in the Horrorfest '89 program book, *2 AM*, *Mediascene*, and the anthologies *Ghosts* (edited by Peter Straub, 1995), *Voices from the Night: 27 Stories of Horror and Suspense* (1994), and *Rise of the Dead: An Anthology of Zombie Horror* (2014), which also features stories from King writers Stephen J. Spignesi and the editor of this book.

At the time of this writing, Blue was editing *Hope and Miracles: The Shawshank Redemption and The Green Mile: Two Screenplays by Frank Darabont* (2018) for Gauntlet Press.

What was your first exposure to the work of Stephen King, and what did you think of him?

It was in 1976. I was out of work at the time and we had moved down to Georgia. I received a letter from a woman who had been our landlady in New Hampshire, and she asked me if I had read a book called *'Salem's Lot* (1975) by a guy named Stephen King. I had seen the hardcover in bookstores when we'd still lived in New Hampshire, but I didn't know anything about it. A friend of hers who lived in New Hampshire was a friend of Steve's, and he'd mentioned it to her. I then made a mental note to pick up the book when it came out in paperback, which I did.

At first I read it, and it was okay. It was sort of a creepy little story. Then I was on my way back from Reading, Pennsylvania, where I had gone to meet a friend of mine. I'd been up all night and I was reading the book, trying to keep myself awake. I kept dozing off and dropping it on the floor. I finally got to the part where the little kid in the coffin is staring up through the lid at the guy who was burying him. As the sun gets lower and lower, the pull gets stronger and stronger. That made me wake right up. It was a really powerfully written section of the book. Oddly enough, after I found out the monsters in the book were just vampires, a little bit of the fright went out of it for me, because, you know, you just get some stakes and a hammer and you're all set!

Shortly after that, the movie version of *Carrie* (1974) came out. I went to see that and made the mistake of sitting between my wife and my sister. At the last scene of the movie they both nearly snatched me baldheaded! Then I read the book, which I really enjoyed.

I've purchased everything of Steve's that I could get my hands on ever since. That actually includes a lot of stuff that not everybody can get their hands on.

What led to your writing about King early on?

I did media reviews for a local newspaper in Georgia just so I could keep my sanity. It was also a neat way to get free books, records, and movies. I had been doing that kind of stuff since 1968. It was always something I was interested in. English was my favorite subject in school, and I had a sophomore English teacher who taught me a lot about analyzing stories and novels. He was an expert on F. Scott Fitzgerald. He loaned me a copy of a book Fitzgerald had written when he was eight or nine years old, and that sort of planted the idea in my head that writers write a lot of stuff before they become published. And we don't get to see that very often, so I was always interested in taking a look at stuff like that.

The first King review that I wrote was a review of Stanley Kubrick's awful movie version of *The Shining*. I also started reviewing Steve's books around that same time. When I found out he was directing *Maximum Overdrive* in North Carolina, which was just a couple of states away, I thought it might be a good chance to go up and meet him. So I contacted the production company, and my local hometown newspaper wasn't impressive enough to get their attention. So I got in touch with the editor of *The Macon Telegraph*, which was about 50 miles away, and they were interested in a piece by me, as well. But even that wasn't enough. Somewhere around this time I found out about the *Castle Rock* newsletter, and I got in touch with them. Their editor was Stephanie Leonard, who's Steve's sister-in-law. She said she wanted to do a piece about the movie but hadn't had the time to go down there and do what needed to be done. So she gave me the job doing it. So I called the production office again, and even *that* wasn't enough!

Then I got in touch with *Twilight Zone* to see if they'd be interested, and the editor asked me, "How did you know we were doing a special Stephen King issue?" I said, "I didn't." So he was interested in me going and covering the picture for them. That finally proved to be enough clout and they invited me up to the set.

The interview kept getting pushed back, and finally ended up happening on Steve's birthday. By that time the magazine was two weeks late—they were holding two pages open and holding up publication of the magazine for me. They had asked me earlier, "Have you ever done anything like this before?" I just told them I had done interviews for newspapers for years, and a magazine piece is just a longer version of the same thing.

I went up there and one of the first people I ran into was Steve. I introduced myself and he said we'd talk later. I basically hung around the set until they broke for lunch at around midnight, and he sat and talked with me and the rest of the journalists who were there that night. It was like we were sitting around a dinner table talking about our day—if our day was working on a movie set! So long story short, I typed up my story in the production office for *Maximum Overdrive* and Fed-Exed it to the magazine, and it got published.

You've met Stephen King several times. What's he like?

I've met him four or five times. He's pretty approachable. He kind of puts you at ease pretty quickly. He's just a regular guy. I've run into him in all sorts of situations. On *Maximum Overdrive* he was the director. He was working, but he sat down and talked to everybody. He signed a lot of my books that night, too. I called his office late one afternoon and he picked up the phone. I've done a couple of letter interviews with him. I've talked to him at Q&A sessions at different public appearances. One time I ran into him at a restaurant in Boston when we were all in town for a Red Sox/Yankees game. Basically we came into the restaurant, and as we were checking in, I looked over and saw Steve just sitting there at a table with Joe Hill and his wife.

When did you decide to write The Unseen King?

It was when I found out about *The Plant* (1982), which was a very limited edition. I may have read about it in Douglas Winter's book [*Stephen King: The Art of Darkness*, 1984]. I obviously wasn't going to be able to read it, so I thought maybe if I did a *Castle Rock* article about it then maybe I'd get to read it that way. Steve did a brief letter interview with me for that. I sent him some questions and he wrote me back the responses in a letter. He sent me a copy of the third book so I'd know what it looked like. When the article was published it was called "The Plant: The Unseen King." That was when I got the idea that maybe since they'd been so generous with *The Plant*, then maybe I could get a look at all of this stuff. And it just happened that Doug's book mentioned all these other unpublished things. People were asking him to see these things all the time, so my idea was that maybe if he helped me with this book then people would kind of go away. It didn't work, but... [Laughs.]

In 1988, I would just get in touch with his office and ask them for things. Then they would send me photocopies of them. There were other ones I could track down on my own. Then I just kind of organized it a little bit. I wrote it and it was published. It did pretty well. I think it sold about 3,000 copies.

It's still a very revered work in King circles.

I'm kind of surprised by that. It was really the first book that examined some of that stuff. "Brooklyn August" was published in that book for the first time in any wide-ranging way. It had just been in a magazine before that. Eventually it appeared in *Nightmares & Dreamscapes* (1993). I've always been surprised by the reaction it got. You can still find it on Amazon every once in a while for about fifty bucks. I don't see any of that money, but it's nice to know people are willing to pay that much for it. [Laughs.] That was from Starmont House, which was one of the first houses to really do a lot of scholarly things on King.

I later contracted with them on my second book, *Observations from the Terminator*, which was an interview and essay collection. It was mostly King-oriented, but it also had interviews with Harlan Ellison and Clive Barker and several other people. But then Ted Dikty, who basically was Starmont House, died and his daughter took over. I had arranged with Ted to handle my own cover artwork. Originally I wanted the guy who did the artwork for the Philtrum Press version of *Eyes of the Dragon* (1987) to do it, but that kind of fell by the wayside. When that fell through, I contracted

Steve Bissette to do something similar to what he did on the cover of Dave Hinchberger's version of *The Shape Under the Sheet* (1991). It was a portrait of Steve circa *The Dark Half* (1989) with a chunk torn out of it and a monster face peering out. He only charged about $75 for that. But the publisher went batshit crazy and said they refused to pay that much.

Finally she just closed down the press. The books were actually printed by somebody in Oregon. Starmont was in Seattle. I guess the guy running the place went out for lunch, and Starmont owned all the printing equipment.... When he came back from lunch all the equipment had been moved out and all the inventory stuff they had in there had been thrown out. He asked a guy who was there what had happened, and he said, "A woman just called and said to throw all that shit out."

In the envelope were several copies of *The Unseen King*, Steve Bissette's original artwork for the cover of *Observations from the Terminator*, all the author photos including ones I had actually borrowed from the authors' personal collections. So the guy asked me if I wanted this stuff and I said yes. He put it all in an envelope and sent it to me.

Then Borgo Press, who has done a couple of Harlan Ellison's books, picked up *The Unseen King* and *Observations from the Terminator*. They got all the way to final proofs on *Observations*, and then they went out of business. That book has never actually come out, although if you go to the Library of Congress' website, it's listed in their collection. Someday I want to go there and see what they've got. As far as I know, beyond this proof copy I've got, it's never been printed. Dave Hinchberger has expressed some interest in doing it as a print-on-demand book, but I've just never gotten around to just sitting down and putting it together for him. But one of these days I hope to do that.

You've worked on several King-related projects with Stephen J. Spignesi. What have those experiences been like?

Working with Steve is pretty easy. I'm trying to remember if I've ever come up with any of the things I've done for him.... Usually he asks me to contribute and I say, "What would you like me to do?" And he'll say, "Well, I've always wanted to see somebody do this or do that." He tells me about it and then I take it and run with it.

You also write fiction. In what ways has Stephen King influenced your writing?

I'm sure the influence is there, but I've been writing fiction since I was eight or nine years old, so I don't know how much of that there has been. I've taken a lot of tips from reading his book *On Writing* (1999)—things to avoid, things to do. I've taken tips from that on the benefits of rewriting, which is something I have never really liked to do. It's usually a good thing to do, although I've found that it doesn't work as good on short stories as it does on longer things. I've usually found that when I revise a short story it gets longer. For instance, the story I gave you for your book *Rise of the Dead*, that was written in one sitting and that was a first draft. That was never revised. That was a lot of fun to write. It's actually my favorite of my short stories.

What do you see as being misconceptions about Stephen King?

I don't think it happens so much anymore with him getting awards and getting a medal from Obama and so forth, but he used to be dismissed as a horror writer. I don't think that's ever been the primary reason people read his stuff. He's a good writer, he's a good storyteller. He creates characters that you care about and are interested in. The rest of the gruesome stuff is just icing on the cake.

I like *It* (1986) a lot. Not so much because of the monster stuff, although that is fun, but more for the interactions between the characters—especially when they're kids. If you want to see what my life was like growing up, then just read *It*. We did all that stuff.

Does that include the orgy scene?

[Laughs.] No, unfortunately.

What King work would you say you've read the most times?

The Green Mile (1996). I've read it at least seven or eight times, and I can't tell you how many times I've listened to the audiobook or watched the movie. That was when I was working on the movie. Well, I obviously hadn't seen the movie yet. The first time I got to see the movie was when it was in postproduction. The opening sequence hadn't been shot yet, but I saw the rest of the movie. The reason I got to see it was because, while we were in there talking about postproduction, Frank Darabont was there talking to Paul Simon about doing a song for the end credits. So he screened the movie for him. The first hint I got about how good a movie it was, was when I was sitting there watching the picture and completely forgot that the guy sitting in the seat in front of me had written "Bridge Over Troubled

Water" (1970) and "The Boxer" (1970). [Laughs.] I like Simon & Garfunkel a lot, and I completely forgot he was there!

At that time you were working on a book about the making the making of the film titled Walking the Mile. *How did you get involved with that?*

I reviewed Frank's student film, *The Woman in the Room* (1983), for *Castle Rock*. I think it was a piece on the so-called "Dollar Babies." There weren't very many of them at the time. I think there were only four or five. And Frank read that and remembered it.

So I got the number for the production office from Steve's office and I called them up. At that time I was just wanting to do a set visit when they were shooting on the East Coast. We had gone to a movie and when I came home there was a message on my answering machine. It was Frank Darabont. He recalled the article I had written with great fondness. He said, "Call me up and tell me what you'd like to do." So I called them up and said I wanted to read the script, have a set visit, do a cameo in the movie, write a making-of-the-movie book. I just gave them this laundry list of stuff, sort of tongue-in-cheek, never realizing at the time that I'd eventually get to do every single one of those things.

I got a call from Dave Johnson, who was his assistant at the time, and he said, "Do you have anything that you've written that you could send us?" I said I could send *The Unseen King* and a piece on a set visit I had just done for *Storm of the Century* (1999). That hadn't been published yet, but I sent them that. I asked, "Why do you want that stuff?" And he said, "Frank wants to do a making-of-the-movie book and he thinks it would be easier to convince them if he could show them something that you've written." I'm slow on the uptake, but the wheels started turning. I said, "You're saying he wants *me* to do it?" "Yeah, he wants you to do it." So I told them yes before they came to their senses.

From there I just arranged to take a week off at a time from my job, and Warner Bros. would fly me out to LA. The shooting days would start at 8:30 in the morning and they would run until 10 or 11 o'clock at night. I pretty much had full-access. I could hang out and do anything I wanted to, as long as I stayed out of the way.

What are some of your favorite memories of that experience?

There's a scene in the fifteenth anniversary edition of *The Green Mile* (1999). There is a scene there in Paul Edgecomb's house where he's telling

Bonnie Hunt that he's got to go to the doctor for his bladder infection. Tom Hanks was eating a biscuit while he was delivering his lines, and at the end it got all muffled like it would when you're talking through a mouth full of food. For some reason that struck Bonnie Hunt as funny, and the two of them just started cracking up. And they laughed for about a half an hour. They were just trying to get that scene in the can, and they had to keep doing it over and over again. They would just crack up every time.

Then in Tennessee, when they were shooting the exteriors of the warden's house, which was actually a very tiny little building with a false front on it, they were shooting in October and the temperatures were pretty mild. But it would get pretty cold at night, and they were trying to get everything done so they could get the interiors ahead of schedule. The picture was way behind. And still Hanks would clown around on the set. He would walk up to the warden's door and knock and say, "This is the INS. Where are your papers?" He would change it all the time.

What are your thoughts on Frank Darabont's work?
I've read several of his screenplays. I've read his two that have been published, and I've also read his *Indiana Jones* screenplay. I like them. They're very readable screenplays. The screen directions are written in a literary style. They're not cut and dry the way a lot of screenwriters do. It makes it easy to read the screenplay as a piece of literature, which isn't always the case.

As a director he's very meticulous. He'll do things over and over and over again to get them right. But his sets are relaxed; everyone feels welcome and feels at ease. They can talk to him about changing their improvisations they want to. He sits down and makes changes in the screenplay by hand. When we were in North Carolina, he figured out that if he chopped the scene where Paul Edgecomb and his friend are going up to the cabin in the woods behind the old folks home, they could wrap production a day early. So Frank sat down on a tree stump with the screenplay and a pen and just started trimming it so that they could finish it that night. He's not worried about editing his own work. I was very impressed by him.

Your Walking the Mile *book was never published. What happened to that?*
I think a couple of things happened. There were three or four revisions. I think they shopped around the first draft, which was the "everything-

including-the-kitchen-sink" version. It might have seemed a bit top-heavy. But I think the main problem was that in order to have a book in the stores by December, you had to have a finished book in the warehouse by September. And the picture had just wrapped in August, so basically we were asking whoever the publisher would have been to typeset, edit, proof, print, and bind a book in a very short time. This was not something you could crash produce. It was going to have photos and storyboards and concept art and production designs. It was going to have a really elaborate layout design, and I think they just realized they couldn't do it in 30 days. So that's kind of why everybody passed on it.

But there remains a lot of interest in it, and I'm hoping this new *Shawshank Redemption/Green Mile* screenplay book we're doing does well. Maybe Gauntlet or somebody else will be interested in putting it out and it might finally see print.

But that was a fun experience and probably the high point of my career. I wouldn't mind doing something like that again.

What do you see as being the finest Stephen King motion picture adaptations?

Those two movies I just mentioned are pretty close to the top. *Shawshank Redemption* (1994) may be a little bit better movie, if I had to be impartial. But I have a big soft spot for *The Green Mile*. Not just because I'm in it, but also because the novel itself is probably my favorite King novel. I think *Shawshank* edges it out just a little. I like the way Frank tells the story—the way he kind of condenses things and changes it in ways that actually make it work better story-wise. In the original *Shawshank* novella, there are several wardens during the time Andy is there. I think Frank's making it just a single warden kind of makes it better because you have just one villain to concentrate on. Although it's not a completely faithful adaptation, it's true to the spirit of King's story. I think it also showcases a thing about King's work that keeps people coming back—the characters and their experiences.

The Dead Zone (1983), which is a really faithful adaptation of the book. Christopher Walken and Martin Sheen are both fantastic in it. I haven't seen it in a long time, although I think I might watch it with a slightly different viewpoint in light of current world events. But I've always liked that film.

I like the TV version of *It* (1990) a lot—especially the beginning part with the kids. I thought they did a really interesting version of it, and I'm anxious to see what they do with it in the new movie version that's coming out.

Of course there's *Stand by Me* (1986) and *Misery* (1990). Rob Reiner is great at directing Stephen King adaptations. I thought the casting in both of those was really well done. *Dolores Claiborne* (1995) was also good. I do realize there's a trend here in that I'm selecting less Stephen King horror movies, but those are the ones I think they did a really great job with. Almost all of the Castle Rock Stephen King movies are in there. I don't think *Needful Things* (1993) was quite as successful, but everybody has an off day.

As far as the more traditional Stephen King movies, I like both versions of *Carrie* (1976, 2013 respectively) for different reasons. I know it wasn't popular to like it, but I actually liked the latest version. And there was a god-awful NBC TV version of it (2002) a few years ago. It was bad, but I thought Patricia Clarkson was really good in it for her very subdued take on Carrie White's mother. I thought that approach to the character worked really well. I also liked that that version concentrated a lot on Carrie's trip from the high school back to her house. The first movie kind of glossed over that.

I have a real soft spot for *Maximum Overdrive*. I would never try to argue that it's the greatest movie ever made or anything, but it's a lot of fun. And for somebody who had never directed a movie before, I thought some of the sequences in it were really well done. Steve told us a story that when the steamroller runs over the kid, he had stuck a baggy of blood down the dummy's shirt because he wanted it to blow up and make a bloody mess. What happened was, when the steamroller ran over it, it wound up looking like the kid's head had popped open. So they had to cut that to avoid getting an "X" rating. I really wished they had kept that footage and maybe put in on the DVD release or something. He said he showed it to George Romero and it made him flinch.

You have been very vocal about your dislike for Stanley Kubrick's version of The Shining. *Why do you hate that film?*

There are the problems that everyone brings up, such as Jack Nicholson's character basically being crazy from the beginning of the film, so it's obvious that he's not driven that way by the hotel. The main thing that bothers me about it is that it's not scary. It's like a lot of Kubrick movies—it's cold and emotionless. It's badly in need of an editor. It has scenes that go on way too long. I think Stanley Kubrick benefited more from the drug culture of the 1960s than any other because a bunch of stoned kids watched *2001* (1968) and thought it was the greatest thing since sliced bread. I think that movie needs an editor, too. I think if they had edited out all of the stuff that was draggy, then it wouldn't have been feature length.

The thing that bothers me about *The Shining* is the scene with the woman in the bathtub. It's supposed to be the scariest scene in the movie, and it actually works really well in Mick Garris' TV version (1997). But at different times they used three different actresses, each in different makeup, in that scene. They cut back and forth. When I'm watching it I'm thinking, that isn't the woman who was there just a second ago. So you're thinking about that instead of being scared by this naked rotting woman coming after Jack Nicholson.

And it's not true to the novel at all. I think if it hadn't been advertised as being based on Stephen King's novel, I might have liked it more. But I think it fails miserably at being a good adaptation. It just wasn't King's book. Sometimes Frank Darabont's screenplays depart from King's original stories, but he does it in a way that either makes them work better as a movie or even improves on the original material to some extent. That's the difference between Frank and Kubrick.

What would you say is the main thing that sets King apart from other writers, such as Dean Koontz?

I think he's a better storyteller, which is not to take anything away from Dean Koontz, who's a friend of mine. I know both of them, but I think King is a better writer. His characterizations are a little better. He can write great characters without spending a lot of time writing about what they look like and what they're wearing. You kind of fill that in on your own. He moves the stories along, even if they're 900 pages or longer. He's able to tell you what you need to know in order to understand and enjoy the stories without slowing down the pacing of the novel. That's actually something that Koontz does, too. But King just does it better. Maybe it's because he dips into this shared well of popular culture that takes things that aren't particularly new—werewolves and rabid dogs—and gives them a twist that makes them new and refreshing.

He sketches in his characters fairly quickly, so that it doesn't slow the story down. Here's an example: In *The Sum of All Fears* (1991), Tom Clancy has this scene where there's a football game going on in the town. Outside, the bad guys have a dirty bomb they're going to set off. The readers know it's there, but the characters don't. Suspense builds up and the bomb goes off, and all of a sudden Clancy spends two-and-a-half pages explaining how a nuclear bomb goes off. He brings the narrative to a screeching halt! But King never does that. I think he knows what to leave out and what to leave in.

RICHARD CHIZMAR

Richard Chizmar established *Cemetery Dance* magazine while still in college in 1988. *Metro Silicon Valley* called *Cemetery Dance* "America's longest running independent horror-themed magazine." In 1992 the company expanded and began publishing books. Today *Cemetery Dance* is widely considered the world's leading specialty press publisher of horror and dark suspense. They are known for high quality hardcover releases and collectible limited edition volumes. They have published books by such respected authors as Stephen King, Richard Matheson, and Joe R. Lansdale.

Chizmar is a prolific writer, as well, having produced three short story collections. These include *Midnight Promises* (1996), *Monsters and Other Stories* (1998), and the much-acclaimed *A Long December* (2016). In addition to this, he has edited more than 30 anthologies and his fiction has appeared in such publications as *Ellery Queen's Mystery Magazine* and *The Year's 25 Finest Crime and Mystery Stories*. He has won two World Fantasy Awards, four International Horror Guild Awards, and the Horror Writer Association's Board of Trustee's Award.

Chizmar is also a recognized screenwriter, having written for (with partner Jonathan Schaech) projects as varied as the TV series *Fear Itself* (2009) and *Masters of Horror* (2007), as well as the feature film *Road House 2* (2006). Chizmar (with Schaech) has tackled two as-yet-unfilmed adaptations of Stephen King novels, *From a Buick 8* (2002) and *Black House* (2001).

In 2017, Chizmar began working on a novella with Stephen King and the two knocked out the work in a mere month. That project, the bestselling *Gwendy's Button Box* (2017), would ultimately elevate the writer's stature to new levels. In early 2018, Chizmar collaborated with his son, Billy Chizmar, on the novella *Widow's Point*.

Richard Chizmar

What was the first Stephen King book you read, and what were your thoughts on it?

Good question, and I should know the answer right off the top of my head, but I'm not sure. I think the first King book I read was *'Salem's Lot* (1975), and I fell in love with Steve's stuff right from the very beginning. It was different from anything I had read before. I can go back even further and say that when we read his short story "The Monkey" (1980) in my 10th grade English class, that's really the moment that changed my life. We took turns reading the story aloud in class. When we were finished it felt as though a door had been opened for me. I can't say I knew I wanted to be a writer at exactly that moment, but I knew that I wanted to be involved in the world of storytelling somehow. It really was a transformative moment for me where I just became hyper-aware that a person sitting at a desk with a pen in hand or a typewriter in front of them could do that—transport a reader to another place. It was King right from the very beginning for me.

You once said, "Stephen King is the reason Cemetery Dance *exists." Would you like to talk about that?*

The story I just told you was kind of the first thing I could point at to reinforce that quote. And the second thing is, when I was in college, I played lacrosse. I went to college on a lacrosse scholarship, so I was very much immersed in that world. I wasn't writing stories yet, even though I had written some earlier as a younger kid. I had gotten away from it because I was so busy between my studies and playing a college sport. But I had been battling through some injuries and my junior year I kind of decided that would be my last year. Lacrosse had stopped being fun for me. I was kind of lost. That had pretty much been my identity, being a student athlete. So when it stopped, I was kind of lost.

It was at that time that Stephen King's novel *It* (1986) was published. I remember reading that in my college apartment and not wanting it to end. I found myself just kind of parceling out the last couple hundred pages so it would last longer. It was a very similar experience to when I had read "The Monkey" in high school. That came along at exactly the right time for me. Something kind of clicked in my brain and it made me realize that I had more than college athletics to lean on.

Perspectives on Stephen King

Within a week or two I was writing for the school newspaper, and within a month of that I started writing fiction again. Within the year I was submitting my stories, and then the year after that I opened *Cemetery Dance*. Without Steve and his work, I'm not sure I would have ever started writing again. I don't know if I would have ever started *Cemetery Dance*. It's a scary thought for me because I think, wow, I guess life works that way sometimes; stepping stones fall into place at exactly the right time for a person.

You've long been on record as saying It was your favorite Stephen King novel. Nowadays more and more people are saying it may be his masterpiece. What are some things you most appreciate about that novel?

Everything. I'm one of those guys that even like the ending. I had never read a book at that point that had transported me across such a great timeline. I grew up in a small suburban town, so we had our own version of the barrens—a stretch of woods with a creek—and we spent endless summer days and evenings there. I've always liked coming-of-age–type books and movies. To me that's the ultimate one. The bulk of the first part of the book is them as adults, and then we go back to them as children. We kind of bounce back and forth.... It just captivated me from page one. I think it has some of King's scariest writing. I personally think he's probably written better books as far as looking at the maturity of the writing and the leanness of the prose.

I've heard him describe the book as being everything but the kitchen sink, and that's what it was for me. It was just, wow. My love for this stuff started at childhood. It started with my childhood friends whom I'm still close with today. So it kind of felt like that book was written for me. There are just so many scenes in that book that work perfectly for me. Still now when I read it, after countless readings, I can't read the scene in the canal where Pennywise is down there and the balloons are floating in the wrong direction. I read that and it still gets me even today.

What do you consider to be King's most underrated work, and why?

I've answered *Hearts in Atlantis* (1999) to that question before. I always think maybe *Hearts in Atlantis* just because the straight horror people have never fully embraced it because it's not terror-based. It's not flat-out scary stuff. It's almost mainstream writing in a lot of ways. I've told Steve this myself. I think the *Hearts in Atlantis* section from that book, where it describes the kids becoming obsessed with card playing and leaving school and getting drafted as a result, is some of his very, very best writing. I've always told him that I'd love to do a stage play even though I have no experience with that. I just think it's so powerful and poignant. So my vote goes to *Hearts in Atlantis* as far as what's underrated.

If I had to think of another one.... I like the *Dark Tower* stuff, and I was late to the game with that one. I didn't read that until sometime in the last seven or eight years. People were after me for years about that. "What do you mean you've read everything by King except the *Dark Tower* books?" I had tried the first one a couple of times and never could get into it, which is weird because I love westerns and I love King's work, so I know it's me. Finally I had Frank Darabont tell me, "Rich, you've got to read it." I finally sat down and read them all back to back and they were wonderful.

A book that's strongly related to that is *Insomnia* (1994). I know a lot of Stephen King fans didn't like it, but I love it. I love reading about the elderly characters. I love the connection to *The Dark Tower*, even though I had read *Insomnia* before *The Dark Tower*. But I think that's an underrated piece of writing of his, too.

What were your earliest interactions with King like?

My earliest interactions were always through his assistant Shirley, who was very good to me. I think via Shirley he gave us a promotional blurb for *Cemetery Dance* magazine. I think that was in year two or three, and it was wonderful. That definitely helped land us some legitimacy. Then I think the second interaction was when he gave us the short story "The Chattery Teeth" (1992) to publish in the magazine. That came from Chuck Verill, his literary agent, so I really had no direct contact there. I know after I read and accepted the story Steve left a message on my answering machine in my apartment way back then, saying how happy he was it was going to appear in *Cemetery Dance*. He said some very kind things. But, as luck would have it, I missed that call.

The first time I actually met Steve was when he invited my wife and I to his big 25th anniversary party in New York City celebrating the publication of *Carrie*. It was a pretty big event and we were surprised to get an invitation. I met Steve briefly there for the first time, and then it just kind of evolved from there. Like I said, my initial contacts were through

Shirley, his assistant, and then from Marsha and Julie, his assistants. He's always just been very gracious and very kind to me.

Then eventually over the years, as we started working on various books, once in a while I would speak to Steve. And then at some point we started e-mailing and again my wife and I were invited up to New York City when he received the National Book Award, which was great. I've since gotten the opportunity to visit with him at baseball games and things like that. At some point the business relationship turned into a friendship. It's been something that I really cherish.

You guys have exchanged e-mails for several years now. I was just curious, what does one of those typical e-mails look like? What kinds of stuff do you guys talk about?

Usually short and sharp and to the point. Often funny and often sarcastic. It just really depends. I mean, the subjects from our e-mails range from family to our dogs to books, movies, a lot of baseball. We take great personal delight when the other person's favorite team is getting their butts kicked. There's a little bit of politics thrown in now and then. Just mainly that type of thing. We e-mail quite often and it could be about any subject. I might send him a movie trailer. Then he'll respond with one of his own and say, "You've got to see this." Normal e-mails between two guys who have a lot of similar interests. We rarely talk about writing. I've always kind of stayed away from mixing business with pleasure, but at some point I started sending him some of my stories. I've always just said, "This one's fresh off the printer." He's sent me stories before that he sold elsewhere and said, "Have a look. What do you think?"

How did you guys end up collaborating on Gwendy's Button Box?

We were exchanging some e-mails like the ones we were just talking about. I brought up round-robin novels because of something we were doing in the office. I referenced these round-robin novels where you have anywhere between four and fifteen different writers contributing chapters or a few pages or whatever. Then we started talking about collaborations. This was in January. We were just talking. In the course of that conversation he mentioned that he had a story he had started the previous year that he had never been able to finish. I just said, "If you want to you can send it my way. I'd love to read it." And then we went on to e-mailing about other stuff.

Then, the next day, I got an e-mail with *Gwendy* attached. The only thing he wrote at the bottom of the e-mail was, "Do whatever you want with it." So I thought, oh boy. I was on my way to my son's ice hockey game. I read the partial that he'd sent me in the parking lot. I loved the character. I couldn't believe it was set in Castle Rock. I wrote him back and said, "I'd love to take a crack at finishing it. But I totally understand if that's not what you want." At that point I wasn't entirely sure what he was wanting. Then he wrote back and said, "Have at it."

We then spent the next month kind of sending drafts back and forth. I sat down immediately that next week and wrote a big chunk and I sent it off to him. Then he returned it right away with changes and a small chunk added to it. Then I tweaked what we had and added a small chunk. We did that three or four times, and exactly a month later we both kind of decided we were finished. Then we said, "What do we do now?" We talked about it and we decided we'd publish it in a somewhat similar fashion to the way we'd previously published *Blockade Billy* (2010). And that's how it came to be. The idea, the thought, the dream, began on January 3rd and then a month later we had this thing with both of our names on it. It was something I never dreamed possible.

The novella seems to owe a small debt to Richard Matheson's short story "Button, Button" (1970). What are your thoughts on that?

I'm a big fan of Richard Matheson and was fortunate enough to have published him several times when he was alive. He was a great guy and I had several phone conversations with him. Obviously this was kind of Steve's take on that story—kind of a more contemporary take—and I think "The Monkey's Paw" (1902) was another influence there. What's interesting to me is that there's a flicker of Matheson in there, but it's the kind of story I really like—a very small story that has very obvious potential global impact because of the power of this mysterious box. It's really just this small story about this teenage girl growing up in Castle Rock, Maine, and it's as much about the daily challenges that she faces as she grows up as it is anything else. I think that was kind of one of Steve's underlying messages there—when you put this kind of power in the hands of an everyday person, you really do have to just cross your fingers and pray that he or she does the right thing.

Was it at all difficult for you guys to write from the perspective of a 12-year-old girl?

No. You know what's interesting from that standpoint? I had never thought about it before, but when I was putting together my last collection, *A Long December,* and I was writing my story notes I realized that a couple of the stories that I really enjoyed working on were both written from a female perspective; one from a young lady and one from a teenage girl. I mentioned that to Steve because at some point a lot of the reviews started coming in and they were pretty universal in saying that you couldn't really figure out who wrote what. It was very seamless, which is something you're always aiming for in a collaboration. But it was not something that Steve and I ever had even one single conversation about, which led me to questioning after the fact. In reading all these reviews Steve actually mentioned to me that maybe the fact we were writing about a young girl allowed that to be even easier for us because we were coming from an outside perspective. There might have been a little bit more bumping heads if he was collaborating with a female because she would have been looking at it from a different perspective. But we both looked at it very similarly and it just all kind of flowed.

I love writing from Gwendy's perspective. That was the first thing for me is that I fell in love with the character. This was a very decent but human teenage girl growing up with all the strengths that any woman you know would have, but also the weaknesses that any human being would carry around with them.

Just to elaborate some: you look at it a little bit later and you're kind of gobsmacked. I never stopped and asked him, "Hey Steve, how did you know this would work?" He's read a lot of my short stories. I know he read a great chunk of my collection. We've e-mailed about various stories that have appeared in that book and some that haven't. So I knew he felt highly enough of me as a writer, but hey, he thinks highly of a lot of writers and he doesn't collaborate very often. But it never occurred to me, and it wasn't coming from a place of arrogance like, "Of course he felt comfortable w riting with me." It wasn't anything like that because initially I was terrified. I was like, what have I done? And even after I got past that I was thinking to myself, I'm going to send him this and he's going to hate it. Fortunately that didn't happen. I thought he might change his mind and decide he couldn't collaborate with me. "We're good friends, but I can't do that." So it wasn't coming from a place of supreme self-confidence on my part or anything like that. It just never occurred to me. I was so immersed in the process and honestly in kind of daze regarding what was happening. It never occurred to me to just say, "Hey Steve, how did you know this was going to work?"

Then we were doing an interview for Simon & Schuster's audio version and the very nice lady who was conducting the interview asked Steve the question. It was great because it was fascinating. But I hadn't thought of it. His answer was very straightforward. He said he'd just finished reading *A Long December*—the title novella from the collection. He said, "I'm a fan of Rich's work, but when I read this novella I really knew we shared a lot of the same sensibilities and I thought we would be a good match." It was a great compliment. It was just very eye-opening to me that I hadn't thought of the question myself. I'm not saying I would have asked him, but maybe I would have.... We are very honest with each other.

Was the Farris character always a manifestation of the R.F. character that appears in so many of King's books, or was that an idea that came up later on?

That was there from the very beginning. That was obviously Steve's.

That had to be fun for you, being a huge King aficionado.

Reading that on that very first day and kind of having the light bulb go off.... It was like, "Wow!" If you look at *Gwendy*, it says "Castle Rock" right in the very first sentence. That was the kicker for me. I could not help but stop and read that sentence over again. And yes, it really was Castle Rock. That and R.F. and the whole thing—it was just kind of a bonus.

You've stated that you originally came up with a darker ending to the novella. What can you tell me about that version of the story, and why did you guys ultimately decide to go a different route?

Again I'm going to pull you back to my collection *A Long December*. I promise I'm not trying to sell a couple more copies, but because of the story notes. Writing those story notes was such an eye-opening experience for me. You know, those stories were written over a period of 20 years, so my memories of them were fuzzy. If someone had sat me down before that and asked me to identify some consistent traits or messages throughout the stories I would have said, "A lot of them are more emotionally horror based. There's not a lot of graphic stuff. It's about family relationships and friendships and about secrets." And that would have been about it.

But writing those story notes and editing those stories all back to back, I realized there were all of these things.... A lot of the reviews mention surprise endings; those twist endings like in *The Twilight Zone* (1959). If someone had said, "You write twist endings," I would have been like, "No, no. I'm not very tricky like that." But then you read the stories and it's like, yeah, a lot of them have these last sentence or last page paragraphs that are just a zinger. That was one of those realizations. Then there was the fact that so many of my stories mention Winter's Run Creek or Hanson Creek—all those things I grew up near. That was a surprise.

So to go back to your question, one of the things I referenced several times in the story notes was that I felt like this character or that character deserved a better ending. But those are the places my mind goes. It tends to stay in the shadows. While I do have a lot of hopeful endings, many times it's hope mixed with real life kind of sadness or tragedy. And sometimes I would say, wow, I just really opted to go very dark there. It almost became a running joke.

So when I wrote the original ending of *Gwendy's Button Box*.... We took a free hand at editing each other and rewriting each other and it never amounted to more than a paragraph or some lines on a page. It was never very significant for either one of us. But we did have a free hand doing that. It was very open and trusting. When I sent him my original ending, it was very dark. The current version ends on kind of an open-ended type of ending with a whole lot more hope involved. Mine was open-ended, but with just a lot of darkness at either end. At the end of one tunnel was the destruction of the entire world—the black button—and at the other end was what was still a very unhappy ending for Gwendy. It was in the present. We didn't flash forward all the way through college. I sent it to Steve and I said, "Oh, boy, here's another one of those Chizmar endings where I particularly feel like our sweet Gwendy deserves a better ending." Steve wrote back and said, "I like it, but you might be right. Let's wait and see."

So we waited a few days and he said, "Let me try this and then you see what you think and you add your own flavor." So that's what he did. He wrote something that was close to what we have now, and I added in some flavoring and changed a few things, and it became one of the most collaborative parts of the book. It was something I was much happier with. Gwendy deserved to have some hope and happiness in her life and my ending just hadn't given her that.

Has there been any talk about you guys collaborating again one day?

We haven't talked about it. After years of people saying Steve should write a sequel to *'Salem's Lot* (1975), I've gotten so many comments that we should write a sequel. But I think I'm smart enough not to go to Steve and say, "There are a couple of thousand people out here who want a sequel." I'm sure he would probably just roll his eyes the way he did all those years when asked the same question about *'Salem's Lot* and *The Stand* (1978). But you know what? The project was so much fun that I'm sure at some point the idea will come up again. Whether it'll happen or not, who knows? He's so busy, I'm so busy. But we always have been and we still managed to do this and it was really smooth. There were no speed bumps or anything. There was no moment where we thought, uh oh, maybe we shouldn't be doing this. To me, there are no real-life restraints like that in the way. It would just be a matter of whether we stumble upon another story to do together. But as I always tell everyone, I'm in! So maybe one day.

Robin Furth

Raised in Upper Darby, Pennsylvania, Robin Furth always had a profound interest in fiction. She read authors as varied as C.S. Lewis and Stephen King, and aspired to be an author and a poet. She attended college at the University of Maine, where her studies focused on English and American fiction written between the end of the Victorian period and the end of World War I. While there, Furth studied under King's old friend and mentor, Burt Hatlen. While still a graduate student there, Furth landed a temporary job assisting Stephen King in sorting through thousands of responses he'd received for a short story competition he was holding. This brief stint eventually transformed into a job as King's personal research assistant, which she would do for the next five years. During that time, her primary focus was on crafting a detailed concordance that King could refer to for continuity purposes while working on the *Dark Tower* series. The work Furth had done for King eventually resulted in the book *The Dark Tower: A Complete Concordance* (2006), published by Scribner.

Furth was then hired (at King's suggestion) to plot and consult on Marvel Comics' *Dark Tower* graphic novel series. In 2009, Furth worked as a writer on the Del Rey Comics adaptation of King and Peter Straub's *The Talisman*. She would later work as a consultant on the Nikolaj Arcel-directed film adaptation of *The Dark Tower* (2017). Furth then published her second book, *Stephen King's The Bill Hodges Trilogy Concordance* (2017).

Do you remember your earliest interactions with Stephen King's writing, and if so, what were your thoughts on what you read?

I've always maintained that I became a fan of Stephen King's work when I was fourteen years old and read *'Salem's Lot* (1975), but actually my obsession with the King universe started much earlier. When I was eleven, my mom took me to see *Carrie* (1976). The film was rated R, so don't ask me what she was thinking; probably she really wanted to see the movie and couldn't get a babysitter. Anyway, I thought it was magnificent. I still remember sitting in the movie theater, watching Sue Snell placing flowers on the spot where Carrie's house once stood. When Carrie's blood-covered hand popped out of the wreckage, I screamed and jumped!

But more important than my reactions during the movie were my thoughts afterwards. I grew up in a family of hardcore rationalists. My father was a microbiologist, my grandfather was a pathologist, my grandmother was a pediatrician and my mother was a nurse. My parents were Quakers, less for religious reasons than for social and moral ones. (They were both pacifists and had demonstrated against the Vietnam War.) Although reading was strongly encouraged, realistic fiction was valued much more highly than sci-fi and fantasy. As you can imagine, as a dreamy kid fascinated by ghosts, vampires, telekinesis, telepathy, and any other weirdness you can think of, I often felt like I'd dropped from another planet. But what I saw on the screen that evening bespoke a world where the dream life was important, and where the powers of the untapped mind were potentially limitless, if also potentially lethal. Although I'd read plenty of ghost stories, I'd never read anything like *Carrie*. I remember standing in the parking lot after the movie ending and feeling such a rush of gratitude to the man who had written that story. For the first time in my life, I realized that there were other people like me in the world and I wasn't alone.

The second big King moment of my life came, as I've said before, the summer I turned fourteen. One of my older sister's friends—who was as big a bookworm as me—lent me a copy of *'Salem's Lot*. I *loved* it. I remember sitting in my grandparents' living room in Maine, reading after everyone else had gone to bed. It was dark outside and bats were flying past the window, nabbing the moths that were drawn to the light given off by my reading lamp. All of a sudden, as I was sitting there with the book on my lap and a blanket over my shoulders, I realized that Jerusalem's Lot wasn't all that far from where I was sitting. It scared me silly but it was great. What I continue to love so much about Steve King's fiction is that he is able to so seamlessly weave the mundane world we know so well with the supernatural, eerie, and downright bizarre. That is an amazing talent.

Perspectives on Stephen King

How did you ultimately become Stephen King's personal research assistant?

I started working for Stephen King while I was a graduate student at the University of Maine, back in 2000. It was the year after his terrible accident. At the time, Steve had already published *On Writing* (2000) and needed somebody to sort through the thousands of responses he'd gotten for his *On Writing* story competition. He wanted to help out a starving grad student so he contacted Burt Hatlen—one of my professors as well as one of Steve's old advisors—and asked him to recommend someone. Burt knew that I was a published poet, that I loved fantasy and sci-fi, and that I was a fan of Steve's work. Hence, he recommended me for the job. (I am forever in Burt Hatlen's debt.) That original project lasted about a month. I did most of my work from home, some from the King office, but all of my contact with Steve at that point was through e-mail. (Most of my work was with Steve's assistant, the wonderful Marsha DeFilippo.)

The job finished up on December 20, 2000, so I went to the King office to collect my final paycheck. It was snowing really hard, and I wasn't certain I would be able to make it to the office before it closed. To make matters worse, there had been a power cut in my town, so I hadn't had a real shower in days. (I felt pretty stinky.) Anyway, I managed to drive on the snowy roads and slid into the parking lot at about 4:28. (The office closed at 4:30.) With two minutes to spare, I ran inside.

You can imagine how shocked I was to see Stephen King sitting in the office, talking to Marsha. Meeting someone I admired so much would have made me tongue-tied under the best of circumstances, but the fact that I was also unwashed left me positively horrified. Lucky for me, Steve was very relaxed and didn't seem to even notice what a mess I was. As Marsha handed me my paycheck, Steve asked me if I wanted more work. He was about to return to the *Dark Tower* series and needed someone to write up lists of characters and places and record the pages on which they could be found. (He wanted to be able to double-check for plot and character continuity—no small job for such a large body of work.) Anyway, when Steve asked whether I was interested in the job I said yes. (Of course!) Then he asked me if I had read the series. Much to my mortification, I had to admit that I hadn't.

Steve wasn't fazed at all. He gave me copies of the four published books as well as a quick rundown about Roland. I started reading them as soon as I got home and was entranced. From that first sentence, "The man in black fled across the desert, and the gunslinger followed," I was hooked. I suppose I am quite an obsessive person, and unbeknownst to Steve at the time, I always secretly wanted to be a folklorist. Not only did I keep track of all the *Dark Tower* characters and places, but I gave each an encyclopedic entry, and made lists of Mid-World games, diseases, gods, lore, and even Mid-World languages. Then I drew a magical door labeled "THE AUTHOR" at the front, so that Steve could re-enter his world, then I bound the whole thing in black and taped a key to the front so that Steve would be able to open the door into Mid-World that I'd drawn for him. I thought that either Steve would find my enthusiasm humorous or he would think I was a crackpot. Luckily for me, he found it humorous. In fact, he liked it so much that he asked me if I would like to continue building my Concordance (as he called it). From then on, Steve gave me chunks of his manuscript as he wrote and I continued to build my Concordance, tracking the histories of characters, baronies, and multiple worlds. I feel incredibly lucky to have been invited to take part in such a magical journey. I think Steve found my work especially helpful since his *Dark Tower* universe was so vast and since it had been written over more than three decades.

What can you tell me about the construction of the Concordance?
Every week I'd go to the office and pick up Steve's most recent *Dark Tower* chapters. I'd read them through once and then back through about six times each, noting page references for characters, places, language, and history, jotting down notes to myself so that I could expand my written entries. I didn't do any computer searches—the chapters I had were hard copies. Besides, using computer searches you miss subtle meanings and indirect references. Every page reference you find in my Concordance was logged in one of an endless pile of spiral bound notebooks and legal pads. I also kept track of things like doorways-between-worlds and magical objects. Because of this I more or less memorized the entire series. I knew characters' backstories, their family trees, their beliefs. I think this helped a lot since I could catch very minute continuity issues. I also drew maps of landscapes and in a couple of instances had to redirect Roland or his ka-mates! (And by the way, when my Concordance was accepted for publication, I re-indexed the whole series for Scribner so that my pages matched their hardback books as well as the trade paperback versions of

the early novels. I then re-indexed the entire series for the UK edition of the Concordance!)

Sometimes Steve would ask very particular and very surprising continuity questions. Some of them were real brain-teasers that sounded straightforward but actually proved to be incredibly complex. For example, one day I got an e-mail that said, "What does Jake Chambers have in his backpack?" Such a question might sound simple, but in truth, to discover the answer meant rereading each and every book, paying particular attention to Jake's backpack. I had to mark every time he opened his bag, every time he closed it, every time he picked something up and toyed with taking the object with him. I even had to pay attention to any time that backpack was lost, just in case someone else slipped something inside.

Between 2001 and 2003 I researched many strange and wonderful things, from the cost of cab fare in New York City in 1964 to what kind of weaponry and body armor Roland's ka-tet might be able to amass if they jaunted back to our version of earth. (I still fear that I might be on a watch list somewhere thanks to that particular bit of research!) One of my favorite jobs was learning how to tan animal hides without any modern equipment. (If you ever want to learn to make a brain slurry, just let me know.)

What made working for Steve so interesting was that my assignments weren't limited to *Dark Tower*. I researched cell phones for *Cell* (2006), and the Dillinger gang for "The Death of Jack Hamilton" (2001). One of the most haunting bits of research I did was for Stephen King and Peter Straub's joint novel, *Black House* (2001). Steve sent me to the New York Public Library to find articles about the trial and execution of the 1930s child killer and cannibal, Albert Fish. (And by the way, Fish's favorite dish to feast on was little boys' bottoms.) As you can imagine, I had some pretty lively nightmares while finishing up that bit of work!

As you know, the Randall Flagg character makes appearances in many King works, always with the initials "R.F." You, Robin Furth, are an R.F. yourself. Are you Randall Flagg?

Roland's nemesis, Randall Flagg, Rudin Filaro, R.F., most certainly shares my initials. Luckily, we are not the same person. (Or at least I don't think we are....) Isn't it a strange coincidence? To tell you the truth, I sometimes think I got my job because of my initials. (It must have surprised Stephen King to find out that the person Burt Hatlen recommended to him was Roland's old nemesis in disguise....) But seriously, there are still a few *Dark Tower* fans out there who don't realize that I'm a real person. They think that Steve King made me up.

But he didn't?

Well, actually he did... [Laughs.]

Are there any aspects of King's work that you have come to appreciate or admire more as a result of your working with him?

Wow. There are so many things. I am constantly amazed by Steve King's fluency with story and with language. While he was writing *Wolves of the Calla* (2003), *Song of Susannah* (2004), and *The Dark Tower* (2004), I picked up his output at the end of each week so that I could continue building my *Dark Tower* Concordance. (I picked them up from the King office, not from his house!)

Those manuscripts were incredibly clean! The language was beautiful and the story was complete. After the manuscripts went to his editors there were a few changes. For example, Steve had to rejig his map of the Fedic Dogan, and the Crimson King lost his cameo spider appearance (I must say, I was sad to see that go), but otherwise, what I got was what remained in the final books.

Stephen King works hard, but that is because he is so incredibly imaginative. He writes every single day and the stories just pour out of him. While we were working together in Mid-World we were both quite literally living there. Although he was one of the world's most famous authors and I was an unknown writer living in a trailer in Maine, in Mid-World, we were equals. We were Roland's traveling companions, and for us, that world was utterly alive and real.

Another thing I admire about Steve King is his generosity. He is incredibly supportive of other writers, and he funds endless local Maine projects. He and his wife Tabby have built library extensions in Bangor, funded small literary presses, saved old movie theaters, built hospital wings, provided grants for writers and artists facing huge medical bills, backed college scholarships and given money to create public parks and baseball fields.

Steve and Tabby grew up broke, and they haven't forgotten what it's like to have no money. What is even more admirable is that they are very quiet about their gifts. They don't make much fanfare about the good causes they support, they just quietly make their donations. The State of Maine is a poor state, and if you live there I can guarantee that Stephen King has touched your life and made it better, whether you know it or not.

What was your reaction to being hired to write and sort of oversee the Dark Tower *graphic novels?*

Co-writing and acting as series consultant for the *Dark Tower* graphic novels was a *huge* responsibility, and to tell the truth I was really surprised when it happened. During Stephen King's initial meeting with Marvel, I was on a phone link. It had already been decided that I would be a consultant for the series, since I'd been working with Steve in Mid-World for so many years. Then midway through discussion and negotiation, Steve said that he wanted me to be a co-writer. I was so taken aback that my first words were, "No, I can't!" And Steve King said, "Yes, you can!" In the end, I was so glad that he had more faith in me than I did. I absolutely loved working on those graphic novels. It was one of the best experiences of my life and I learned so much about the art of storytelling. I've always loved graphic fiction, so to be able to take part in such an important venture was incredible.

What were some of the difficulties you faced in trying to tell these stories?

The biggest problem I faced when transforming Stephen King's *Wizard and Glass* (1997) into graphic novel form was that I had to take this huge, wonderful, complicated book and boil it down to seven issues. As you know, moving from novel to graphic novel is an act of translation, since a story previously told in words alone now has to be told in words and images, though the images are foremost. Originally, I broke the story into eight issues and then Marvel said they wanted me to squeeze the story into six. In the end, we settled for seven.

For the later *Dark Tower* comics, the biggest challenge was remaining true to Steve King's vision. *The Gunslinger Born* (2007) was a straight adaptation of a *Dark Tower* novel, but for the other comics, Marvel wanted new and original material to weave through the stories that longtime fans already knew. Being asked to add to the universe of an author you love is incredibly scary. Luckily, I was able to mine the many seed stories that Roland shares over the course of the series. By seed stories, I mean those little glimpses you get into his past, and into his many adventures. Being able to flesh those seed stories out was an amazing experience.

Robin Furth

It must have been quite a bit of fun having the opportunity to delve in and explore those "seed stories."

Looking back, I realize that I spent about twelve years co-writing the Marvel *Dark Tower* comics. Even though the first comics weren't published until 2007, we started work back in 2005. That's a hell of a long time! To tell the truth, between traveling with Steve King through Mid-World and creating the Concordance, co-writing the *Dark Tower* comics, and working as a consultant on the recent *Dark Tower* film (as well as on Universal's proposed film which never came to fruition), I sometimes think that I remember the events of Roland's life better than I remember my own. That's a pretty scary thing to admit, but it's actually true.

Tell me about your role in the development of the Dark Tower *(2017) movie.*

It sounds kind of funny, but my involvement with the *Dark Tower* film began with an e-mail. I already knew that MRC was interested in making the film and that Nik Arcel—a director I greatly admire—had been hired to direct. I thought that the project sounded wonderful, but I wasn't initially involved in the loop of it all. Then one day I checked my e-mail and there was a note from Nik Arcel. At first I thought it was an advert for one of his films. As I said, I've been a fan of his films for many years.... I almost deleted it. Thank God I didn't! My involvement with the film began as a series of e-mails between me and Nik, talking about Mid-World. After a couple of months, Nik got me involved as a consultant for other aspects of the film. My job was really to give background information on Mid-World and on characters/costumes/landscape, etc., as needed. I was also involved with Sony and with the creation of fun, fan-based Internet outreaches such as the SHINE test. I really wanted fans to be able to test themselves for the Shine—or the Touch as it's called in Mid-World—so I was thrilled when that test went live.

A lot of fans were disappointed with the Dark Tower *film. While I understand some of the reasons for this, I think it was sort of baked into this particular cake. I don't think there was any version of that series that could have completely satisfied fans.*

Personally, I really loved the *Dark Tower* film. It was different from the novels, but I felt that it captured the feel of Mid-World and the energy of Roland's quest. I also thought that Idris Elba did a great job as Roland and Tom Taylor was absolutely fantastic as Jake. Matthew McConaughey played Walter with humor and style. Choosing to make a sequel to the series rather than beginning with an adaptation of *The Gunslinger* (1982) was a risky venture, but I'm glad they did it. In years to come, I think that film will be appreciated a lot more and will finally get its due.

Your most recent book on King's work was The Bill Hodges Concordance. *How would you assess the Bill Hodges trilogy? As you know, there are critics who say King has recycled a lot of previous themes and motifs in those books.*

I really enjoyed the Bill Hodges trilogy and building that Concordance was great fun. I even ended up creating entries for all of the serial killers that are mentioned in the first novel. Talk about giving yourself nightmares! I really liked the fact that Steve King moved into thriller and suspense again, since I think he is really skilled in those genres. I also love the fact that the Bill Hodges books begin with thriller/suspense and then move into the realm of the supernatural.

In the Bill Hodges trilogy, King played with many of the themes and images from his supernatural novels, but I love that kind of cross-pollination and I think a lot of other King fans do too. Brady Hartsfeld—the Mercedes Killer—is a monster, so isn't it fitting that he almost begins to meld with the monsters of our shared dream-world?

How do you believe history will look back on King and his literary legacy?

Stephen King has earned his place in literary history, and as far as I'm concerned he's right up there with Poe, H.P. Lovecraft, and Shirley Jackson. I don't think that anyone can predict what future readers will value most, but his literary output has been so vast and so diverse that it will contain something for everyone. Unlike any other contemporary writer, Stephen King has defined the horror novel. His characters and hauntings—from Pennywise to the Overlook Hotel, and from the super flu to Carrie—have molded the nightmares of several generations. What more of a lasting influence can any writer hope for?

LEE GAMBIN

Hailing from Melbourne, Australia, Lee Gambin is a noted writer, author, and film historian with a focus on the horror genre. He has written for a number of publications including *Fangoria*, *Scream*, and *Diabolique*, where he serves as an editor. He also runs the Melbourne-based film society Cinemaniacs and lectures on film studies.

In 2012, Gambin wrote his first book, *Massacred by Mother Nature: Exploring the Natural Horror Film*. The book, published by Midnight Marquee Press, examines the subgenre of ecologically-themed horror films, such as *Jaws* (1975) or *Cujo* (1983). The book dissected fundamental stock standards of the subgenre, offering anecdotes, critique of specific narrative devices, and analysis of performance, audience appreciation, and filmmaking craft. Gambin's second book was *We Can Be Who We Are: Movie Musicals from the 1970s* (2015), which focused on films like *Phantom of the Paradise* (1974), *Saturday Night Fever* (1977), and *The Rocky Horror Picture Show* (1975).

For his third book, Gambin would return to the subject of the ecologically-themed horror film with a thorough examination of the underappreciated Stephen King adaptation *Cujo*. "I think it's essential to balance idiosyncratic analytical thought and film criticism with a heavy emphasis on production history," Gambin told *Four Three Film*. "I will always champion the voice of people who worked on these films: they deserve to be heard. As a film historian and devotee to cinema, I always approach the artists who were involved—and that is part of the fun." Based on interviews with everyone from director Lewis Teague to actor Danny Pintauro, Gambin's thoroughly researched and meticulously detailed *Nope, Nothing Wrong Here: The Making of Cujo* (2017) would receive critical praise from just about every horror publication and website in existence, as well as a Rondo Hatton Award nomination for Book of the Year.

At the time of this writing, Gambin was hard at work on similar volumes dedicated to the making of John Carpenter's King adaptation *Christine* (1983) and Joe Dante's *The Howling* (1981).

Do you remember your earliest brushes with the work of Stephen King?

There were two pivotal moments. One of them was the movie *Carrie* (1976) and the other was the novel *'Salem's Lot* (1975). I was very young when I saw *Carrie*, probably four or five. I remember Channel Seven here in Melbourne aired it, and I remember being drawn in straight away, right from the opening sequence with the girls in the shower room. There was this beautiful sort of maudlin music, and I remember being like, "What the hell is this film?" Then all the chaos starts to happen and Sissy Spacek starts to bleed and all the girls turn on her like a lynching.... I was just instantly attached. Stephen King started out as a film thing for me as opposed to the books, which came later. After watching *Carrie* and being able to stay up for the whole thing—I was very lucky because I was allowed to watch whatever I wanted, which is great—I really got into horror.

Then I went in my early teens and read all the books, or at least most of them. As far as *'Salem's Lot*, it's become one of those things I go back and reread or at least read passages from every year. I think it's one of the best works of horror fiction ever written. I remember my grandmother lived next door to a place that had been abandoned. The guy who had lived there had been taken away to an asylum, and his house was just sitting there disheveled. So me and some cousins went there and snuck in to see the place, and lo and behold there was a copy of *'Salem's Lot* on the floor. It was the one with the girl on the cover with the blood dribbling out of her lips. So I grabbed it, and I was hooked. Absolutely hooked. It's the only novel I've ever read and turned around in shock and had goose bumps. I don't really get scared, per se; the real world scares me, but horror films don't. I remember reading the part where Mike Ryerson is found in his rocking chair, and I was like, "Fuck. That's really creepy."

So for me, those are the two big discoveries regarding Stephen King. And I became addicted. *Cujo* became a favorite; *The Dead Zone* (1979);

Firestarter (1980); all of that stuff from the early period. Then in the late eighties when I was renting videos I would always rent all the Stephen King adaptations. I remember when *Pet Sematary* (1989) came out as a film. That was a big deal for me. *Misery* (1987) was a massive deal. The love of Stephen King was definitely a formative thing for me. It helped me cultivate my love of books and films and horror.

What are some elements you most appreciate about Stephen King's work?

What I love is his understanding of character. He really understands people. He understands the human condition, and he understands character. That is definitely his strongest point. He writes really rich characters, and regardless of whether they're leading roles or just characters who pepper his little towns, they're all really well-structured characters. And he complicates them. For instance in *Christine* with the character of Dennis Guilder, he's another sympathetic jock character. That's something you never really got in the history of literature or film. With Tommy Ross in *Carrie*, you've got the same deal. He gives them depth instead of just making them cardboard cutout two-dimensional characters. He enriches them with characteristics that make them very, very real and very human. I think that's amazing.

I also really appreciate the way he deconstructs things that are supposed to be benign institutions. For instance, he turns America's prom into a hell on earth in *Carrie*. And the love affair between people and their automobiles becomes this sort of perverse, sick sort of obsession in *Christine*. On top of that he does this beautiful stuff where he captures character dynamics and relationships. Like in *Firestarter*, which is essentially about a father and his daughter; a father who will do anything for his daughter.

I love that. I feel like King really loves kids and elderly people, although he definitely does not like religious zealots. They're always fucked up. [Laughs.] He does this fatherly puppeteering with his characters that's really lovely to observe. It's like Carrie White's mother. If you look at it, she really does love her daughter. It's like a Rapunzel thing where she doesn't want her daughter to be hurt by the outside world. That's wonderful and something that should be treasured about his writing.

You wrote a book titled Massacred by Mother Nature: Exploring the Natural Horror Film. *That was sort of a precursor to your book about Cujo.*

What do you think it is about nature-themed horror that appeals to audiences? What is its appeal for you?

That's a loaded question because there are lots of answers there. I'm always championing that horror is not one specific thing; horror is a vast thing that has spawned a lot of subgenres. I believe that people who say they don't like horror are actually morons because they don't really recognize the complexity and diversity of the genre. In saying that, eco-horror is one of my absolute favorite subgenres. I just gravitated toward the notion that animals will attack humans. As an animal lover, I love the idea that animals will get their revenge on humans that have done them wrong. Or maybe they'll just straight out kill them. I think that's a guilty pleasure, watching for that aspect.

Growing up and starting to write film criticism, I started to pay attention to tropes in eco-horror films. So the seed to write this book was beginning to take shape. I realized that there was always an innocent character who would be killed off in the first scene. There would almost always be government officials who would turn a blind eye. There would be haunted policemen. There would be sympathetic specialist women who would come in and talk about how well they knew the animal. All these character tropes were happening and I saw all these connective tissues linking these movies.

Then I saw different trends in eco-horror. In the early days, movies like *Frogs* were all about environmentalism and pollution. Then you get to the late seventies and early eighties and it becomes more interpersonal and about character. You had *Cujo*, which is basically a family melodrama with a rabid dog. That stuff is personally very interesting to me and I absolutely love it. I love the idea of animals acting in response to different character situations. In *Orca* (1977) you basically have a haunted seabee who does the whale wrong, and then the whale avenges his partner's death. Then countering that you've got *Nightwing* (1979), which is basically about Native American Indians having to deal with a white settlement and having to coexist. Then you have this religious leader controlling bats to spread around the bubonic plague. It's sort of this political and social message film. I love that aspect of ecological horror. It's a subgenre I really responded to.

Have you always been a fan of Cujo, *and do you consider it to be an underappreciated film?*

I loved it from the first time I saw it on television. Then I stole the video from a local video shop and kept it. I think it's a perfect film. It's definitely one of the best King adaptations. It's tight. It's strong. It moves swiftly and it has a really lean story. King's novel itself was also very lean. I would love to have seen what Peter Medak, the original director, had in store for it while using Barbara Turner's original screenplay before it was turned over to Don Carlos Dunaway. But Lewis Teague's film is incredible. He does a beautiful job. A lot of Barbara Turner's script is still in the movie, thank God. The siege sequence was all her. You forget that writers are actually writing action sequences, as well. I love that movie very much.

It's definitely underappreciated. I think people write too much about *Carrie* and *The Shining* (1980). Even things like *The Shawshank Redemption* (1994), which I don't really have much of an affinity for. Maybe it's because it's not horror. But I love *Cujo*. I think it's a smart novel, and I think it's a smart film. King says he wrote it because he was addled or whatever, but I really don't think I believe that. And if he was, well, then he did a fantastic job! It's extraordinary. The book is just so rich and beautiful. It's profound and moving. It's got this sort of somber tone. It's all about their domestic unrest and also commerce in Reagan era America. It's an incredible story, just the idea that this dog becoming rabid sort of justifies this family falling apart.

I have to commend you on your book, Nope, Nothing Wrong Here: The Making of Cujo. *I don't think I've ever seen such participation in a non-official movie book. You managed to interview just about everyone conceivable. That hardly ever happens on these types of projects.*

Thank you. That's very kind of you to say. I don't go in half-assed. I like to go in and go crazy. I remember when DVDs started in the late nineties, one thing I really loved, aside from being able to see the films in their proper ratio and without pan-and-scan tracking, was that they loaded these with supplementary material and documentaries. I thought, "This is incredible." I felt like this was what should happen in books. If you're going to do a making-of book or a critical assessment book, do all of it. Get as many people as you can. Take the time and give it the justice it deserves.

So with *Cujo*, I wanted to go out and get as many people as I could. Being the kind of completist that I am, it really irks me that there are a couple of people missing. But I tried. [Laughs.] Dee Wallace was an easy one. Lewis Teague, as well. But then there were these amazing stories of how I got certain people. For instance, Gary Morgan, who was a stunt guy who wore the dog costume—I got him through Barry Pearl. I had done a book on seventies' movie musicals in 2015 and I had covered *Grease* (1978). Barry Pearl, who was Doody in *Grease*, seems to know everyone in Hollywood. I asked him if he knew the producer of *Cujo* because he had also done *Grease*, and he said, "He's off the radar. I don't really talk to him, but I know Gary Morgan, who was the dog." I said, "What?" So there was this beautiful kind of connection there between my musicals book and the *Cujo* project. Then it turned out that Gary Morgan was actually Shelley Winters' son in *Pete's Dragon* (1977), which I also covered in the musicals book. I thought all those connective tissues were amazing. Then it went from there to Jean Coulter, the stunt double who lost her nose in one of the stunts. I got Danny Pintauro, I got Danny Pintauro's parents. Robert Clark and Kathie Clark, who built the animatronic dogs. I got Therese Ann Miller, who's the daughter of the late great animal trainer Karl Lewis Miller. They all shared photos, they shared experiences. It was great.

As far as my approach, I feel it's very important to marry film journalism and film criticism. I feel like that's your job when you write something like this. You kind of do analytical writing, which is where you have your own idiosyncratic thoughts and feelings about the film, and then you need to provide a platform for people to talk about the actual production itself. I've interviewed lots of people throughout my career, and when people hear your criticism and analytical insight into the way they read, and they agree with you, it's quite interesting. Or maybe they say, "I've never thought about that in that way." Or they just completely disagree, which is also fine. Everyone's got a different opinion, and that's cool. But as a film writer, you should try to marry those things because it's important in a book like that. Anyway, that's what I was attempting with the *Cujo* book, and hopefully it achieves that.

You've read Stephen King's original unproduced screenplay for Cujo. *What are your thoughts on that, as opposed to what ended up in the film?*

He was first hired by Warner Bros. to adapt the screenplay. One significant change is that it opened differently. It opened with the Trentons watching a slideshow in their living room. And Cujo has already made an impression because he's in the slides. We'd already met him. His script had a lot more of the friendship between Cujo and the Cambers. The script was, I think, a little bit convoluted. It's sort of all over the place. It ends with Vic having plans to sue Charity Camber for not vaccinating the dog. There's a lot of stuff that relates to the Sharp Cereal campaign. There's one great scene that I wish was in the film, which is the little girl vomiting up what she believes is blood but is really food dye. It sort of moves into Vic Trenton's dilemma of having to deal with the Sharp Cereal campaign, instead of what's in the film, which is sort of an economically-written script where you just have a journalist talking about how scared people are around Castle Rock. In the King version, there's a mom on the phone and she's talking to a friend, and all of a sudden this kid is vomiting up blood in the bathroom. It's sort of a shock thing.

Beyond that, the script really is a bit convoluted. There's some stuff in there involving the small town people, but there's nothing really in there relating to *The Dead Zone* (1979). In Barbara Turner's script, she really played on the idea of the dog being a reincarnation of Frank Dodd, who is the psychotic killer in *The Dead Zone*. But that was all pushed aside in subsequent drafts of the script as well. It's very interesting to look at the progression of the filmic transition in adaptation. Like in *Christine*, one of the main things is the character of Roland LeBay, the former owner of the car, not being in the car anymore. In the book he's sort of this E.C. Comics–style decaying corpse sitting in the back seat and influencing Arnie. But in Carpenter's adaptation, he decided to keep the car at the forefront. I think that's much better and much stronger.

Your next book is going to be about the making of Christine. *What do you have planned for that one?*

You can expect the same treatment as the *Cujo* book. It's going to be loaded with interviews. I've got John Carpenter, cinematographer Donald M. Morgan, Alexandra Paul, Keith Gordon. I'm about to contact Roy Arbogast, who did the special effects on the film. There will be a whole bunch of people. Again there will be a scene-by-scene breakdown and analysis, all loaded with quotes. I've gotten lots of great photos already. Also, the producer, Richard Kobritz, who was the producer who is amazing and who also produced *'Salem's Lot*, sent me a lot of never-before-seen photos. It should be a very nice companion piece to the *Cujo* book.

Perspectives on Stephen King

What are some other Stephen King films that you feel are underrated?

Underrated as far as critics go, I would say all of them. [Laughs.] As far as fans go, I really, really like *Pet Sematary*. I wish there were some story elements that had been changed in it. One of the main things that irks me in that is the character of Ellie's sudden ESP. Also, I don't care for the Pascow character. I don't like him as this friendly helper character. But ultimately I think Mary Lambert's vision, as well as the mood of it, is great. Fred Gwynne is just outstanding. I love him. The score is just gorgeous, the look and feel of it.

I really love the first part of the *It* miniseries. I know people poo-poo it, but I really love all the kid stuff. I think it's really moving and touching and sweet. I think King really understands kids. I also really enjoyed *Silver Bullet* (1985). I produced some featurettes for the Blu-ray, so I just re-watched it recently. It's a really fun watch. I like that King uses the werewolf as a sort of moral judgment. The reverend is a werewolf killing off people who are sinners. I find that quite interesting, because it goes back to that recurrence of these corrupt religious characters in King's stories.

You know what I really love that's underrated? *Sleepwalkers* (1992). I think that's a lot of fun. It has that fantastic finale with Alice Krige.... It's just so demented and fun. And I love Mick Garris. I think he's one of the nicest, smartest filmmakers. His film knowledge is insane. As much as he is an epic filmmaker and storyteller, he's an incredibly important film historian. What he knows about film is incredible. He's just this incredible fount of knowledge, as well as a great support for other artists. I don't like to use the word community, because I don't really believe in community, but in this world of horror film folk there's just so much support. There are really only a couple of people that I won't mention that aren't that nice, but the rest of us are really lovely and support one another. I think that's fantastic.

It seems like a lot of Stephen King projects that have potential turn out to be bad movies. Why do you think that is?

There's nothing problematic with the writing of the novels. What happens is, a lot of the stories don't really have clear endings as far as what a screenwriter thinks is a clear ending. So when you look at one of his books and it doesn't really end the way someone would end a film, I think problems start to arise. I think things get lost in translation. What I've found is that a lot of King adaptations start really strong. They start so strong that you don't know where it's going to go. You're so invested in the first two acts that you're inevitably let down in the third act because the screenwriter or the producer often doesn't know how to handle that. That open ending in a novel works, that ambiguity, because it leaves the reader wanting more. But with the films a clear ending is more frequently required, and that can be a problem. There are a lot of problems with endings in Stephen King adaptations. Look at *Children of the Corn* (1984), which I love and think has some good qualities. It has an ending that should have been something different. In fact, it would have actually been better if the adults had been killed. But people don't want to see that, which is why they saved Tad in *Cujo*. I think that's often a problem when the ending of the original work is interpretive rather than clear cut.

Zak Hilditch

Perth, Australia, native Zak Hilditch dreamed of becoming a professional screenwriter and director. He spent almost a decade fashioning short films and trying to get his name out there. He spent this time developing his craft as both a writer and director. During this time he came close to landing several feature directorial jobs, only to see them fall through at the end of the day. Finally, Hilditch's struggle paid off, and he made his writing and directing feature debut with the apocalyptic thriller *These Final Hours* (2013). The film received glowing reviews and screened at the Cannes Film Festival. Since then, there have been talks with Hilditch to helm an American remake.

Hilditch began reading Stephen King at the age of eleven, and quickly became a fan. Many years later he would read King's novella collection *Full Dark, No Stars* (2010). When he did, he would find himself particularly impressed by the collection's first novella, *1922*. The novella, about a father and son who conspire to murder the family matriarch, has been described as a "Midwestern riff on Edgar Allan Poe's *The Tell-Tale Heart*" (Tasha Robinson, *The Verge*). Hilditch wanted his second feature to be an adaptation of the novella, and he eventually found funding to make it for Netflix. "I never thought in a million years that I'd be the one to do *1922*," he says. "The planets aligned, and I was the one who was given the opportunity to do it."

Hilditch's *1922* (2017) would star Thomas Jane, who'd previously appeared in the King adaptations *Dreamcatcher* (2003) and *The Mist* (2007). The film would be released on October 20, 2017. It would receive critical acclaim, and King himself would praise the film and help to promote it.

Zak Hilditch

You first discovered Stephen King when you read It (1986) *at the age of eleven. What do you remember about that, and what was your reaction to what you'd read?*

I watched the miniseries and I wanted to know more, so then I followed up by reading the book. Reading the book was quite the epic journey! [Laughs.] Then after that, I guess I just led myself down a path of King. I started watching and reading anything I could get my hands on.

What stood out to you when you first read that novel that made you decide to read more of King's work?

Those were some of the first things I'd both seen and read, and I came to realize how completely different those two things can be. That blew my mind, because I was absolutely obsessed with the miniseries, being a kid who loved movies. I had the movie on VHS and I would watch it with my friends, and we could all quote the thing by heart. Then reading the book it was like, "Wow, this is actually very different!" That was the first time I'd ever considered and actually realized what an adaptation was. It's such a wild story. It's a very dense book for an eleven year old. [Chuckles.] I had to sort of commit to that.

I think Stephen King just has a way of getting under his characters' skin. That was again the case with *1922*, which was why I really felt like it was something that needed to be made into a film.

When did you first read that novella, and what elements of it really spoke to you?

It had honestly been a while since I'd read any King, and I was trying to get financing for this Australian film called *These Final Hours*. My producer and I had sort of done everything we could at that point, so we were just kind of waiting for the governing bodies here in Australia to give us the green light. I was just kind of sitting on my hands. I don't remember how I stumbled across *Full Dark, No Stars*, but I thought the cover was striking with the girl all contorted with the red letters and the black background. And *Full Dark, No Stars* is one of the most badass titles I've ever heard in my life. I was like, "Oh, wow, a collection of four novellas by Stephen King!" This sounded like the sort of thing I should devour right then. I bought it and I opened up the book, and the first story was *1922*. It just completely transported me to another place and time. It kind of took my mind off the fretting I was doing, waiting to hear if our film was going to be financed or not. When I finished the novella I thought, Frank Darabont is gonna make this into a great movie one day! [Laughs.] I wonder who's gonna play Will? Then I went on and made my film *These Final Hours*, and that opened up doors for me in the U.S., and I got agents over there. So when it came time to find my next project, my mind kept coming back to *1922*. I started looking around. "Does anyone have the rights to this? Is anyone planning to make it?" It was such an obscure King title that no one even knew what the hell I was talking about. So I just sort of swept in and got my hands on it. I'd never done an adaptation before, and this was a great one for me to learn how to do that given that it's just in Will's head the whole time. And those are my favorite kinds of movies—ones that are told from a particular point of view, from a single person's narrative. It worked really well, and King's novella was just written in such a cinematic way. It was a pretty quick period of time that I was playing around with it and adapting it into a screenplay.

I sort of get obsessed with things when I fall in love with them, and with *1922*, once I got the go-ahead to adapt it, I just immersed myself in that world of the Depression era of the 1920s and 1930s, and that whole Americana vibe. I surrounded myself with as many images and whatnot from that time as I could. This was my first crack at adapting another writer's work, and I had a lot of fun doing it.

When you were adapting the novella, what were some of the challenges you faced?

Nothing, really. King's story was pretty much written for my sensibilities as a filmmaker, so that's why I fell in love with it. It sort of took it to other levels.

You know what was probably one of the biggest challenges? How we were going to handle Arlette's return with all the rats. In the story, she is literally surfing on a sea of rats. The way King describes this nightmare vision that Harlan has of this visit is the big climax crescendo of the movie. It's just so chilling. But we didn't have a crazy amount of money to make this movie with, but I really wanted to do this story justice when it came to the bigger horror elements that inevitably evolve. I had to be very specific about the decisions I made, given that they're going to be timely and costly. "How do we strip things back but still retain that sense of horror?"

But with Molly Parker, a lot of it was done in her performance. Once you put the makeup on her, she just did it in an almost sexy kind of way when she comes down the stairs; she's a ghoul, but this is his wife. There used to be something there between these two, and the way she sort of fucks with him is really interesting. And that was just sort of something that happened on the day. Molly was kind of playing around with ideas.

I guess the main challenge was just doing the really big horror elements and doing the story justice. As far as doing horror, this was my first horror film. So I was trying to figure out the rules and also figure out how to make things as creepy and full of dread as possible. This isn't a film full of jump-scares. This is a film about a very slow-burning psychological horror, which is the sort of horror I enjoy watching.

Another challenge was replicating 1920s Nebraska in Vancouver in 2017. That was no easy feat either. But we had a really great crew, and they were all very excited about working on this King film. They were all pushing themselves and trying their hardest to make the best film possible.

Molly Parker really is incredible in the film. But then, truthfully, all the actors are.

She was my first pick. We didn't go to any other actress. The weird thing is, she actually grew up in Langley, which is the area where we shot the film. Not only is she Canadian, but she actually grew up in that area. But she was the very first actress that came to mind, and she said yes, which I couldn't believe. And she got a kick out of it because she'd never done a horror film before, so she wanted to know what it was like with all that shit on her face, sitting there in that chair. She just wanted to experience that. However, I don't know if she'll ever do another one. [Laughs.] But she really went the extra mile for us on this.

I read that Tom Jane was actually your first choice for his role, as well. What was it about Tom Jane that made you say, "This is the guy"?

I didn't really write Wilfred with anyone in mind in particular. So when it came time to start having meetings, he was the very first actor I had a meeting with. He responded immediately to the material. We had a lunch, and I sat down across from him. He just pleaded his case and explained how much he really wanted to do it. He understood the character, and he was determined to do it. And right then I realized I was sitting across from Wilfred. I could just see it, the way he talked about farming and what it was like to be on the land, and how everything moves at its own pace. Sitting across from him I realized that all of the work was already done. I knew this was someone I could trust with this material. He got it, and he was so passionate about exploring his character. It made my life a lot easier, knowing that there was someone who absolutely *was* Will.

This was Tom Jane's third Stephen King adaptation. Is he a big fan of King's work, or does he just keep getting these roles by chance?

He really digs King, but it's just a wacky coincidence that he's now done three of these films. He doesn't really go out of his way to pursue King material. I think it's more of a coincidence than anything else. But yes, he does love the writing of Stephen King. He's attracted to dark subject matter, as am I. He really responded to this material in a big way.

One thing that's interesting about 1922 *is that it actually ties in with some of the other works that you mentioned. For instance, Mother Abagail from* The Stand *goes to Hemingford Home, where* 1922 *takes place. It also has ties to* It, *because the Ben Hanscom character eventually moves to Hemingford Home as an adult. Did that excite you to be making something that's a part of that same universe?*

It was exciting. If you had told eleven-year-old me that one day he was going to make a Stephen King movie, I would not have believed you. I'm still pinching myself that I got *paid* to make a Stephen King movie. And I'm pretty proud of it. I think it turned out pretty well. It achieved everything I set out to do, which was sort of a slow burn psychological examination of this amazingly-rich King character, Wilfred James. But yes, those were nice little Easter eggs, having it be loosely linked to those stories, although once you're immersed in the story, you don't really give those things a second thought. But it is a cool thing to have it in that zeitgeist.

Your film was one of four Stephen King movies that were released in 2017. One of those was the remake of It. *As a movie buff and also a fan of the original miniseries, what were your thoughts on the newest adaptation?*

I really dug it. When I heard they were going to adapt *It* again, I thought, you can't out-Curry Tim Curry. [Laughs.] But then, sure enough, they made this newest version of the film and the character Pennywise something new and fresh. That Bill Skarsgaard guy.... Just from that opening sewer scene I was like, "Oh, shit, this is gonna be pretty incredible!" I guess his performance—just every time Pennywise was on the screen—was my favorite part of the movie. I thought that everything he brought to that role, just that whole creation, the performance, the lazy eye, the whole thing, was just wonderful. His drool…. His entire performance was just done so well.

You've talked about both Frank Darabont and Tom Jane, so I have to ask: what were your thoughts on the ending of The Mist (2007)? *As you know, it really made a lot fans angry. I personally believe it's brilliant, but that's just one opinion.*

That visceral experience of *The Mist*—you don't see it coming. You don't think it's going to go down this godless path, and then it does all of a sudden. [Laughs.] Hats off to Frank Darabont. It would have been very easy not to have done that. And the fact that it added that little kick in the gut certainly does what good horror should do, which is to horrify. In that sense, I think it was a good call.

As you know, Stephen King praised Tom Jane's performance in your film.

King has been a great champion of both myself and this movie, from day one. I've never spoken to the man, and I've never corresponded with him, but through his interviews and through Twitter he's expressed that he's a big fan of *1922*. And that means a lot. Even showing him a rough cut, he was very positive about it. His feedback was "yep, keep on keepin' on." It was great. He's very hands-off when he lets his babies go out into the world, and I think he was just really happy that this was one of the films that turned out well.

He actually compared the movie to There Will Be Blood *(2007), which is remarkably high praise.*

There was a lot of *There Will Be Blood* blood in this film. That was obviously another big influence on everything. That's how I saw the movie, but then we added our own element to that. We actually used *There Will Be Blood* music in the temp score when we were editing. That movie resonated a lot with me, so I thought him saying that was really great.

From a filmmaker's perspective, what are some of the other King adaptations that most resonate with you?

The Shining (1980) was a huge influence on *1922*. I love *Misery* (1990).

Misery is the kind of movie that, whenever it comes on TV, you have to watch it again—at least a little bit. But then you end up watching the whole thing again. *Shawshank Redemption* (1994) is another one. What's interesting is that I think there are elements of all three of those films in *1922*. My favorite King adaptations kind of found their way, through osmosis, into *1922*.

I was also obsessed with *The Stand* (1994) miniseries as a kid. I must have watched that thing a million times, as well. I'm kind of excited; there's been some talk of them doing a *Stand* remake. I think that would be incredible to watch.

Let's talk about the music in the film. Mike Patton's score for 1922 *was sublime. It just keeps ratcheting up that sense of dread. It's just so effective.*

I worked really closely with Mike once it was time to focus on the score, so we spent a few months with me in Perth and him in San Francisco, just going back and forth and working on each cue as we needed to. He just came up with some amazing stuff. Hats off to him. He's a musical genius, and I just love that we basically went in with the idea of antique psychedelia, and I think it's exactly that. I definitely wanted Mike to bring his own craziness to it, and he did that in spades. It's a very unique score. It definitely feels like a Mike Patton score, but kind of a different take on a Mike Patton musical arrangement. It definitely elevates everything in the film.

As we mentioned previously, 2017 was a big year for Stephen King movies. There were four King adaptations released in the past year. With an 86 percent on Rotten Tomatoes, your movie beats out two of them and comes pretty close to the other. That must be satisfying for you as a filmmaker.

Oh yeah, it was a crazy year for sure. Who knew that between the films and the television series there would be six or seven Stephen King properties coming out all at the same time? It's crazy to have come out around the same time as *It* and *Gerald's Game* (2017). Those two were, I think, the two that really took everyone's attention. I kind of feel like we were the Little Engine That Could. We just sort of went out there and did our own thing, and it's great that it's on Netflix because there are lots of people discovering it on a daily basis. It's kind of a slow burn where every day there are more and more people who are becoming aware of the movie.

Zak Hilditch

Your film came out on Netflix almost immediately after Gerald's Game. *Did that intimidate you at all? Was there ever a sense of competition where you felt like you had to have a really strong product in able to compete?*

Not really, because you're just so busy trying to get the movie finished in time. And I always knew that *Gerald's Game* and *1922* were going to be a sort of double header and that they were coming out at roughly the same time. Even down at Fantastic Fest in Austin, where we both premiered.... I got to meet Mike Flanagan, and he was just a really lovely guy. Having the opportunity to watch *Gerald's Game* at the Alamo Drafthouse when no one had seen it before was terrific. Experiencing that de-gloving scene with a packed audience was unlike anything I had ever experienced before. People were losing their fucking minds. It was really great to be able to be there and witness that. After that initial screening, it's up to people in their own living rooms to experience that. To have seen it in a group like that was a great experience.

C. Courtney Joyner

C. Courtney Joyner grew up just outside Pittsburgh, Pennsylvania, an avid reader of both comics and novels, and he was a voracious film viewer from an early age. His tastes in all these areas ran the gamut, but he turned frequently to crime novels and lurid pulp paperbacks. He longed to work in the film industry, and ultimately succeeded in doing so. His work in film began with his appearing as an extra in the films *Dawn of the Dead* (1978) and *Murphy's Law* (1986). He got his first screenwriting credit—the first of more than twenty—on the cult shocker *From a Whisper to a Scream* (1987), starring Vincent Price. He then wrote the screenplay for Renny Harlin's *Prison* (1987). He followed that up with *Vietnam, Texas* (1990), *Class of 1999* (1990), and *Doctor Mordrid* (1992), before making his directorial debut with the Charles Band-produced *Trancers III* (1992).

Two years later Joyner would write and direct the H.P. Lovecraft adaptation *Lurking Fear* (1994). He would dabble in video game and animation writing for a bit, while still churning out screenplay after screenplay. He frequently collaborated with both Charles Band and *Firestarter* (1984) helmer Mark L. Lester. Joyner's subsequent screenplays include *Public Enemies* (1996), *The Base: Guilty as Charged* (2000), and *Stealing Candy* (2003). He also wrote for the short-lived William Shatner–hosted television series *Full Moon Fright Night* (2002) and directed a vignette in the anthology film *Tomb of Terror* (2004).

A member of the Western Writers of America, the Horror Writers Association, and the International Thriller Writers, Joyner has written his fair share of short stories, novels, and non-fiction books. He has been nominated for the Peacemaker Award twice for his short stories. His has written for numerous publications including *Famous Monsters of Filmland*, *Fangoria*, and *Cinema Retro*, and his nonfiction output includes *The*

C. Courtney Joyner

Westerners: Interviews with Actors, Producers and Writers (2009) and *Warner Bros. Fantastic: A Guide to the Studio's Horror, Science Fiction and Fantasy Films* (2012). His novels include the popular *Shotgun* western series and the *20,000 Leagues Under the Sea* sequel *Nemo Rising* (2017). He has also worked on several comic books and wrote the graphic novel *The Saga of Billy the Kid* (2012).

I understand Stephen King's writing played an instrumental role in your ultimately becoming a novelist yourself. Would you like to talk about that?

Even without cracking a single Stephen King novel, to deny his influence on horror—on popular literature of the time—is to deny the air around us. The first King novel I ever read was a dog-eared paperback of *Carrie* (1974), with that fold-in cover, that I snatched from my sister's bureau.

I was fourteen, and not a reader of novels for pleasure, because I hadn't grown into it; the books we plowed around for English lit class were of a different stripe—*A Separate Peace* (1959) and *The Good Earth* (1931)—so when I went to the paperback racks at my drug store, picking up *Conan* or *Doc Savage*, or a movie or TV tie-in—lots of *Rat Patrol* (1966)—because I loved the covers, and would read a few paragraphs here and there, then open an issue of *Vampirella*, and drool.

Robert E. Howard and Edgar Rice Burroughs would sink in, through scattered pages, Frazetta paintings, and comic adaptations, but it was piecemeal absorption of fantasy, science fiction, and horror writing, before I ever attacked the original books full-on.

The first novels I ever read completely—just because I wanted to—were *The Barbarous Coast* (1959) by Ross McDonald and *Valdez Is Coming* (1970) by Elmore Leonard; strictly cops and cowboys. And then *Carrie*.

Until I'd taken in King's prose—I hadn't read any of the short stories—what I was used to was "classic" horror, short stories in Alfred Hitchcock collections; or, a real favorite was *The Ghouls*, offered by the Science Fiction Book Club, with all the short stories that inspired movies. So I'd read Bloch, Lovecraft, and Poe. Small dollops—including poetry—and none of them wrote the way my friends and I talked. I was used to the formality of the Gothic tradition, no matter if it was coming to me from Universal or Hammer Films, or an issue of *Creepy*, there seemed to be rules to the storytelling, and with King, I didn't find any. He was writing as if I was yakking with a buddy about monster movies who suddenly launched into a scary story.

That was the eye-opener, and brought me to horror literature in a new way. But, I didn't always follow King. There was so much, the output so huge, I couldn't keep up—especially if I wanted to get anything down on paper myself.

And the movies? *Carrie, The Dead Zone* (1983), *Creepshow* (1982), *Misery* (1990), *Stand By Me* (1986), *The Shawshank Redemption* (1994), *Apt Pupil* (1998), *1408* (2007), *Christine* (1983), and Tobe Hooper's miniseries of *'Salem's Lot* (1979). Those are the ones that immediately come to mind—that were just what I needed to see when I saw them—and we could add others, including some of the biggies, but I loved this bunch of flicks. And there are some doozies, too...

As the years moved on, for King's writing I drifted towards *The Green Mile* (1996) and other works, even as I didn't get through *The Tommyknockers* (1987). With *Mile*, he also tried a new way of publishing, and I admired that.

Lots of King books, lots of King movies, running the gamut of quality. But, I was still drawn to crime, and Westerns—so I loved it when King wrote for Hard Case Crime.

The influence on writing? It was everywhere, in every bookstore, on every screen, and King wasn't the only one, but that first exposure to his style showed me a different way to put down horror; to write about people who lived down the street, or worked at the burger joint. King brought horror home. But, with it all, ultimately, it is his non-fiction book *On Writing* that I return to the most. I was steeped in screenplays when it came out, lots of movies behind me, but it's one of the best essays on the writing process I've ever read, because there are no quick fixes in its pages. Just experience from an astonishingly successful author. It's just the way he did it; revealing his own basics of structure, what he liked and hated, favorite films, favorite writers, and most importantly, how he's shifted his own focus and interests over the years, especially after the terrible accident, when he found the strength to heal, and write. A lot.

But how did he write all of this? Informally. Like we were sharing a couple of beers, and the talked turned to favorite books, then authors, another round of drinks, and finally, to writing. The kind of talk you have after midnight, and I devoured every word.

For me, Stephen King took the pretense out of authorship, and by so doing, encouraged writers. Of all kinds, in all genres. He let the rest of us think that maybe, just maybe, with hard work and a sense of purpose, we could write a novel, too.

If that's not inspiration, I don't know what is.

As an accomplished author yourself, what do you see as being King's primary strengths? Would you like to talk a little bit about that?

Growth. King established himself with horror—becoming an icon—and although he returns to the genre, he moved away from it, to create different, personal works. Expanding. Of course, he had the money and reputation to do it, but I believe he would have done it anyway. He needs to explore.

Elmore Leonard started with great Westerns before finding a voice in the streets of Detroit. James Clavell was banging out scripts for Lippert Pictures, focusing on screenwriting, before devoting himself to *Shogun* (1975). Remember when John Jakes was writing *Brak the Barbarian* (1968) before he took on epic history? It's always great to have this commercial success, but to move beyond it, going into writing areas that aren't keeping with your established image, that's tremendous, and tremendously inspiring.

What are your favorite Stephen King works?

My favorite King novel is *The Stand* (1978). It's an epic achievement; even with the works outside of horror, this remains an incredible feat of structure and pure writing skill.

As for the movies.... As we said, there are lots to choose from, so to narrow it down might be tough. The DeLaurentiis period's pretty tough sledding, but I'll always love *The Dead Zone* (1983). *Creepshow* remains a great King/Romero collaboration. I also like *The Dark Half* (1993). *1408* was a great little surprise—and also, King is sometimes best when he is adapted by someone else, like William Goldman's gorgeous script for *Misery* (1990). Also, it's great that he gives filmmakers the chance to adapt his short stories, to show what they can do; that's a real commitment to filmmaking and filmmakers. The King catalog is so huge, the favorites really do shift around, depending on what's grabbed from the shelf, or pulled from behind the couch cushions. Recently, I was taken away by *The Mist* (2007), when I sat down with the black-and-white version, and what I saw was—*horror*.

When you mentioned the King film adaptations, you referred to some of the lesser ones as "the doozies." As an experienced screenwriter yourself, what do you think are the biggest reasons for the failures of so many of these films?

That's a tough one because the making of any movie is a singular experience unto itself, and all sorts of factors come into play that can really affect whether it turns out well or not. But the amount of work involved is always tremendous, starting with the crafting of a screenplay. But, that special alchemy, that lightning strike, when a movie is really great is about the hardest thing in the world to achieve. This is why great movies are so rare, but good ones happen frequently when hands come together with talent and experience.

I'm kind of old fashioned, but that's why I love so many of the flicks—all genres, all sorts, and all budgets—made by the old studio systems. People knew what they were doing, and came together and applied that experience to everything from Universal horror to an MGM musical. I guess this finally leads us to your question…

I think the best of the King adaptations, for me, always started with a screenwriter who understood the attitude of King's story, and that's often a veteran. Not just getting the structure—we all know book adaptations sometimes have to take liberties with original material, compacting chapters, making cuts, etc.—but the attitude of the piece, especially from someone who puts it into his prose the way that King does, is vitally important to a good adaptation to film. That attitude is King's alchemy; his word choices. His defiance—but to do it for film. Capture that and I think you capture King, and the skill to do that well comes from screenwriting experience. Turning pages into film.

Interestingly, King himself had to get a few scripts under his belt to do his own best work for film and TV, even his own adaptations. We saw the learning curve.

I thought Brandon Boyce did a great job on *Apt Pupil*, and he wrote it when he was a newbie, but he really caught the King feel, and from one of his works that didn't have extreme violence or horror; it was the horror carried around inside the characters. That's a tough thing to dramatize, and I think *Apt Pupil* did it beautifully, and the movie was made in the right way—small and sinister and disturbing.

Jeff Boam? Wonderful work on *The Dead Zone* for Cronenberg, which is certainly the best of the Dino flicks. But, I'll admit, that for most of the Stephen King films, I'll always lean toward the screenwriters with miles and miles of film behind them as the writers who did some of the best King adaptations. Not all, but most. And there are a hell of a lot of movies.

Paul Monash's work, adapting George Higgins' *The Friends of Eddie Coyle* (1972) was brilliant, as was his miniseries of *'Salem's Lot*. A vet from the 1950s, and some of the best TV, he made such dynamic and dramatic choices, and really brought the spirit of King's work forward. And amazingly, this was for TV. Probably the best overall script that Tobe Hooper ever had to work with (and yeah, I know what I'm including).

And then there's *Misery*. There are few screenwriters with the pedigree of writing brilliant adaptations as William Goldman. *Harper* (1966), *All the President's Men* (1976), *The Right Stuff* (1983), and also taking his own stuff that he wrote first as novels and then turning them into films, gives Goldman a remarkable skill set. And record. Cranking the tension he did on *Misery*, while being so careful with King's characters, and keeping them true to King's original pages.

I love what Lawrence Cohen did with *Carrie*, finding a way to keep the tone in synch with King, but also DePalma, with the major change from the novel being the ending and the death of Carrie's mom. Some brilliant choices were made and executed by top filmmakers, and it all felt like Stephen King; even the filmmakers' inventions, just as it should.

The glories of *The Shining* (1980) are so extraordinary, and so soaring, but they feel to me more like what Kubrick did once behind the camera, rather than his work with Diane Johnson. But that was a first impression when I saw the film in its opening week. Of course, the film haunts, and stays, and rises again; flashes of imagery that have now become iconic horror images. It's as if we can't unsee what Kubrick shows us at the Overlook, and that power, the sense of dread that won't leave us no matter what the film's failings, makes it one of the great adaptations.

Of course Stephen King has been critical, and reassessed, and changed his mind, to dismiss, then honor, all the movies made from his work, including the ones he wrote himself. So, perhaps we're all in the same boat, trying to nail down the King favorites, or the best, because judgment about horror can be such a liquid, changing thing.

You've worked quite a bit as a screenwriter with Mark Lester, who directed Firestarter. *It's been years since I've talked to Lester, but he had some very "interesting" things to say about King. Did you guys ever talk about his work on that film?*

Actually, not very much. I think Mark was a little disappointed that King took after *Firestarter* the way that he did, because he felt they had a good relationship when the movie was being made. Mark's an action director, and that was the approach that was taken with the material. Popcorn time, with very little darkness to it, which it could have used. But, drive-in popcorn time. I honestly do think that Mark's own *Truck Stop Women* (1974) was an inspiration—certainly a fuse-lighter—for *Maximum Overdrive* (1983) (along with a zillion other movies, but I bet it was in the King rotation).

Stanley Mann was still involved with Lester when I first worked for Mark, and we talked about *Firestarter* a bit. I loved Stanley, and he was a top-flight writer. *Theater of Blood* (1973), *The Mark* (1961), and adapting *Eye of the Needle* (1981)? Big stuff. But he also wrote *Meteor* (1979) and the *Conan* sequels. Still, an old school pro, and he was very happy that King's reaction to the script was so positive. In fact, King had said he loved the idea that Stanley had Charlie making toast with her powers, and wished he'd included that in his book. Sadly, the final movie changed his opinion, which is understandable in a lot of ways, but I think Stanley was bothered by the change of heart. Still, they were all working for Dino DeLaurentiis, and Dino stayed in the Stephen King business for a long time.

In your Shotgun *novels, you updated the familiar trope of the crippled warrior found heavily in Asian films and movies like* Rolling Thunder *(1977). King also does this; taking familiar themes and tropes and updating them in new and refreshing ways.*

The crippled warrior is one of the great visuals, on film or on the page. I've always loved it, and have always been drawn to it, because it puts the hero at a disadvantage. He'll always be the man with one arm or one leg, who can't fight his own fights, and then, *wham!* He comes back with more ferocity than his opponents. They're old tropes, but they have instant conflict and drama. I think that's why Stephen King is also attracted to these things. Besides, when these things work, they're very cool.

You've written a lot of film analysis and about the history of cinema. What are your thoughts on King's Danse Macabre *(1981), which focuses on his own cinematic and literary influences in great detail? That seems like something that would be right up your alley.*

I love *Danse Macabre* because, like his book on writing, it's written in such an informal style, but gives us the insight into King's inspirations and influences, and he wanders around in his opinions, does some exploring, like a really good interview. Very open. Just talking horror movies with a buddy, and some opinions you agree with, and others…. Jesus, you have to be kidding! That thing sucked!

JOE R. LANSDALE

Joe R. Lansdale has written more than forty novels and thirty short story collections in a variety of genres, including Western, horror, suspense, crime, and science fiction. He has also written chapbooks, comic book adaptations, and worked on *Batman: The Animated Series* (1992). Lansdale is perhaps best known for his offbeat Bram Stoker Award nominated novella *Bubba Ho-Tep* (1994). The novella, which depicts Elvis Presley and John F. Kennedy battling an undead mummy in a nursing home, was later adapted into a successful film by Don Coscarelli of *Phantasm* (1979) fame.

He is also the author of the bestselling *Hap and Leonard* series, which (to date) includes nine novels, three novellas, and three short story collections. The crime series, which focuses on the exploits of best friends and private investigators Hap Collins and Leonard Pine, has also been adapted into the popular Sundance television series starring James Purefoy and Michael K. Williams.

Lansdale has won an impressive ten Bram Stoker Awards and has been nominated for another nine. He has also received the American Mystery Award, the Horror Critics Award, and the "Shot in the Dark" International Crime Writers Award. In 2011, he received the Bram Stoker Award for Lifetime Achievement and in 2012 he was inducted into the Texas Literary Hall of Fame. He has been nominated for the World Fantasy Award eleven times.

Lansdale continues to churn out books at the speed of light. In addition to his usual output of novels and short stories, he published the memoir *Miracles Ain't What They Used to Be (*2016).

Joe R. Lansdale

You once said, "Stephen King was the first writer I read that I felt was of my generation. He had similar experiences so many of us had. He had grown up on the same music, books, magazines, television shows and films, and he had a natural conversationalist style." Would you like to talk a little bit about that?

I had read other writers who had either written about our generation, or at least appealed to our generation, like Kurt Vonnegut. When I read Stephen King, I had this unique feeling of, "Yeah, I was there, too. I lived through those same events." I knew what it was like in the late sixties, early seventies. When we refer to the sixties, that actually goes until about 1974. Really, when the Vietnam War ended, there was a switch in the way people were seeing and dealing with things.

When I read Stephen, he had that kind of style that felt like people just sitting around and talking and having a good time. He was also a regional author. Although his region was very different from mine in many ways, there were other ways they were very much alike. People have a misunderstanding about all of this; rural places have their own rednecks everywhere, and they also have their own sort of folklore and wisdom. All of those things that were in Stephen's writing appealed to me, and I think it's probably how people felt about Mark Twain when they were reading him in their own time. They were thinking, "This is the guy from our time that writes about our time." They probably didn't get all of the satire and the different things he was doing, but they at least felt comfortable reading him. And he kind of has that way—well, both King and Twain—of making you comfortable with them even when you disagree with them.

I always felt that if I had any strength at all it was in writing about my background and my region. The kind of writers who have always appealed to me were conversational and it was the kind of thing that made me feel that I was on the right track. We do very different kinds of work, but I'm a great admirer of his. The early novels and some of the later novels are among my favorites, but I always loved the fact he was willing to go out there and try different things. I always felt like having "horror writer" as a handle is nothing to be ashamed of, but it's not entirely applicable to Stephen King—he's a writer with many different talents.

In the 1970s, you were a struggling author working a full-time job as a janitor and occasionally selling short stories to the pulp markets. This is very much like Stephen King's story around that same period. Do you feel a sort of kinship with King because of that?

I was kind of late to the Stephen King party to tell you the truth. In the seventies I had read *Carrie* (1974). I liked it, but it kind of hit me in a funny way because it was so unlike all of the other so-called genre novels at the time. I liked it, but I didn't know what to make of it then because I wasn't as experienced a reader back then. I didn't really get started reading Stephen King until the late seventies, early eighties. I think he had been around since the mid-seventies. I had been aware of him then, but suddenly there was a boom of his stuff in the late seventies and early eighties. I became aware of what he was doing and it took me a while to arrive there. But as he began to talk in some of his introductions about his past, I found that I related to him.

Neither him nor I really published in the pulp magazines—in the strict sense—because they had died out long before he and I were writing. But we wrote for pulp-like magazines. I wrote for *Mike Shayne Mystery Magazine*. I wrote for a couple of skin mags under pen names. I had no idea the extent of his background previous, but he had been around for a while just like I had. When I discovered that, I found more of a kinship to his background and to his work.

From the perspective of an author who has written your fair share of horror short stories, what are your thoughts on King's short work? Do you have any favorites that stand out?

I love King's short stories. You know, I really love all the ones in *Night Shift* (1978). They were very much of the pulp era. The thing is, he and I both grew up on things like *Thriller* (1960), which was a TV show that was based on the pulps. And we probably both grew up reading old anthologies of stories from the pulps. But by the time his second collection came out, he had transitioned from the pulps. Looking at the bookends of his career, which is very similar to my own, is that the early stuff is the best of the pulp ideas sort of transitioning into the digest-type stories. Then when you get into *Skeleton Crew*, I think he had had enough experience and success that he was more comfortable writing the more personal stories.

I think one good thing that made his pulp stories stand out is that there was a personal experience feel to them no matter how outrageous they were. He knew the people of which he spoke, he knew the places he wrote about, and I think that's always been a key for King. If I have any attribute of my own, I think it's feeling like I have a sense of place and knowing my characters. If you really know your characters and your places and you have a style that is somehow able to make people comfortable, they'll believe most anything. That's what you're trying to do—you're trying to make the reader believe the absurd by writing in such a way that it makes sense and seems common.

You mentioned King's sometimes writing about the absurd. One thing that has always impressed me about King is his balls-out audaciousness, whether it's something absurd like a killer car, or telling a story from a dog's point of view, or killing off a beloved child character like he did in Pet Sematary *(1983).*

Those are all things I've done, as well! [Laughs.] I admire it, you know? I feel a kinship to him more than I feel an influence. I feel like we were kind of coming along in the same way at the same time. I was impressed with that. I wrote a lot of short audacious stories like that, and I'm sure he's made me feel comfortable enough to do it. I think his work has influenced me in that way. His work said, "You can write about where you come from, you can be audacious, you are of that same era." I was born in 1951, so I'm a little bit younger than Stephen King. "You can bring all of those elements to your work and it will stand." And that's exactly what I did. I owe him for the security that his work gave me to do that. Before I read Stephen King, I was already writing and selling my work, but his stuff said to me, "Guess what? You're wanting to write about your own region? I'm doing that and it's working." That's the main thing I got from his work. I think it gave me the comfort zone to pursue the things I wanted to do.

Speaking of comfort zones, like King, you're a writer who isn't afraid to use profanity when you deem it necessary. Do you feel that Stephen King played a role in making that kind of vernacular more acceptable to a mainstream audience?

He may have, although a lot of mainstream I had read—like King I was influenced by both the pulps and mainstream—a lot of the writers who wrote in the era following Hemingway did that. Guys like Henry Miller. But I think he introduced a lot of genre writers to that. Before that, a lot of genre fiction was written for a juvenile audience. Science fiction, fantasy, and horror... a large percentage of it was written for 12-year-old boys.

I also think it's a generational thing. I think those of us who were coming up during that time were more open to that kind of language. I think it was a more provocative period where we were trying to break barriers. And in some ways I think we overdid it. I think so much of the youth background that was trying to change things got caught up in trying to use the word fuck than with things like women's rights and those sorts of things. I think that may have affected that negatively. But I think it changed the way people spoke, but I think sometimes you can also lose the impact behind certain words by overusing them. They no longer have the impact they once had. So it's a trade off. But I think that people in our era—in King's era—were already loosening up in regards to that anyway, and it was bound to seep over into genre fiction.

You once observed, "I think Stephen King has a tremendous voice. That's his biggest asset." Would you like to talk about that?

Well, I think it goes back to that conversational style. And Stephen King writes with a confidence. He writes with a "I'm putting this out here and you can take it or leave it" mentality. That appealed to me. I think there were many writers from our generation who were doing that—guys like Hunter Thompson and Kurt Vonnegut—but his voice is so powerful, it has such an impact.... It's so courageous.

A lot of people coming along now can't remember or understand the impact that Stephen King had on not only popular fiction, but on fiction itself. He actually changed the way books were published after that, both negatively and positively. He doesn't need to take blame for the negative aspects, but he can certainly take joy from the more positive ones. All of a sudden every publisher wanted to have their own Stephen King. People now wanted bestsellers or near-bestsellers and that's all they wanted. Every publishing house had its own horror writer who specialized in that. Most of them did not have King's staying power or his ability. It's been many years since he first impacted the publishing industry and he's still going strong. And that voice is what carried him through.

A lot of people keep returning to his work. Stephen King once said something that I completely disagree with. He said, "It's not the storyteller—it's the story." No, it's the storyteller. It's just like telling a joke. Some people can tell a good one, and some people can't. The people who have the biggest impact are actually the storytellers. They can make a banal story seem interesting. Look at John D. McDonald, who could make a banal story magnificent just with his style and his conviction. I disagree with Stephen on that. I don't believe it's the story, it's the storyteller. And that's not to make the story seem less important, because it is important. But a storyteller can take something like *Huckleberry Finn* (1884), which is all over the place and goes everywhere, and it's brilliant because of Mark Twain's voice and his characters and his ability to keep you engaged. Otherwise it's just a boat trip down the river.

I believe you excel in two areas where King frankly struggles—crafting well-drawn, multi-dimensional black characters, and writing engaging dialogue. How do you think King manages to not only succeed as a writer, but often times really hit that big homerun ball despite his shortcomings?

Because the other things are so strong. We all have shortcomings. I'm not great at scope. That's one thing Stephen can really do well. If you take something like *'Salem's Lot* (1975) or *The Shining* (1977), even though they're isolated to a town or a hotel, there's this feeling of scope—this sort of great map that's out there. I think he writes conversational, real dialogue most of the time. But dialogue is one of those things that, for me, I'm not necessarily trying to write the way people actually talk. I'm trying to give the illusion of the way people talk. And I'm heavily influenced by the old novelists and the films of the thirties and the forties. People had snappy dialogue and a great exit line. That's important to me.

As far as writing black characters, I think I may have an advantage in that I grew up in the South and I was around a large number of black people. It's one of those things where I had constant awareness and constant association. I was involved in being a voice for civil rights. Being in the South and having this different attitude put me in a different place. And also being poor like a lot of black people in the South were, I saw the connection there. I think it may well be that. Because there's no way I could write New Englanders. If King and I both saw country people where we were from, we would see tremendous similarities between them. But there are certain aspects about where these people are from that I wouldn't get, just the same as there would be certain aspects of the people where

Perspectives on Stephen King

I'm from that King wouldn't get. I think that's a lot of it—proximity. There aren't as many blacks in Maine as there are in the South.

Don Coscarelli once called you "the Texas Stephen King." What do you think about that?

I love Stephen, but I don't like that label. I think the reason I don't like it is because I don't want to be Stephen King. I want to be Joe Lansdale. We do our own thing. It's a compliment and I accept it as that, but it's limiting. I've been compared to everybody. It's the funniest thing. I have a list. Part of it is because certain novels echo certain other kinds of novels. If I write Southern Gothic I'm going to be compared to Flannery O'Connor or William Faulkner. I've read them both and I don't doubt that they've been influences, but by the same token I've read Stephen King, but I also read lots of horror fiction as a child. I get those kinds of compliments, but I don't like those types of limitations. I write like Joe Lansdale and he's who I am most like.

You write in a lot of different genres, which I think keeps you from being pigeonholed as a "horror writer" or a "crime writer." As you know, King has been nailed with that "horror writer" label despite the fact that he's written in a lot of different genres. Is that something you consciously wanted to avoid?

Absolutely. I didn't want that. There's a plus to that tag, and there's also a negative. The plus is that people recognize you for doing a certain thing that they want and they return to it. I think Stephen King has written plenty of other types of stories, but he got tagged so early in his career with that label. I think one thing that saved me from that is because a lot of my horror is short stories rather than long-form novels. In the eighties there was a group that came to be known as splatterpunk, and I was briefly tagged with that label. But I always hated it. I refused to accept it as a label, and to this day when someone mentions it I say, "I hate that." I love my friend David Schow who invented that term, but I've always hated that moniker. I think it's destroyed a number of people's careers or put them in a position where they weren't able to transition to other things.

But I was writing novels like *Cold in July* (1989) and the *Hap and Leonard* series, as well as a tremendous number of short stories that were not horror. So there are some people who loved the horror fiction early on who do not read my other stuff. They have tagged me with that label. I do return to horror fiction frequently. I haven't been labeled as heavily as King has. It might have been better to have been either a horror writer or a crime writer in terms of the market, but I've had tremendous success. But the most important thing to me is that I have been able to do exactly what I want to do.

I had a friend who was a fairly popular horror writer who did everything he could to embrace that label. I told him, "I think that's going to hurt you in the long run, because you may find that your voice is more adequate to expand than you think." And in time, that's exactly what happened, and he couldn't find his way out of that. He ended up putting his career on hold. And I think a large part of it was because he so heartily embraced the horror writer moniker. I never was against it. When people say, "You write horror stories," I say, "Yeah." But if you call me a horror writer I don't say anything about it because I'm proud of that, but what I'm trying to say is that I do other things as well.

Today, despite your history with horror, you seem to be more closely associated with the crime genre. As I'm sure you know, King has dabbled in crime writing a couple of times, perhaps most notably with his Richard Bachman novel Blaze (2007). What are your thoughts on King the crime writer?
When you really think about it, if you take *The Dead Zone* (1979), even though it has elements of the supernatural in it, it's a crime novel. It's so much the structure of a crime novel with the mystery.... I think you could go through a number of his books and you'll find that often times the feeling of crime is actually more prominent than the feeling of horror. At least for me it is. So yes, I think he's quite good at that.

Obviously you're a very original writer, but I wondered if you've ever seen anything pop up in your writing that seemed like it was influenced by King or that you were aware might be interpreted by others as having been directly influenced by King?
I can't think of anything at the moment. I often see things in my writing that I think are reminiscent of other people's work. I see that in King's work, as well. I see Richard Matheson in there, I see some Ray Bradbury, maybe Charles Beaumont.... But if you make it your own it doesn't matter. We're all parts of other writers. A good stew uses a lot of ingredients. There's a difference between plagiarism and influence. I think there have been two or three of my stories which I felt may have been influenced by King, but I really can't be certain because I have such a big pot of stew

with many different things in it. I'm sure that's part of it. I can feel Flannery O'Connor moving around in my bones sometimes. I can feel Bradbury for sure. But I feel this sort of potpourri of all these different writers I read growing up. The writers I still read influence me. I read a tremendous amount. I think that's another thing that Stephen King and I have in common—we are both voracious readers. We have to constantly be reading. We also watched films and listened to radio shows. We're both media-influenced type writers. In my case, art has played a role, as well. I'm sure it's the same with King. Music. I never listen to music when I write, but music is a big influence on the rhythm of my prose. There are so many influences out there.

I think one of the reasons Stephen King can appeal to so many people is that there's a way of sort of referencing these things and letting them run through the strainer of his imagination and then putting it out there where people can feel a relation with that. It's like hearing a song that has a loop from Lightning Hopkins, but it's not a Lightning Hopkins song. But you can feel that same reverberation, that same special moment, you first felt when you heard Lightning or Robert Johnson or any of those blues players. And now hear them super-electrified with all sort of other things going on, yet you hear that influence. I think King was much more influenced by the hard, heavy rock than I was. But I think we both have a folksy element. I think I have a lot more rockabilly/blues/country—things of that nature. It's sort of that weave-in-and-out that our culture has been influenced by. I think that's his ability to assimilate so many different influences and put them into fiction.

You mentioned Bradbury. Like Bradbury and King before you, you've been honored with the Bram Stoker Lifetime Achievement Award. You're in pretty good company there.

My friend Bill Paxton, who died recently, had a saying that he just wanted to have a place at the table. And that's all I wanted—to have a place at the table. I never had grandiose ideas. I just wanted to be able to write and sell and maybe make a living at it. And then I wanted to be better at it; I didn't know I had the talent I had. To what degree that may be is for others to measure, but I know I had more than I expected. When I got in, I finally felt like I had my place at the table.

I'm incredibly honored to be listed alongside people like Stephen

Joe R. Lansdale

King and Ray Bradbury and Robert McCammon. They're all magnificent writers that have heavily influenced this field. And for me to be there alongside them is surprising to me, because I'm just a boy from East Texas with just a high school education and a few hours of college. And I have a lot of miles of work behind me. I did physical labor until I made it as a writer. I worked at it very, very hard. I generally only work three hours a day, and I've done that for more than 20 years. Because that's what works best for me. I had to learn all of that through that process of which those writers taught me a lot. Bradbury had that thing about writing a story a week, and I started out doing that. And then it kind of evolved into something else. Some writer would give me a little tidbit here or there. To be on that list with so many writers who influenced me in so many ways—to have my seat at the table—that's pretty nice.

Have you ever read anything by King and thought, "Man, I wish I had written that?"

Constantly. I do that with a lot of writers, and Stephen King is certainly one of them. I have always thought that *'Salem's Lot* is one of the top three vampire novels ever written. It's more than just a vampire novel. It transcends. When I read it, I thought, this is just like *Peyton Place* (1956) with vampires. Then later I saw that he said something very similar to that. And I thought, well, he certainly nailed that. That novel was so strong on characterization. It reminded me of John O'Hara a little. It had a lot of those same feelings. But the style came at me differently in the beginning, when I first started it. I initially put it down three or four times. At that point I had read only *Carrie* by him, and I thought, this is slow. It was because I had only been reading genre fiction at that time. So I went in finally and said, "I'm going to give this a real run." And I got it. The thing I think I need to give him credit for is I think he transformed the way I looked at fiction. It broadened my readership ability. I started reading a lot of writers that I didn't normally read. I started reaching out beyond the genre, because I recognized immediately the reason he was so good and so different—the reason he had the impact he did—is because he wasn't just working in one little pond.

Like Stephen King, you're no stranger to having your work adapted to film and television. Do you share King's view that whatever the filmmakers do will ultimately be okay because the book will always remain at the end of the day?

Perspectives on Stephen King

James Cain originally said that. A woman said, "Isn't it terrible what they did to your book?" And James Cain said, "They didn't do anything. The books are still right there on the shelf." I agree with that, but I do believe that the films have more of an impact than people think. Because a lot of people, if they see a bad film, they won't read the book. We'd like to think that isn't true, but it is true. But it doesn't change the nature of the book. It's still your book. It's still how you wrote it. I haven't had as many films as Stephen King. I think a lot of the films they've made from his work have been magnificent, but I think a lot more have been terrible. It's because they just go for the horror element, and they don't understand the character element. They don't understand what drives the stories.

That's why *The Dead Zone* was really good. Because Cronenberg understood the characters. He had a magnificent view that captured the style and tone of the Stephen King novel. Not just like there's a booger bear and we're going to have it happen here and then it's going to get scary and then it's going to attack them and then they're going to defeat it. Those things are all fine, but what makes Stephen King Stephen King is kind of the motor that drives it, but it's got a special chassis built around it and it has really cool upholstery. It's got a lot of special things you can get and you can't get with every other novel. With Stephen King you're getting the whole package. I think that's why so many of the films fail. Because they don't understand what really makes the stories work. King, like a lot of writers, myself included, gives the illusion that you can take our stuff and just kind of stuff it in the camera, but there's so much more than that. It's an internalization that's hard to depict purely through visuals.

I've been very lucky with my adaptations. Of course I haven't had as many as Stephen has, so I'm sure my turn is coming for that.

You've talked in the past about directing. As you know, Stephen King directed Maximum Overdrive *(1986). What are your thoughts on King having actually taken that plunge, and what advantages do you see to an author choosing to go that route?*

I admire him for doing it. I don't think it was a very good movie. Even movies like *The Shining* (1980), which I know people revere, I don't like. I think Stanley Kubrick missed what Stephen King was doing. I don't like the television version either, which is very literally the novel. The problem with it is that it was television in an era where they couldn't do what they could now. I thought the actors were bland in that. There were a lot of things wrong with it. I think it's worse than the Kubrick version. The Kubrick film has impact—it has moments that I really, really love—but that was one of those novels that was so dear to me that I wondered why in the hell Kubrick felt obligated to change it so much. I'm one of those people who believes if you're going to do a novel, you should try to do it as close to the source material as is reasonably possible. I think there are some exceptions. I think there are some novels that are really just ideas, but it seems like in a lot of cases there are just people who feel like they have to stick their fingers up their asses and rub their shit on your stuff. They feel like they can't stick to the original material. Visually, the Kubrick version is great. But one of the problems is that in the book, Jack Torrance is a regular guy and he eventually evolves into what he becomes. But in the film you've got Jack Nicholson playing Jack Nicholson, and he's crazy almost from shot one. So there's nowhere to go with that because you know he's crazy.

Has your perception of Stephen King or his own trials and tribulations, either personally or professionally, changed in any way since you yourself have become a popular mainstream author dealing with a lot of the same things he does?

He has kids like I have kids. We had families about the same time, which is another reason I personally relate to him. I met him in St. Louis one time with my wife and my son. He carried my son around because he missed his kids, but I also think it was because he didn't want to sign autographs. But I also thought that was funny.

But what I would say is, I admire the way Stephen King has been in this for the long haul. And I love the way he's always had an honest way of dealing with things. I've met his son, Joe, whom I like a whole lot. I've exchanged some e-mails with Owen, and I love his work. My kids are both in the industry now. It's funny how these same kinds of things have happened to us. I think it's mainly because, when you get right down to it, we're just a couple of country boys. And we're family boys. We come from the late sixties and early seventies. We both had strong mothers. I also had a strong father, but unfortunately Stephen's father left when he was young. We both believe in family. And we both believe in hard work. We both believe in trying to be diverse. So I relate to him.

RICHARD CHRISTIAN MATHESON

Richard Christian "R.C." Matheson was born the son of legendary science fiction-horror writer Richard Matheson in 1953 while the author was working on his masterpiece, *I Am Legend* (1954). The younger Matheson soon fell in love with the horror genre and dreamed of following in his father's footsteps. He was not only interested in writing novels and short stories, but he also had an interest in writing for film and television. In 1978, he earned his first screenwriting credit on the TV series *Three's Company*. He continued writing for television and was hired to work as a story editor on the TV series *Quincy, M.E.* He would eventually write for many notable series, including *The Incredible Hulk* (1978), *B.J. and the Bear* (1981), *Knight Rider* (1982), *Hardcastle and McCormick* (1984), and *The A-Team* (1983).

Matheson got his first feature credits with *Three O'Clock High* (1987) and *It Takes Two* (1988). He then collaborated with his father on a screenplay titled *Face Off*, which was ultimately transformed into the comedy *Loose Cannons* (1990). Matheson would later call the film a "big-budget mess." In 2000, Matheson was tapped to adapt Dean Koontz's *Sole Survivor* (1997). He then wrote two popular episodes of the horror anthology series *Masters of Horror* (2005) and adapted the Stephen King short story "Battleground" (1972) for the miniseries *Nightmares and Dreamscapes* (2006). The episode would win numerous awards, including an Emmy for Outstanding Music Composition. The episode would prove to be so popular that Matheson would later produce the book *Stephen King's Battleground: A Commemoration of the Emmy-Winning Television Adaptation* (2012). He would later return to the land of King, adapting the novella *Big Driver* (2010) into a 2014 film directed by Mikael Salomon.

Matheson is also an accomplished author. He has written many short stories, and he has three critically-acclaimed collections: *Scars and Other Distinguishing Marks* (1988), *Dystopia: Collected Stories* (2000), and *Zoopraxis* (2016). He published his debut novel, *Created By*, in 1993. It was later expanded in a 2007 edition.

As you know, Stephen King has frequently cited your father as being one of his biggest influences. What elements do you see in King's work that you can recognize as your father's influence?

The psychological exploration of the characters. Stephen typically explores a story with more characters than my father typically does, with something like *Misery* being an exception to that. I also think that my father focused on horror in suburbia in his early short stories and novels. He did not focus on the usual settings, backdrops, and tropes that had previously appeared in horror. I think Stephen was very taken by that. Stephen's settings, like my father's, are misleadingly mundane.

What did your father think about King? Did he ever talk about him or his work?

Sure he did. They had an active correspondence together. I have found, since my father's passing, in his archives, letters from Stephen about the things that are going on in his life, as well as books he was working on at the time that have since gone on to become iconic works in Stephen's oeuvre. It was interesting to read, because it's one writer talking to another writer, saying things about the book he's dealing with and the concerns he has with it.

My father had the highest opinion of Stephen as a person, as a family man, as a friend, and foremost as a writer.

As an accomplished writer yourself, what do you see as being King's primary strengths?

I'm currently involved with the fourth King adaptation that I've worked on. I adapted "Battleground"; I rewrote a screenplay for *The Sun Dog* (1990); I wrote *Big Driver*, which was adapted into a very good movie that Steve loved. Now I'm doing something I can't really talk about at this point that will end up being a six or eight hour miniseries.

I've given a lot of thought to Steve's work because when you adapt another writer's work, you have to look at it very closely. I also adapted Dean Koontz's *Sole Survivor* into a four-hour miniseries. And I looked very, very closely into his work. You don't read it as you would a fan of that author. Instead, you're going through to see what you can eliminate, as well as to see what you can enhance. With Steve, he is very easy to adapt because he keeps the story moving along. To comment on his prose, he's also a superb prose writer. So the writing itself—the actual language—is propulsive, it is intense, and it is poetic. I also think Steve has a remarkable ear for dialogue; how people think; how people speak. It's an observational level about the human experience. You could be a wonderful prose stylist and not have an ear for dialogue. I've known writers like that. You may have a wonderful ear for dialogue, and have no real talent for how to keep a story moving along. Steve really has it all, and I say that as someone who has examined his work closely. I've examined it as a fellow prose writer and as a person who has adapted his work into screenplays. All of the adaptations I've done have shared a level of perception of people that are psychologically honest and deep. They all share a momentum in how the story is told, so that the stories don't get bogged down in that psychological insight.

You mentioned the Sun Dog *adaptation. Would you like to talk a little bit about that?*

Sure. The guy who wrote it and did the original adaptation was unavailable to do one more draft. I believe he went on to do the stage adaptation of *Carrie* (1974). So the producers of *Sun Dog* asked me if I would do a rewrite, and that's how that came to be. At this time it remains unproduced, which is amazing to me just in that anything of Steve's is unproduced at this point. But there are some, and *Sun Dog* is one of them. But it's a fantastic project that I believe will eventually be produced.

Stephen King, like yourself, is a believer in the supernatural. Do you believe that belief plays any role in the work? Does it have any effect on the authenticity or overall effectiveness of a horror writer's work?

I don't think people who don't believe in the supernatural write it as well. I think if you do believe it you are able to convey it, whether it's to be lyrical and beautiful or to be frightening, in a way that a writer who doesn't have those beliefs won't be able to convey it. I'm not saying they couldn't convey it. I believe it could be conveyed if a writer has an essential grasp of the idea, but like anything as a writer, the more deeply it is within you, I believe the more deeply it affects the work.

As you mentioned, you adapted "Battleground" for the television miniseries Nightmares and Dreamscapes. *I realize the original story doesn't contain a lot of dialogue, but there is some there. Yet you chose to excise every last word of dialogue. What were the considerations you made in wanting to write it that way, and what was the initial reaction to that decision from the powers that be?*

I was working on it and it was going to be a one-hour story. I believe there were going to be eight episodes with each one containing an individual adaptation of a Stephen King story. So they asked me if I would adapt "Battleground," and as I began to work on it, I thought the dialogue was functional in getting ideas across, but I thought maybe it could be done without dialogue. It was just an interesting thought. The dialogue was fine; Stephen never writes dialogue that isn't really, really good, but when you're adapting something and writing the script you are constantly moving things around and cutting dialogue so you can re-examine the overall effect.

One of the tricks of screenwriting is that you never start a scene at the beginning or finish a scene at the end. You always try to focus on the middle of the story so it gives it more of an urgency. In following that kind of approach, I thought cutting all of the dialogue might make it intriguing. So I added a few little screenwriter tricks, like putting a CNN newscast crawl when the character is sitting in the airport. You have to get some exposition across, but not very much. There was a movie made in the 1950s that had no dialogue, and that was an entire movie. Most of what is bad, in my experience, and I've written probably 750 to a thousand scripts, is the exposition. That's what kills you. So the more you can get your story across without exposition, the better it will usually be. You need really good actors. You need a story that has a sort of strange inevitability to it, so you can kind of follow it. But with "Battleground," it fit perfectly. The only thing I needed to do with "Battleground" was extend it, so I added this other character that the hit man didn't know was in the box of Army soldiers. He didn't see it, he didn't know it was there. And that one was more fierce. So that created the opportunity to extend the story without being repetitive.

As for the second part of your question regarding the immediate reception of my idea to write the piece without dialogue, I will say that the network was unconvinced that it could work. But then when they read the script they quickly decided that it could work, and then we hit the jackpot by getting William Hurt, who was able to get everything across because he's a wonderful actor. I think in the hands of a lesser actor, the effect might not have been as dynamic.

How difficult is it to write an entire screenplay containing only scene directions?

It's not hard at all. You have to have a story that is simple enough that the twists are visual. If the twists are plot-driven, then it gets trickier. If the twists are an idea, then it gets trickier. If the twist is that the soldiers come at you from a different direction than where you thought they were going to come at you from, then it visually explains itself. If it's information, it gets a lot trickier. That's why I front-loaded the information. The exposition about how this guy is, who was he killing, why was he killing him, why did the soldiers get sent to him, all had to be accounted for. I couldn't just say absolutely nothing about it, but it didn't have to be in dialogue. If the story is telling itself visually, you don't need a lot of dialogue. For instance, I don't remember much dialogue in *Mad Max*. That's a pretty straightforward dynamic. Once they're on the road and they're all fighting, there's not a lot to say. You can see what's happening. Or look at my father's film, *Duel* (1971). There's not a lot of dialogue there, but it's clear as a bell what's going on there. So it has to be visual and not information or plot-driven.

You mentioned your father's work again, which leads me to another question. There are a couple of nods to his work in "Battleground." How did that come about? What made you decide to do that?

It was just a lark. I think we all got a kick out of the idea of putting the devil doll from "Prey" in there. There was also a reference to his *Twilight Zone* (1959) episode "The Invaders," which also had no dialogue. And you know what? One person who particularly appreciated "Battleground" was my father.

That episode of Nightmares & Dreamscapes *is frequently hailed as the greatest of the series. It also snagged two Emmy Awards. All of that had to be pretty rewarding.*

To be associated with anything that is singled out and celebrated like that is very fulfilling. I was very proud of the way it turned out. I felt personally very, very blessed to have had a great story to work with, a great director in Brian Henson, and of course William Hurt.

You later edited a book to commemorate the episode. How did that book come about?

So many people loved that episode, and then there were the Emmys that you mentioned. I thought filmmakers and screenwriters would be intrigued by how it got put together. So I began to think in terms of maybe interviewing some of the key people and just putting something small together. And then I was given access by TNT to the original film, and it just started to grow. I started getting set photos that were not released to the public. Everybody was so proud of the episode that I just thought, why don't I see how much more I can add to this thing? So I thought, I'll add some of Jeff Beal's score, which I thought was an interesting thing to do. And then more people wanted to be interviewed. It just kept getting bigger and more interesting.

What were some of the challenges specific to adapting the Stephen King novella Big Driver *(2010)?*

The first challenge was when I got the assignment they wanted to get into production really quickly, and they wanted to know how fast I could write it. So I said I could adapt it into a script in two weeks, but that I did not want to write out the story, which is usually the first step when you adapt. When I adapted *The Chronicles of Amber* my story outline before I even wrote the script was sixty pages long, which is reducing the story down to something that could be discussed as a story. Once you got past that, then you could move into the script. With *Sole Survivor* (2000), the story outline was thirty or forty pages long. So I told the executives I could do it in two weeks, but I didn't want to write the story because that would waste valuable time. I said, "The script itself will let you know how I want to take this piece that Steve wrote and turn it into a screenplay. I'll give it to you in two weeks and then we'll talk about it." So I stepped over the story phase, and all the decisions I would have made in changing the story would be reflected in the script. So they said fine. I wrote it in two weeks, turned it in, and they loved it. We then shot it up in Halifax, and it turned out great.

Perspectives on Stephen King

Do you think there was a real-life inspiration for novelist Tess Thorne, or do you think it was basically just modeled on King himself?

That's an interesting question. It's always hard to tell if a character is the author. It's tempting to figure that some amount of the character has to be the person who wrote it. I don't know. Steve has gone down that road before with other things he has written, like *Misery* (1987) and *The Dark Half* (1989). It's hard to say. There are so many different philosophies that are expressed in Steve's work. I think if you had to sit down and thematically assess it all and try to figure out who was the man who wrote it all, I think you'd have a difficult time. It's so eclectic, and there is so much to look at. All of Steve's characters are expressed with such depth and authenticity, how would you know without seeing Steve interviewed? If Steve was long gone and we were looking at his work without any way of knowing anything about the author, I don't know what you could determine. Was he a religious man? Was he not a religious man? Was a cynic? Was he a romantic? There are many different tonalities and philosophies that are articulated in Steve's work, and they are articulated so eloquently and with such a reality that you think, that must be what he thinks. And then you read the next story in the collection with a completely different character, and you think the same thing again. He is not just chameleonic, but he is able to get into these people in a way that is very, very deep. And as to whether Steve had any of the feelings that Tess had in *Big Driver*, I couldn't really tell you. There are inside jokes about being an author, and I certainly jumped on them and added to them.

When the mother is there and there's a confrontation between Tess and Big Driver's mother, part of what the mother is so upset about is that she just thinks Tess's work is subpar. [Laughs.] She's taking great personal offense. That's what happened in *Misery* also. She takes it personally. What I saw happen with my father and other friends of mine who are well-known writers, and I've seen it happen in my own life, is that people take your work personally. Some people. If it's just the wrong person, they could be problematic in your life. Steve has explored that in *Misery*, and I can't think of anyone who has explored that better.

I understand that you performed with Stephen King's band, the Rock Bottom Remainders. What was that experience like?

It was not only fun, but it was a good thing for me. They had put a band together where all the players were published novelists. I had just published my first novel, *Created By*, which was about a writer who has problems. The band found out I was a drummer and that I had studied with Ginger Baker. I wasn't just some new drummer, I had been at it for a while. I flew up to San Francisco with some of the guys, and then I got invited to join the band. My house burned down in Malibu not very long after that. I think it happened in that same month. My house burned to the ground, and all of my stuff got destroyed, including my drum set. We were going to do this gig in Miami, and they sent me the set list. I went through it and learned all the songs. About three or four days after my house burned down I was in Miami playing a gig with these guys at this big dancehall that was like an old-style movie theater. That's where we did our set. Then I remember there was a party after. Steve doesn't drive, so we just rode in the limo together to this party. It was just he and I.

It was really wonderful. We practiced at Dave Barry's house down in Miami. Ridley Pearson was there, too. It was really fun and they were great guys. We had a lot of fun and went to the movies together. It was the perfect thing to do after your house burns down. It would be the perfect thing to do even without that happening, but that was a very healing process for me.

As I recall, Al Cooper was sort of the official guy who was keeping an eye on the band since none of them were full-time musicians. The slogan of the band was "we make music as well as Metallica writes novels."

Stephen King has had some very positive things to say about your writing. What is it like to receive that sort of praise and validation from him?

My father and I were at a writer's event. I think it was at the World Fantasy Convention. It was probably about six years ago. Steve wasn't there, but Mick Garris was there speaking for him. Steve had won something from the organization, and he took the moment to look at the overall landscape and say some nice things. To a room full of people, King said by way of Mick Garris, "To Richard Matheson, for being Richard Matheson, and to Richard Christian Matheson, for being a brilliant chip off the old block." That was awesome. I was like, "Whoa!" My father had to leave early because he was having some health issues, so I was at the table by myself. I remember it feeling like everyone in the room's heads pivoted to look at me. It wasn't like I hadn't published stuff or that there was anybody in the room I didn't know, but that was a major comment. It was pretty heavy-duty.

He also loved my script for *Sun Dog*. And he loved my script for *Big Driver*. I will also say, and this is something I can take with me to my grave, when I was riding in that limo with Steve after playing that gig, two things stand out in my mind. One, the radio was playing very softly, and Steve knew the lyrics to every single song that came on. This was one of those stations that plays all kinds of music, but Steve knew every lyric to every song. I thought, I think this guy's got a photographic memory. People ask writers, "Where do you get your ideas?" It struck me that with Steve, so much comes into his mind, whether he's reading the paper or watching CNN or whatever he's doing, everything goes in there. And Steve's predicament is, "How do I get rid of it? How do I put it into some kind of a paradigm that will accommodate it?" I believe that's how his mind functions.

The other thing about the ride is that he said things about my work so astonishing to me. It was beyond validating. And that's something I will hold onto in my mind forever. It was profound about my writing. Not that I was Richard Matheson's son who had started writing and was making a name for myself, but rather about my writing specifically. It was about my talent. And that was nothing he had to say. He didn't owe me a word of that.

Considering your similarities and interests, I was wondering if you consider King to be a bit of a kindred spirit?

Completely. His love of music. By comparison, again, when you're adapting a fellow author, you notice things; I don't think music plays quite the same role in Dean Koontz's writing as it does for Steve. There are always references to popular culture and music in Steve's work. I think Steve could have been a happy rock-and-roll musician if he had no writing talent. Music plays a huge role in my life. I've got a new album coming out next month with my band. I've had other albums. If I had had no writing talent, I'm sure that's a path I would have seriously pursued. I think we're also in sync when it comes to issues of life after death, issues of mortality, issues of fear, issues of anxiety, issues of betrayal and deception, and how those things fall into the narrative of our stories. And with both of us, as was the case with my father, we have an absolute love of stories with a strange premise and a strange twist. Steve has a very original, surreal streak, and I think we certainly share that.

Patrick McAleer

Patrick McAleer teaches writing and literature at Inver Hills Community College in Inver Grove Heights, Minnesota. His primary scholarly interest is Stephen King. His first book was *Inside the Dark Tower Series: Art, Evil and Intertextuality in the Stephen King Novels* (2009). With this book, McAleer sought to provide a "focused look at the center of King's fictional universe," examining it against King's horror work, while also exploring audience expectations at the times in which they were released. He later wrote a second King-related book, *The Writing Family of Stephen King: A Critical Study of the Fiction of Tabitha King, Joe Hill and Owen King* (2011). The book's descriptive text boasts, "This is the first extended exploration of the works of three authors who have too long been overshadowed by their proximity to 'the King of Horror.'"

McAleer then teamed up with co-editor Michael A. Perry on *Stephen King's Modern Macabre: Essays on the Later Works* (2014). The book collected thirteen essays by a variety of writers analyzing King's more recent output, dividing them into three categories: "King in the World Around Us," "Spotlight on the Dark Tower," and "Writing Into the Millennium." He, along with Philip L. Simpson, co-edited a second collection of essays on the work of Stephen King. This volume, *Stephen King's Contemporary Classics: Reflections on the Modern Master of Horror*, also focused on King's later works (post–1995) such as *Duma Key* (2008), *Joyland* (2013), and *Dr. Sleep* (2013).

McAleer has also penned several articles for *The Los Angeles Review of Books*, all of them focusing on the work of Stephen King.

You've said in the past that The Colorado Kid *(2005) is your favorite of Stephen King's works. As you know, that novella has divided a lot of readers, primarily because of its unresolved ending. What is it about this work that speaks to you?*

My primary fascination with the book is the ending. I absolutely love what King did. I will admit after I turned the last page and saw there was no resolution, I think I, like most readers, got a little cramped, if you will. But when I read his explanation with that line, "I told all the story there is to tell," that really resonated with me, especially as a teacher of literature. I frequently have students coming to me wanting answers. They'll say, "What does this mean?" or "Why this color, or why this symbol?" I just kind of roll my eyes and say, "Sometimes there are no answers." That's the beauty of literature. I think it's part of King's genius, and also his impish side, to say, "Hey, I gave you ten bucks worth of story, and that's all you're going to get." I think it's fantastic to challenge us to do more than just passively read the text. As a teacher and as an individual, I think it's great to kind of boomerang that sense of responsibility back onto the reader, to make him say, "What do I want to get out of this?," and kind of take some of the pull and power away from the author.

Additionally, there's so much mystery surrounding what happens to the Colorado Kid. How does he get to Maine? What's up with these Russian coins? I think that's great for those who have read all of King's other work and can speculate a bit and think about these magical doorways that appear in the *Dark Tower* series. I think that's part of the fun and the marketing that King employs to say, "Hey, there are answers all throughout my canon. Pick and choose. Read your way through and figure it out." That's fun. Also, that story between Stephanie and the old men is just one of those pieces that has so much going on ... so much subtle witticism and ambition. *The Colorado Kid* just really tickles me in a good way.

I think that ending also speaks to King's desire to be somewhat of a slave to the story as opposed to a writer who simply writes things his audience will like.

That's one of the things I've seen with Stephen, and his sons, as well. I think they all prescribe to this idea that real life is not plotted. "Let me take this idea and kind of see how it branches out." The minute you have an ending in mind, you start forcing your way there. "I want to see the couple get together at the end and live happily ever after." Sometimes that doesn't happen in real life. I absolutely applaud King for how he's very brutal in his honesty sometimes and his aspirations of the story. "This is the way the story's going to go. You may not like it, but that's the way I imagine its reality to be. If you don't like it, go read something else." I love that challenge that he gives. That description of him being a slave to the story is just perfect. You tell the story, and as the author if you feel you've done your job, then pack it up and send it out. Whether or not people like it, you've lived up to your responsibility. I think King is satisfied with that.

I read an interview where you talk about academics still dismissing Stephen King as a lowbrow hack, even today, some twenty years after his receiving the prestigious O. Henry Award. What are your thoughts on this, and why you think academics sometimes have that knee-jerk reaction to dismiss King's work?

    I can only generalize to a degree here, but I think the knee-jerk reaction comes from the notion of merit. Some people look at King as a horror writer, and see that as an automatic relegation to low status. Or "He's popular, so there can be nothing profound there." There are these senses that because King is appealing, particularly to the middle class, a worldly author as opposed to a highfalutin individual, some people look at that and say, "How can there be merit in something that comes so easily to someone and is so easily read by others?" It's almost as if some academics think that literature has to be something out of a *Saw* (2004) movie—just a complete and utter torture device. When I think of King sort of playing with his audience and torturing them in one way or another, I think he realizes that literature doesn't have to be this blown-up, overly-emphasized sense of value. Of course value is subjective and whimsical. I think because King challenges what a lot of people get kind of defensive about, I think it's almost kind of a pissing match. They're like, "You're trying to devalue us by writing this mainstream popular literature? Fine. We'll devalue you." And it kind of ends up in this really bad volley.

    I think a lot of academics get defensive and when pressed to define what they think has value or merit, and they can't necessarily nail it down, they're quick to say "not King." When they can't define it, it comes back to this very basic, almost visceral sense of, "I just know that's not literature." It's an almost childish response. I think it's because King doesn't take himself too seriously. I think that's seen as one of the biggest strikes against him, and I think that snowballs from there. But I think you can get a lot of value out of things that are not serious on their surface. For me, some of the most valuable lessons I have learned in life have had a candy-coating. When you ease someone into something in that way, they kind of come to things on their own terms. They realize things, as opposed to being beaten over the head. I think a lot of academics have that sense of self where they're like, "This is important. Let me beat it into you, and once you've accepted that I can go home feeling superior and everyone else will fall in line." But Steve doesn't fall in line, and I think that rankles a lot of them.

You've taught King's work in a variety of collegiate courses. Would you like to talk a little bit about that?

I'm fortunate to work in a community college, where scholarship is encouraged but it isn't pressed upon you. I can experiment a little bit. I don't have to have the perfect class. I can come back a semester or two later and make a few tweaks. One of the first opportunities I had to teach a King novel was in a Contemporary Fiction course about ten years ago. The book I chose was *The Gunslinger* (1982). It was one of my favorites and I thought it would be great to get a modern Western-romance with all the other genres thrown in. I thought I might also be able to get other people onto the *Dark Tower* train. That first reaction was really one of rejection. The kids didn't like it. It wasn't *Harry Potter*. It didn't work with them. I tried to tell them, "This is part of a series, and there's much more to it. I'll admit it took me reading the second book to really get engaged in the series." But that book did not work very well.

So I changed it to *The Mist* (1980). I think the movie from 2007 really helped because it was still in the cultural memories of a lot of the students who were maybe 16 or 17 when the movie came out. It was still kind of with them, and the ending of the movie still resonates with a lot of students regardless of their age. That helped with that particular class.

In my Introduction to Literature classes, where I'm supposed to go from Shakespeare to Michael Chabon or whomever, I'll often have an extra credit assignment where I'll have them look at a short story by Steve, Tabitha, Joe, and Owen, and offer up their thoughts. I'm trying to get a little exposure and see what the students think. For the most part people like King, and not because of name recognition; when they compare him to his wife and his two sons, they see some of that *je ne sais quoi* that the others don't have. I think it's genuine when they say there's a greater engagement or enjoyment they get out of Steve as opposed to his family members. So that's interesting to look at and watch to see how that might change throughout the years.

Probably the most interesting class I had with King was a focus on his novels a few years ago. It was kind of a yin/yang class in that I had half who were high school students doing the Running Start program, and the other half sophomore folks who were getting ready to transfer and had been through the rigors of other classes. That divide was very noticeable in the class. The more experienced students were ready to come to class with discussion questions and ideas, ready to rage in debate, where the high schoolers did not have the same level of engagement, awareness, or even passion.

From that experience it seems as if age or even just experience might have something to do with the Stephen King experience. Especially if you're picking him up for the first time. I started reading King when I was about 12, so by the time I got to college I was waiting for Stephen King to be in the college classes. I was disappointed, but I was ready. I think because some of the college kids who had been here for a year or so had already been exposed to some of the harsh elements that King covers, like family abuse or alcoholism, they were more ready to talk about it and make connections with some of their other classes, like Psychology and Sociology. So those who were fresh-off-the-farm, so to speak, just didn't know quite what to do. That suggests to me that reading for pleasure and reading for deep intellectual engagement is still something that needs to be fostered. It doesn't seem like it's being done in a way that I would prefer at the earlier levels and high schools. So I think for me, having King as a sophomore would be great in preparing one for future levels because of how complex he is.

He has a great sense of humor, he is very engaging and fun, but he almost always gets really deep and really insightful. It's nice that his writing makes connections to all sorts of other departments, and I think the more experienced students are ready for that, whereas the newer students are not quite ready for that nuance. Older students love King. Experienced students are ready for him. Those who have basically been spoon fed literature most of their lives, they don't know what to do because they're expecting fun, games, a little bit of gore, and dead babies or whatever. There's a little more to him than that.

I read that you used Rita Hayworth and the Shawshank Redemption (1982) *in a class as a means to discuss prison reform?*

One of the things I do in my Writing II class is I'll have the students read *Different Seasons* (1982) and I'll invite them, if they're going to go down a Humanities or a Psychology route with their career, to write about one of the stories and how those things apply to it. With *Rita Hayworth and the Shawshank Redemption*, a lot of students really get into the issues of prison reform, especially in regards to solitary confinement. A lot of these kids have no idea what it's like to be alone somewhere with no cell phone, no Wi-Fi, with nothing but your own thoughts. When you try to get them to even imagine that—

That's the real horror for them!

Absolutely. So when they get confronted with that, they are able to expand this text and apply it to other concerns. Even with *Apt Pupil* (1982) ... I had one student a couple of years ago look at that and channel her emotions from the sense of genocide and mindless murder, and she looked back at all sorts of acts of European genocide that history has largely missed. I thought, "I'm glad King inspired you to inspire us to do more research and realize there's a lot more horror going on than we're even aware of." She looked at how these things get buried and how people ignore them, what gets focused on in classrooms and what gets set aside. I think in that regard, King is great for the literary folks, but also those looking more into Social Justice or psychological standpoints. I'm sure you could find something in Engineering to make a connection to something like *The Tommyknockers* (1987).

That's why I still have such a passion for King. I believe that he can, in one shape or another, speak to just about everyone.

*You wrote a book entitled I*nside the Dark Tower Series: Art, Evil and Intertextuality in the Stephen King Novels. *What was your motivation for writing that book, and what was your experience like working on it?*

I think my motivation was, if I'm being extremely honest, as a young gentleman who had just finished a Master's Degree and was moving into a doctoral program, "How do I get myself on the map?" [Laughs.] I don't know if that was just youthful arrogance, hubris, or just something kind of natural. It was something I just really wanted to do.

As a side note, I was talking with one of my colleagues, and we were saying that it seems like a lot of people tend to either read King's older stuff and then slowly gravitate towards *The Dark Tower*, or they'll start with *The Dark Tower* and go the other way. I was the latter. I started with *The Dark Tower* in junior high, and by the time I got finished with the series I was like, "Look at all of these other connections. Let me branch out." So by the time the entire series was finished, I thought, "I want to be the first to write about this." And then of course Bev Vincent came out with *The Road to the Dark Tower* (2004).

McFarland & Company had approached a colleague of mine for a book on King, but she was swamped with various things. So she kind of passed that on to me. I thought about *The Dark Tower*. It's my favorite series and I think there's a lot to say, so I thought I'd just try to get the ball rolling. I had chapter ideas for eight or nine chapters. One of the criticisms of the book was that it just scratches the surface. I know that's true, but it kind of starts the conversation. So it was like, what really stands out for me at this time? The intertextuality was a big theme for me—how King pulls all of these stories together, and how he sometimes does it deftly and at other times how it kind of falls apart. One thing I've noticed sometimes, and I don't fault him for this, is that King will get an idea and write a book. Then a few years later he'll be like, "What did I just write?" It's always fun to see what he tried to do and what he did well. Even in the book *Insomnia* (1994), when he writes that the Crimson King is pent at the top of tower. Then ten years later when he finishes *The Dark Tower* they explain it away as, "That's just King being misleading with his subconscious."

At that time the graphic novels were coming out, and I wanted to see how well they adapted the story. In the book I was highly critical of the graphic novels the same way I'm going to be highly critical of the film at a conference I've got coming up. But I will say, if I was to revisit the book now, the graphic novels actually gave root to a much better story than the film. The writer Robin Furth eventually came out and told folks, "I realize I'm playing fast and loose with a lot of the story threads. I had to make some changes." When she finally announced that it was like, "Okay, I can forgive that now." Now I see what you're doing. But I still wanted to explore what the graphic novels were doing at the time with the first two story arcs, how they were building bridges or crumbling bridges in some respects. I also looked at who my favorite characters were in this and what was the basic dichotomy.

I really enjoyed looking at Randall Flagg because he's such a fascinating character. He is, at least for me, kind of a lovably evil guy. He's always very smug, smiling and laughing. Of course I don't approve of or dismiss any of the horrible evil things he's done, but for me, when I read *The Dark Tower* series and we got some of those little snippets of his backstory—especially him being a rape victim—so many things clicked into place. "Wow! That potentially explains a lot about this guy." I know I've harped on that in various places, but that little piece of important information possibly explains the smile in front of the evil. He's like, "I've been burned before, but I'm going to burn you one better!" It's not necessarily something I want to emulate, but it's just a wonderful, deep, empathetic character sketch. I think we have to applaud King for making us love and hate someone so extremely. I wanted to look at Flagg and say, "You know what, people? He may not be as bad as you think." I kind of like stirring the pot a little bit like that.

As you know, there are a lot of King fans who, for whatever reason, still haven't read the Dark Tower *series. Why do you think that is? What do you think it is about the series that repels some King readers?*

I think it has to do with a level of expectation. When I teach my King classes one of the first things I do is try to challenge people and say, "Stephen King is not a horror writer." And they'll say, "What are you talking about?" Let's define horror. Let's get to some of the subtleties and take a look at what he does. Let's look at supernatural horror; let's look at American gothic horror; let's look at techno horror. I think people get it in their minds that something bad has to be happening from page one all the way to the last page. With the *Dark Tower* series there is a drastic departure. Yeah, you have Roland as a kind of antihero right away, killing all those people in the town of Tull. We're like, "We've got to root for this guy?" But he's not really bad. It's a matter of survival. We have that whole scene with Sylvia Pittson. "Interloper! Get him!" It's almost like bad Fox News politics. You know, "There's the bad guy! Everyone get him!" Then the whole town rallies against him, so you kind of feel bad for him. So I think that expectation of horror is something that kind of pushes people away. They're not getting what they want. Here's a bad analogy: people who go to IHOP and order the same style of pancakes every single time. Then there's a wrinkle, like, "We're out of bacon today. You'll have to have sausage today." And they're like, "No! We've got to go to Perkins today!"

I think I can safely say this was the case with one of the top King scholars, Tony Magistrale. I met him about 13 years ago at a conference and *The Dark Tower* had just finished up. He admitted to me, "I haven't read it." I was like, "Tony! Why the heck not?" It was kind of the same thing. "It's not as good as *The Shining* (1977)." I said, "It's gonna be good for different reasons, but you can't make that judgment until you read it." Part of his explanation (as far as my memory goes) was that departure. I think the multigeneric approach seemed to be too much for people to chew on. For me, who has kind of an inner-geek, that's really appealing. I love that. But for others, who maybe did not grow up with *The X-Men* or who shunned *Star Wars* (1977), they probably looked at *The Dark Tower* and thought, "Whoa! Nerd central. I don't want that." Also, I think it can be kind of scary to invest yourself into something you don't know where it's going to go. It's like *The Colorado Kid*—people despise the unknown. When something is beyond categorization and beyond what people consider to be safe, a lot of people don't like that. Even though books like *'Salem's Lot* (1975) or *The Stand* (1978) are not necessarily safe, people kind of have an idea of what to expect from them. That gives them a certain level of control. But with *The Dark Tower*, control was tossed out the window around mile one.

Let's switch gears and talk about King's later work. As you have pointed out in the past, there are echoes of works like Rita Hayworth and the Shawshank Redemption *and* The Dead Zone *in* End of Watch *(2016). In a review you wrote for* The Los Angeles Review of Books, *you even suggest that* Finders Keepers *(2015) could be seen as a sort of reboot of Lisey's Story (2006). Some critics might say King has hit a point in his career where he's just recycling old material and revisiting familiar tropes. Do you believe this is true, and if it is, do you believe it's necessarily a bad thing?*

I'm really torn on whether or not it's a bad thing or not. One of the first things that pops into my mind is the old adage "write what you know." When I teach King I tell the students to expect something from Maine, something with blue collar characters, and something a little bit strange. That's what King knows. So if you were to get the same book from someone like Bill Gates, he's not going to know the blue collar world as well as King does. So I think in some respects his going back to the well is kind of normal. With *Under the Dome,* a colleague of mine called it *"The Stand,* only in one location." And *Cell* could be seen as a twist on *The Tommyknockers* in that its a weird alien influence that somehow zombifies us or changes our essential humanity. So "write what you know." I can appreciate that.

Everyone recycles on some level. A lot of my own work on Stephen King almost always ends up cycling back to a central theme of failure. In looking at Stephen King's writing, it seems that he's quite the cynic. Maybe I'm reading too deeply or too selectively, but that's something I keep coming back to. So I would easily accuse myself of going back to the well. I'd like to think I'm writing about these themes from different angles, but on the surface they look similar. I think there are enough variances where King does those things, but I think you can really justify it as his attempt to update something or to exorcise certain demons or had things he wasn't able to fully flesh out in the things he worked on back in the seventies or eighties. I'd like to give him the benefit of the doubt and think that he is re-exploring old ideas, but with new locations and new characters, as well as fresh angles and fresh language. And in some respects, these things may also be for fresh audiences. He may be trying to capture them with some of those larger concerns. "Hey, if you like this I've got a whole slew of books you can get back into."

But at the same time there could be a level of him sort of petering out. When I read *Sleeping Beauties* (2017), a lot of that book seemed to be his son Owen writing. I like Owen well enough as a writer, but it was my perception that King started to pull back on that book. It seems maybe he's getting a little bit tired, but doesn't know what else to do. I think we all understand that. Once you get into a career, a hobby, a fandemonium of a certain sports team, you just kind of get stuck. Is King stuck? Maybe. But again, I like to give him the benefit of the doubt because I generally don't see a lazy or indifferent writer. Maybe a forgetful one or a tired one, but I think that's forgivable.

You mentioned Sleeping Beauties. *That was one of two collaborative stories he had coming out this year, with* Gwendy's Button Box *(2017) being the other one. Do you think that says anything significant about his career?*

Patrick McAleer

I think his collaborating more frequently is significant. I remember when he collaborated with his son Joe on the Richard Matheson homage *Throttle (2009)*. I thought that was really fantastic because Joe only had two books out at the time and people were still trying to get a measure of his voice. And that was a really good collaboration. I thought that was significant because when I read "Throttle," I couldn't tell one voice from the other. It was the same way for me with *The Talisman* (1984). But when *Black House* (2001) came out, once I got past the first fifty pages, it seemed like King's voice took over. I thought, "Well, I'm sorry, Peter Straub. At least your name is on the cover and you get some royalties here."

To see him work with all of these other individuals like Richard Chizmar or Stewart O'Nan, I think he's helping to buoy them with name recognition. I think that's a great favor, but at the same time trying to keep fresh with his craft. I think he's trying to ensure that he doesn't get stale. With *Gwendy's Button Box*, it was a lot like *Throttle*. I could tell it was a King piece, but I couldn't tell where King started and Chizmar ended. I thought that was very smooth. So I think him being able to meld his voice into others', I think that helps him to pull back on some of his trademarks. As writers or teachers or whatever role we take on, once we get into a routine we kind of tend to stick with that. It's what we know. So here's King at 68, and he's still going strong. Where most people are retiring, he's trying to find his next phase. So I think with his collaborations or even some of his recent poetic work, I think it's good to see him trying to play a little bit. One short poem that he did for *Tin House* a few years ago called "Mostly Old Men" (2009) was fantastic. That was absolutely beautiful, just a simple and elegant poem. I think King is kind of playing darts with his career right now. "Let's just throw and see what hits. If I find something that works for me and gets me out of my routine, let's play it up." I have to tip my cap to him for that. I think that sense of freshness and that sense of vigor for the craft of the story is something that people may not necessarily give him credit for—especially in those outsider circles we talked about.

You wrote a book called The Writing Family of Stephen King, *which looks at the writings of King's wife, Tabitha, and his sons, Joe [Hill] and Owen. I'm sure there are people who believe they only got published because of their connections to King. What would you say to those people?*

I would say absolutely not. I know that Owen struggled with whether or not he should adopt a pen name or use his own name. And even in going with his own name, if you go onto his website and look at his C.V. you'll see that he took the route that most young writers take. He submitted to college journals and other publications and wrote articles for magazines. "Let me get my own name out there as opposed to just dropping a brick in the pond and hoping my career takes off because I'm Stephen's son." I think Owen is like Joe, who has a handful of short stories he published very early on and will never see the light of day again because he's embarrassed by their young quality. I think both of these individuals understand that you don't just write a book, get rich, and live a happy life.

When I see the bibliography of both Owen and Joe, I see people who understand that writing takes a lot of time and that name recognition alone won't get you an audience. When I think of Owen, this is somebody I see with a great level of wit, a certain level of brevity, and someone who has very good ideas. I see him expanding and exploring with more detail in his storylines. In some respects he is a little too ambiguous for me, but at the same time I appreciate that he's trying to let the reader do a little work on his or her own part. I see growth. I see someone who is attached to the craft. It's the same thing with Joe. You look at his short story collection, *20th Century Ghosts* (2007)... That very first short story, "Best New Horror" (2007), has a surprise ending that you don't see coming. You're like, "Wow! That's pretty damned good!"

Joe is kind of aligning himself with his dad in the horror genre, but he goes so far beyond that. I see someone who's able to go to those horror places, but also if you look at some of his Twitter posts or that wonderful *Locke and Key* (2008) graphic novel series, you see that this is a guy who understands how to craft a story. So even though I think when Joe was writing *Locke and Key* he knew how he wanted it to end, he didn't really know what the stopping points between A and Z were gonna be. That comes back to that plotting issue we talked about earlier. Joe says, "I know where I want to go, but I'll let the story take me there." This was something that probably could have been done in three or four volumes, but it took him six. I'm glad he took the time to flesh it out and see where the story took him.

So I think the King name is a good thing, but I don't think it's the raft they rode in on.

Tabitha King is a good writer also. I think her being King's wife does her a bit of a disservice because it causes some people to automatically discount her work.

Absolutely. I'm with you. I like Tabitha's work. I've been critical of *Candles Burning* (2006), which she took up when Michael McDowell passed away. I think that was a project that she just completed out of the goodness of her heart. But when I think of Tabitha's work, namely *The Trap* (1985) and *One on One* (1993), I think she's terrific. In *One on One*, I really like her take on two teenagers navigating adolescence, cliques, different family backgrounds, and the main character Deanie who has to avoid physical and sexual abuse at home. I appreciate how the persona she puts out at school is actually a defense mechanism. These are how kids act and react. Just like her sons and her husband, Tabitha has done her homework. Instead of just presenting us with a weird-looking kid and asking us to pity her, she gives us reasons why we should pity her and why she acts the way she does.

Tabitha has a certain rawness, especially in terms of sexuality, that Stephen doesn't have. It might sound a little mean to say, but when I think of Stephen King and sex, I think of very puritanical, like bad coloring books you give to a seven-year-old who's just learning about the birds and the bees. With Tabitha I think of Cinemax; it's not pornography, but you get a pretty good idea of what's going on. She has remarkable honesty. As she's described herself in various places, "I'm not a lady. I'm a writer." In that sense, she will tell you exactly what's going on, what's in her head, and what people will do in X, Y, and Z situations. I think that's the mark of a wonderfully honest and very bold individual. I think Tabitha, if she didn't have Steve's shadow or were to have a renaissance of her own and starts putting out some of these things she's set aside, I think she might get a little more credit this time around.

Stewart O'Nan

Stewart O'Nan was born and raised in Pittsburgh, Pennsylvania. Pursuing a career as a writer, he attended Cornell University, where he graduated with a Masters of Fine Arts degree in 1992. O'Nan then taught courses at the University of Central Oklahoma and later the University of New Mexico while working on a novel and publishing short stories in a variety of publications, including *The Threepenny Review*, *The Nebraska Review*, and *The South Dakota Review*. He then published his first book, *In the Walled City (1993)*. This short story collection was later awarded the Drue Heinz Literature Prize.

He then landed a publishing deal for his first novel, *Snow Angels* (1994), after the manuscript was awarded the Pirate's Alley Faulkner Award. (The novel would later be adapted to film by David Gordon Green in 2007.) In 1995, O'Nan became a writer-in-residence and taught creative writing at Trinity College in Hartford, Connecticut. He has since published many novels, including *The Names of the Dead* (1996), *Everyday People* (2001), and *West of Sunset* (2015), which focused on the final days of writer F. Scott Fitzergerald.

O'Nan collaborated with Stephen King on the non-fiction book, *Faithful: Two Diehard Boston Red Sox Fans Chronicle the Historic 2004 Season* (2004). In 2012, O'Nan and King collaborated a second time on a novella entitled *A Face in the Crowd*, which was released exclusively as an e-book.

What was your first introduction to Stephen King's work, and what were your thoughts on that?

I read him as a teenager as his first books were coming out. I was a fan of horror comics and movies and *The Twilight Zone* (1959), so I was ready for the great early novels and the stories in *Night Shift* (1978). There may not be a more brilliant stretch in American writing than his output from 1974 to 1983, and I had the first hold on each one at the lending library in the drugstore near our house. It cost ten cents a day to borrow a book, so I'd take *The Dead Zone* (1979) home and read it straight through.

Since you were reading King in your formative years, would it be safe to assume that he's had some influence on your writing?

Stephen King's influence on my early writing is both direct—enjoying his work as well as studying how he achieves his effects—and indirect, in that his *Danse Macabre* (1981) sent me back to the library (and the video store) to find writers like Charles Beaumont and Shirley Jackson and Ira Levin. And he still influences me both ways. I read his new work and reread the classics. Meanwhile he's recommending books I otherwise would never find. Like Jonathan Lethem, he's a book hound, always digging.

Since you would ultimately write a book with King about the Boston Red Sox, I wondered how your love of baseball and the Sox began. Was this around the same time you were discovering King's work?

I grew up a Pirates fan—I still am—and the fall I moved to Boston, they won the World Series. Since I lived two blocks from Fenway Park, once spring rolled around I paid my two bucks to sit in the bleachers. I discovered that the Sox weren't your typical, anemic American League team like the Orioles, all pitching and defense. No, the Sox were decidedly like the Bucs—no pitching, no defense, no speed, just a ton of lumber. They'd win and lose games 10–8 or 14–11. So it was a perfect fit. Obviously I had no idea what I was getting myself into. I'd learn the hard way in 1986 when I was living on Long Island and the ball went through Bill Buckner's legs.

What do you see as being King's primary strength as a writer?

As a storyteller he delivers on his promises, but also tosses in lots of surprises. He's great at suspense and dread, and when it comes to big set-pieces—say the siege of the grocery store in *Under the Dome* (2009)—he details them fully without losing pacing. And look at the plotting in *'Salem's Lot* (1975); just unstoppable. Plus the concept: he jams together *Dracula* (1897) and *Peyton Place* (1956) and comes up with a brilliant hybrid. Or *The Stand* (1978), where he takes the conceit of *The Andromeda Strain* (1969) to its logical end—and that's just the starting point. He can write the short story, the long story, the novella, the short novel, the serial novel, the long novel, the epic—and he's done it in multiple genres, occasionally, as in *Different Seasons* (1982), in the same book. And he's hitting it every day. Beyond talent, curiosity, and drive, he's got a truly consuming love of writing and reading.

You mentioned all the different writing arenas in which King excels. Is there a particular format in which you prefer to see him perform?

While he's done brilliant work in the short story, the novella, and the epic, I favor his medium-sized novels like *'Salem's Lot, The Shining* (1977), *The Dead Zone*, and *Pet Sematary* (1983). In 300 to 450 pages he still has room to move, but the focus and pressure on his main characters is more intense.

What are your favorite of his works?

His Castle Rock work still feels like home to me, and I'd include *'Salem's Lot* in that. Small-town Maine, where everybody's up in everybody's business, and then the rocky farms and stand-alone ranch houses, all surrounded by dense forest cut by game trails and train tracks. And life-threatening weather.

Do you have any King reading experiences that stand out to you?

Re-reading *Pet Sematary* in line at Disneyworld/Epcot with my children when they were little. I took the paperback with me because it would fit in my back pocket, not remembering this was where Dr. Creed daydreamed of ending up. There we were, surrounded by kids Gage's age, all having the time of their lives.

I remember being so shocked by the audacity of Gage's death scene when I first read Pet Sematary. *As a writer, King doesn't pull any of his punches.*

Pet Sematary is as scorched earth as he gets with a sympathetic character. It reminds me of the newlyweds in *Night of the Living Dead* (1968). When they get torched in that pickup, we understand that the rules of the horror movie have fundamentally changed. Of course, in the real world, the rules changed long ago. Genocide and cannibalism have been around forever, well before mechanized warfare and bombing civilians. But there's always been a kind of poetic justice in our weird tales. From Poe to EC

Comics, it was always the wicked who reaped what they'd sown. And typically, that standard appears in almost all of his other work. Which is why Tabitha King didn't like *Pet Sematary*. Gage, like the newlyweds, was an innocent, and a beloved one at that. But you can't take on "The Monkey's Paw" (1902) without losing someone who was truly loved and worthy of risking everything to bring back.

What do you see as being the finest of King's film adaptations, and why?

My favorite movies from his work are David Cronenberg's *The Dead Zone* (1983), Rob Reiner's *Misery* (1990), Stanley Kubrick's *The Shining* (1980), and Brian DePalma's *Carrie* (1976), with honorable mentions to Bryan Singer's *Apt Pupil* (1998) and Tobe Hooper's TV movie of *'Salem's Lot* (1979). I'm leaving out a few really solid ones—the Darabonts, surely, and a quieter film like Reiner's *Stand By Me* (1986)—but these leap to mind. All great directors with strong, idiosyncratic visions who drew brilliant performances from their leads. Christopher Walken, Kathy Bates, and Sissy Spacek inhabit their characters fully, and Kubrick's sense of dread and use of space and music is still the standard for the haunted house flick.

You're no stranger to being adapted to film yourself. Do you share King's attitude regarding film adaptations—that the novel will, in the end, stand alone on its own merits regardless of how the film turns out—or are you more affected by the outcome of an adaptation?

I've had just one novel turned into a film, *Snow Angels* (2007), and was lucky in that David Gordon Green was both the screenwriter and director, so the film has a singular vision. He nails a mood and gets great work out of his cast. He uses a fair amount of my book, but, like Kubrick's *The Shining*, it's its own experience, its own world. As with *The Shining*, I'm glad that both the novel and the film exist. Of course, I worry that readers may see Sam Rockwell as Glenn when they read *Snow Angels*, but I never see Jack Nicholson as Jack Torrance when I read *The Shining*.

You and King have both had the experience of having had Sam Rockwell bring one of your characters to life in a film. Have you guys ever talked about this?

I suppose I knew this, but we've never talked of it. Sam Rockwell really melds with his characters and whatever world he's in rather than trying to stand out and be a movie star. I don't know if he's a Method guy, but when he was playing Glenn in *Snow Angels*, he supposedly carried around a Bible. I especially like his performance in *Moon* (2009).

Is King aware of your opinion on Kubrick's The Shining? *I just wondered if you had ever talked about it, and if you had, what he had to say about it.*

No, we haven't talked at length about Kubrick's version of *The Shining*, but I know Steve feels it's not scary enough. Too cool or cerebral, based on dread rather than all-out suspense. Imagery rather than energy, every move too obviously calculated. And I'm sure the casting distracted him, as it distracted all of us at the time. Nicholson's too recognizable as a movie star, and Shelly Duvall's Wendy comes off as too soft and dithering. Like all Kubrick, it's not about the characters but the situation they're in. "The Marines do not want robots," Private Joker says robotically. And there's the easy cheat of the walk-in cooler door being opened (by Delbert Grady, we surmise, or just the Overlook).

When and where did you first meet Stephen King?

We first met in person at Fenway Park. We'd been e-mailing for a while, and one day he called and, knowing I'm a big fan, asked if I wanted to catch a Red Sox game. Sometimes when you meet someone you know online in person, it's awkward, but immediately we were riffing off each other and having a big time. He's genuine and generous, irreverent and incredibly smart. We're both fans and products of the same American pop culture—lovers of big bug films and noir, rock-and-roll, punk, baseball, politics.... Simpatico.

When did you guys first consider collaborating? Was Faithful *the first of such ideas, or were there others?*

We didn't consider it—we just did it. In 2003, we got excited about the Red Sox and started a private blog to talk about the team day by day—and not just the two of us, but also Joe and Owen. We were crushed when we lost in the American League Championship Series on Aaron Boone's walk off, and when spring rolled around, an editor at Doubleday who was a big Yankees fan asked if I wanted to write a book about the Sox. I said yes, but only if Steve could write it with me. He was busy finishing up *The Dark Tower* and couldn't promise how much he could contribute, but his yes was enough to get Scribners in on it.

When you guys were preparing to write Faithful, *did you look at any other baseball books to get a sense of how they had been written?*

No. I knew from the beginning that it would have the diary format, and none of my favorite sports books have that structure. I did want it to have some of the depth of Nick Hornby's *Fever Pitch* (1992), and I definitely didn't want it to have the heavy literary bent of the *New Yorker*'s coverage. This would just be two overexcited fans watching the games and talking about them.

What could you tell me about the collaboration process on that book?

Faithful was supposed to be an immediate account of how it feels to be a Sox fan across one season. The high hopes and low lows, and the generations-long yearning for an impossible championship and what it means to New Englanders. The idea was to react the same way we did on our blog and let people see how obsessed and superstitious we are about the team. Every day there was a game, we'd write our coverage of it. I'd choose what I felt were the best or tastiest parts and add them to the growing manuscript. Since it was supposed to be a diary or emotional record of our fandom, I didn't go back and rewrite pieces after the fact. As the season progressed and Steve finished *The Dark Tower*, he added a few brief essays to the game coverage. I included these whole. One great pleasure of collaborating with him is that he writes so quickly and cleanly, and his mind works so differently from mine.

Early on in the draft of *Faithful*, I realized the book was a conversation between one fan who believed the Sox would eventually win and one who believed they never would. With that in mind, I incorporated our e-mails. With spring training, 162 games, a ton of off-field issues and a full postseason, the hardest part of putting the book together was keeping it under 500 pages.

You guys dedicated the book to Victoria Snelgrove, the college student who was killed during the 2004 ALCS celebration when she was shot in the face by pepper pellets by Boston police officers. What made you guys decide to do that?

After she was killed in the celebration after the ALCS, we felt it fitting to remember her. For everything the championship meant to people in New England, her death put things in perspective. We didn't want other Sox fans—or anyone for that matter—to forget her.

Looking back on the finished product, what are your thoughts on the book today?

I haven't revisited *Faithful* in a while, but the last time I dipped into it, it felt like a time capsule, chock full of stuff even I'd forgotten. The diary/journal format prevents it from being all about finally winning the World Series, and in that respect it's more honest than the dozens of books written after the fact. The club's problems in the first half of the season—the angst of Nomar Garciaparra's ankle injury and him being traded to the Cubs at the deadline—is presented fully rather than relegated to the background. It's a true record of the season and how it felt to day-in day-out fans, which is what we were shooting for.

At one point HBO was planning to make a six-part miniseries based on your book. What happened to that?

They just decided not to pursue it. Maybe they felt the moment had passed, or they thought they could do a doc on the season without using *Faithful* as source material. A six-part miniseries seems a little long to me.

Like King, you've rarely written non-fiction books. Is that something you enjoy working on?

For me, writing non-fiction isn't as much fun as writing fiction. I love doing legwork and interviewing people, but I also like the freedom of just sitting and daydreaming, making things up. In non-fiction, the writer's allegiance is to the reader. You have to answer any reasonable question the reader has about the material. In fiction, you're at the service of your characters, figuring out the most powerful way to get their emotional world across to the reader, and that always involves point of view—getting into someone else's mind and skin, and that's what I love to do most. In non-fiction, you don't have as much leeway or as many tools at your disposal, and there's just not as much discovery.

How did collaborating on Faithful *affect your relationship with King?*

Being friends and colleagues is one thing. As writers, there's a whole different level of trust when you're working with each other's prose. His openness and generosity during our back-and-forth while putting together and shaping *Faithful* were a perfect example of selflessness. But at that point, it really wasn't surprising. The longer I've known Steve, the more I respect him.

Tell me the story of how "Spectators" eventually evolved into your novella A Face in the Crowd.

I think it was 2005, the year after *Faithful*. We were at Fenway, and between pitches he leaned into me and said, "Here's an idea for a story: A guy's sitting at home watching the ballgame, and behind home plate he sees his best friend from childhood who he knows for absolute certainty is dead. Go write it." I was working on a novel, and didn't pursue it (he has story ideas all the time), but one night, years later, I was half-asleep and the story came to me. I scribbled some notes on the yellow pad by my bed, and in the morning they still looked good. I e-mailed Steve and laid out the basic premise, and he said, "We'll write it like that. You start."

In what ways was it different collaborating with him on a work of fiction rather than a non-fiction book?

Collaborating on fiction is like having a second brain to figure out the story's problems. It's exciting, partly because someone else is helping with the lifting. You send your pages off, and a couple of days later they come back with changes, the story's moved ahead several scenes, and you've got a fresh set of problems and clues to work with. Again, with fiction, your loyalty is to the character. With non-fiction, it's to the reader; you need to answer any question the reader reasonably has about the subject. There's more freedom and mystery in fiction, and for that reason it's much more fun to see where your partner takes the story. Let's face it: it doesn't hurt when your partner is Stephen King.

Have you guys talked about collaborating again in the future?

We've casually run story ideas past each other—notions, really—but nothing substantial. But you never know. Writing *A Face in the Crowd* was such a blast, just waiting to see what he'd come up with and then taking that a step further. We were hot on it, in a way that doesn't come along that often.

What kind of feedback have you received from the novella, and do you feel that it's given you access to a wider fan base?

I haven't heard too much feedback on *A Face in the Crowd*, but that's not surprising. No doubt the story, like *Faithful*, reached a wider (and different) fan base than my other work, and if some of them are curious and pick up *A Prayer for the Dying* (1999) or *The Night Country* (2003) or *The*

Speed Queen (1997), that's great. That's how I discovered a lot of my favorite writers—by association.

How do you assess Stephen King's legacy?

He reinvigorated horror, stealing it away from the candelabra and harpsichord dramas of Hammer Studios and transplanting it here in modern day America. Most great writers are lucky to write one or two breakthrough books that outlast the heat of their initial release. With *Carrie* (1974), *'Salem's Lot*, *The Shining*, *The Stand*, *Different Seasons*, and *The Dead Zone*, he published six of them in about as many years, with *The Gunslinger* (1982), *Pet Sematary* (1983), *Christine* (1983), and *Misery* (1987) right on their heels. And because the movie of *Carrie* was such a success, he also influenced the horror film in a way that no other writer has. He set the benchmark for a whole era.

Most people agree that scholars and readers will still be reading King's work a hundred years from now. The work will live on well beyond our deaths. How does it feel to be a part of that legacy?

While no writer aspires to be a footnote or a passing mention in someone else's biography, as an avid Stephen King reader, it's an honor to be part of the catalog, even if just in a small way.

Kevin Quigley

Kevin Quigley grew up in the suburbs of Boston, bouncing around various places like Taunton, Quincy, and Braintree. He had a love of literature and a desire to write from an early age. "I've always known what I wanted to do," he explains. "I remember writing full stories when my teachers would give me vocabulary words and ask me to just write sentences using them. I made a lot of my teachers tired." He first fell in love with Stephen King's work at the age of nine when he read *Cycle of the Werewolf* (1983). After that he was hooked. He later found influences in the writings of people like William Goldman, Robert Parker, Dennis Lehane, and J.K. Rowling, but he remained most passionate about King's work. In 1996, he established Charnel House, a website devoted to all things Stephen King.

In addition to his work on the website, Quigley self-published a novel titled *Spare Parts* (1989) and wrote poetry. In 1999, his novel *I'm On Fire* was published by Cemetery Dance. He contributed to George Beahm's King-based newsletter Phantasmagoria and the website FEARnet, both of which have since disbanded. Much of Quigley's subsequent work has focused on Stephen King. He is the author of *Wetware: On the Digital Frontline with Stephen King* (2010), *Blood in Your Ears* (2011), *Chart of Darkness* (2011), *Ink in the Veins: Writing on Stephen King* (2011), and is the co-author of *The Illustrated Stephen King Movie Trivia Book* (2013). He has also contributed to other King-related works, including Brian James Freeman's *Reading Stephen King* (2018) and Stephen J. Spignesi's *Stephen King, American Master* (2018).

How did you first become aware of Stephen King, and what was your reaction to his work?

Perspectives on Stephen King

My very first exposure to King was when I was nine years old and I was at sleepover camp. A friend of mine brought *Cycle of the Werewolf* because the pictures were cool. He passed it around to all the kids. We didn't read the book, we just looked at the pictures basically. Then this same friend slept over at my house one night and he brought *Creepshow* (1982), and we read that, and that was really cool. I was nine-years-old and this was horror, so I was just really excited. Then when I was twelve, my Dad took me and my brother to see *Pet Sematary* (1989). That was not necessarily the best choice for a twelve-year-old to watch. My little brother got scared, so my Dad took him out and took him to another movie. I sat and watched *Pet Sematary* and I loved it, so my Dad bought me the book.

We were on vacation and I read the book in a cabin in the woods' attic during a lightning storm. [Laughs.] It was really the best exposure to King I could have had. I was very excited to read it because it was my first real adult book. What had happened was, my grandparents had sent a box filled with my uncle's old books to us after my uncle went off to college. There were a bunch of Stephen King books in there, so after I read *Pet Sematary*, I read *Rage* (1977) and *Night Shift* (1978). Then I read *It* (1986) for the first time when I was twelve years old. That was the thing that really hooked me.

What was the first thing you wrote about King?
The first thing I ever wrote about King was when I was fourteen and I wrote an oral report about *The Bachman Books* (1985). That was really fun and I was super nervous. But the first thing I wrote professionally was starting Charnel House, my Stephen King website, around 1996. I wrote essays there about King. My first one was on the Rock Bottom Remainders, because I had gone to see their concert and I decided to write about that. Then I eventually started writing book critiques. I had read Michael Collings' King critiques in George Beahm's *The Stephen King Companion* (1989). I was fascinated by how in-depth they were, so I was trying to do my own interpretation of those when I was twenty-one. My initial critiques weren't very good. I skimmed the surface on a lot of things. Like my critique on *The Shining* (1977) was "three people go into a haunted hotel and it's really scary." [Laughs.] I didn't get really, really critical until much later when I read more books on criticism and how to critique and deconstruct things.

Kevin Quigley

Since then I've written plenty of essays. George Beahm asked me to write an essay for one of his books. Hans Lilja asked me to write something for an upcoming book of his. And I've done a bunch of stuff for *Cemetery Dance*.

You've written extensively about King. What is it about his work that draws you back time and time again?

It's the voice. He has a very conversational voice, so when you're reading a book of his, no matter how smartly written or how scary the book itself is, the tone is conversational and when you come back to it, it feels comfortable. I recently reread *Firestarter* for probably the seventh time, and you know, those events are horrific, but you get in and you get drawn into these characters and you get drawn into the way King talks about them. It makes you feel like you're reading about old friends.

I think that on the first read of any Stephen King book, he has this way of drawing you in and making you feel like you already know these people. But on a reread (and then a re-reread) it doubles down almost; you feel not only like King's relaying these stories about old friends, but now they are legitimately your old friends because you've gone in before.

It's very difficult to find other writers like that. I think John Irving is one. But otherwise it's very difficult to go back and reread a book and have that same feeling multiplied and magnified. I think that's an exciting thing about King—I never go back and then get bored during a reread. It's just the feeling that I got when I first read the book and it's almost tripled.

As a writer, what are some lessons you've learned from Stephen King?

One of the most interesting things I've learned is foreshadowing and how important that is. And the basic structure of books—how best to lay things out so that everything flows together.

One of the coolest things, and I don't think it's talked about a lot, is where King takes a secondary character and has the whole focus of the first part of the book on that secondary character. Take *The Dead Zone* (1979) for instance, where you read all about Sarah's life at first, and she's looking in at Johnny.

And in *It* you hear from Ben Hanscom's bartender, and some other people, and Beverly Marsh's husband.... So you see them from the outside before you get into the inside, and I always thought that was really smart. That's something I have tried to bring to my own books. Because when you're a reader, the first thing you're doing is approaching the character from the outside, and then you get more internal. I think it's a really smart way to be introduced to a character before you get really deep into their heads and their lives.

You mentioned It, which you have frequently called King's masterpiece. What makes you label it as such?
Part of the reason is the multiple timelines—you follow the kids and you follow the adults at the same time. And the structure of the book is so smart the way it folds in on each other. What was exciting to me in that book is the whole thing about history and how it has a way of repeating itself. King does so many audacious things in that book where you go back to the beginning of time—at least the time of the dinosaurs—in that book. He shows you that this where it started ... before humanity. And then humanity has always been affected by what *It* is and humanity also affects what *It* is.

It's exciting to me to have that structure and that timeline. He also balanced seven main characters, and did it quite deftly. It never feels like, "Oh, man, I have to read this other back story." It always feels so rich and so different, and he basically wrote a historical novel. Nowadays when you read it again it's a history of two different time periods that aren't now, which is also very exciting. King has lamented the fact that he's always been a writer of his time, and I don't think that.

You know, you go back to *It* and even though it's set in the eighties and it's a time capsule of that time, it still feels fresh and new. But you also go back in there and see what life was like in the 1980s. He captures the zeitgeist. It's also very interesting that he positioned it as the final statement on children's monsters.

He dialed back on that a little bit, but there is a very clear demarcation line in his career, all the books leading up to that one and then right after that you've got stuff like *Misery* (1987) and *The Tommyknockers* (1987)—more adult books with adult concerns. I think he doesn't get as much credit as he deserves for positioning books at certain times of his career. You know, musicians do that. The Beatles did that, Springsteen does that, where you have this one record and then here is a second record that is a reaction to that. King does that all the time, but he does it with books. After *It* you have this very small personal book *Misery*, which is completely different from everything that had come before and he retained his audience.

Structurally, character-wise, *It* is a book that has this scope. For any other writer it would have been the capper of a career; it would have been a final statement. And here it was he wasn't even halfway through his career. He'd only been writing for 10 years. Michael Collings has a statement that basically said, "As you're reading the writing transcends itself." And I feel like that. Sometimes the words get in the way when you're reading it. You're reading it so greedily because it's so well written and so easy to access. But it's still extremely intelligent and has a lot to say about humanity and time.... The way people get set in their ways, and the way cycles never really end.

How did you come to work on The Illustrated Stephen King Movie Trivia Book*?*

That was very exciting. I was out of work. I had been laid off from my job. This was back in 2009, and Brian Freeman and Lilja were working on it, but it was sort of on a backburner. Then Brian Freeman wrote to me and said, "I've read your critiques on your website and I like them. Would you be interested in doing some quiz questions on Stephen King movies?" And I said, "Sure, that sounds like fun." I was laid off and I had literally nothing else going on in my life. I had been depressed and this was sort of a clarion call out of the sky like, "Here's something you can do to make yourself feel better." So I attacked it.

I set up some rules for myself. I said, "I'm not going to ask any questions that involved dates or numbers, but everything else is going to be fair game." I went back and re-watched all these things. I sort of filled my life with this book. Then I got it turned in pretty quickly. I think Brian was a little amazed at how quickly I turned in all my quiz questions.

It was a little bit of torture because I made myself watch *Graveyard Shift* (1987) again, and all those *Children of the Corn* movies again. They're just terrible, terrible movies. But it was fun just the same. The most exciting thing about it is that Brian realized how fast I wrote and how well I wrote about King—how accurately. It's really because of that book that got me all these other books on King from Cemetery Dance. So I couldn't thank Brian enough for taking a chance on me.

What are some of your favorite King film adaptations?

Perspectives on Stephen King

A lot of them are the same as what a lot of people's favorites are. You know, *The Shawshank Redemption* (1994), *Stand by Me* (1986)... The movies that are proof that Stephen King didn't have to have horror to be effective. And there's a lot of speculation as to whether King works best on screen when he's not doing horror. But if you look at those two—or even *Misery*—which is more of a thriller, you can have an argument for that. Or *Dolores Claiborne* (1995). But there are some really effective horror movies. *Christine* (1983) is one of my favorite movies of all time. I've watched that more than any other Stephen King movie, I think. And *The Dead Zone* (1983), which is more of a political thriller with supernatural overtones, is a terrific film.

Those films are just exciting and I think the danger with a lot of King movies is that they focus on the horror before they focus on the characters. But the good ones—the ones I mentioned—focus on characters first, so you get more involved and then when the horror comes it's more surprising.

I used to love *The Stand* (1994)—the four-part miniseries. Then I went back and tried to re-watch it and I just can't watch it anymore. I find it unwatchable. I don't know why. It might be the acting, or just the way it's adapted. The first two hours of it are brilliant—focusing on the kids was brilliant. I think the adults in that movie didn't really take it as seriously as the kids did, so came across as hokey in the second half.

Silver Bullet (1985) is a weird favorite of mine. It's one of the first ones I ever saw, and I just love werewolf stuff. What's interesting to me is that King wrote the screenplay for that, and it has glimmers of King—the way he writes, such as the brother and sister dynamic, the stuff with Uncle Red. That stuff does feel real, but I think he focused a little too much on the horror in his own screenplay. But I still loved it. I loved the interaction of the kids, and the uncle I thought was really well done. But mostly, I think the creature effects were really, really cool. So that one's my guilty pleasure, but I think the other ones are top notch.

Dolores Claiborne is one of the best movies I've ever seen. It's both a great book and a great movie. And Kathy Bates, any time she's in a Stephen King adaptation she just raises the bar.

Everyone loves *Shawshank Redemption* now. I don't want to be one of those hipsters, but I saw *Shawshank* in the theater when it came out, and I saw it three times. I knew about it way before it became a huge phenomenon. I was sort of "in," you know? I don't usually get in on things before they become popular, but I did with that.

What are some of the common mistakes you see filmmakers making when adapting King to film, particularly in horror?

I think there's a lot of emphasis on the gross-out. I mentioned *Graveyard Shift*, which tried really hard to be scary but wound up just being kind of a gross movie. It doesn't really lend much to it. There are some gross-out moments that work. It's funny but it's also cool in *Sleepwalkers* (1992) where she takes the ear of corn and jams it through the cop's head. That's cool and gross, but a lot of these films rely too much on moments like that. I think a lot of filmmakers approach Stephen King in the way that they're looking at a *Nightmare on Elm Street* (1984) sequel, where it's all sort of quips, gross, and jokes while forgetting what made the original *Nightmare on Elm Street* really good. You know, where it was creepy and character based.

Cujo (1983) is a great film. It's very well done and I think very underrated. But then right after that you have something like *Firestarter* (1984) and it's almost an exact replica of what happened in the book, but it's boring on the screen. I think what makes a good director and a good screenwriter is knowing how to edit for the screen. You have to know your source material well enough to know what's going to work. Frank Darabont does that every single time he goes out. Rob Reiner also does that.

Look at *Misery* (1990). They cut a whole bunch out of that—most of the stuff about writing Misery, which is an integral part of the book. But it's not a part of the movie because that makes for a better movie. Then you look at *The Dead Zone*. There's a lot of stuff they cut out of that, but it makes for a better movie. *Carrie* (1976) is the same way. All the external stuff that King added to make the book bigger—the interviews and all that other stuff. Most of that is not in there. It's just the straightforward story of Carrie White. So I think that's a problem with the films a lot—that they try to put the entire book up on the screen and it's dull.

That same thing happened with *Dreamcatcher* (2003) unfortunately. I mean, I went back and reread the book and it has merit. King doesn't like that book anymore, but I think it has merit. I don't think it should have been made into a movie. All the stuff that worked in the book ... there's a lot of anger in there ... doesn't make for an interesting or pleasant movie. They even tried to focus on the characters in that one, but I think it just fell flat.

What do you believe are King's greatest strengths as a writer?
That's tough because there are so many. His characterizations are spot on. That's what always brings me back—the people in his books. He can draw them so deftly that they don't feel like they're characters. Like I said, you feel like you already know these characters. A recent book of his, *Joyland* (2013), felt like a relic of my past. I read the book and I was like, "Did King write this back in the seventies?" Because it felt like that. It had the same feeling as *The Shining* or *Firestarter*, where you go in and you immediately know these characters. Look at *11/22/63* (2011); you get into Jake Epping's story so much that for a long time he doesn't follow Oswald and he doesn't care about JFK at all. He's just falling in love with Sadie and living in the past, and it doesn't matter because it's so well done.

I've noticed King has been doing that a lot more lately, where the main thrust of the story is his characters. The plot becomes secondary. It happened in *Duma Key* (2008), where Edgar Freemantle has this scary stuff happening, and it's all important, and it's all interesting. But the main thrust of the story is him and Wireman and Elizabeth on the island, and talking about art. And he makes that fascinating. I'm focusing on more modern examples because I think a lot of people only go back and think about, "Well, Stephen King was good then..." I think he's still great, and he still fashions fascinating characters. You know, *Finders Keepers* (2015) is great. They're all great. The first book in the *Mr. Mercedes* series is very good. The third book, *Finders Keepers*.... I had some troubles with it, but *Finders Keepers* is a masterpiece. But what's interesting is that he takes this little kid who discovers these books in his backyard, and then you get involved in that life.

It's the same thing that happened in *Duma Key* and *11/22/63*. You get involved in this kid story that is sort of tangential to the whole plot. I love that. King will draw a character and you will follow them, follow their ways of being, and whatever they want to do even if it doesn't relate to the plot because you're so excited to find out what's going to happen next to this person.

I think that's his greatest strength. He does a lot of great things. He structures books in such a way that it feels effortless, and he always writes by the seat of his pants. He doesn't really outline unless he's doing stuff with Peter Straub. He has some issues with endings, and that's fine. But he also will have something happen on page three that will later become super important on page 300 and you don't ever feel like you have to leaf back and say, "Wait, did he say this?" Because he makes it in such a way that you remember, and that everything feels important, and everything feels effortless.

What do you consider to be King's most underrated works?

I think the more recent ones get the short track. I think people basically focus on his early and mid-career. Let's see.... Well, *From a Buick 8* (2002) is the number one most underrated novel he's written. It's well-made, very smart, and I think the problem with that book that a lot of readers had was that it didn't have an "ending." But neither did *Pet Sematary* or *'Salem's Lot*. I didn't really find a problem with that. There was a lot of stuff during that period, like *Cell* (2006), where he decided to leave the ending ambiguous.

With that one I thought it was just a really interesting take on what fathers give to sons, and what sons take away from that. It's a theme he hasn't tackled since *Pet Sematary*, really, and I thought it was just really smart and really kind of sweet in a way. There's definite horror there, and the horror is scary, but it's also got a sweet side. It's a really cool structure; the book is told in an epistolary way, and King hasn't really done that in a novel before. I thought it was a really interesting take on doing it that way.

I also think *Blaze* (2007) doesn't get talked about a whole lot, which I find baffling. It's a wonderful book. And when I was first reading about Stephen King way back when, *Lost Work of Stephen King* (1998) and Tyson Blue, you know, they talked about *Blaze*. George Beahm talked about *Blaze* and I was like, "What is this novel I'll never be able to read?" Stephen Spignesi said, "The chances of ever reading this book are zero. You have to travel to the University of Maine." And then it came out as a Bachman book. It's just so well-written and smart. It's the same feel as the earlier Bachman books except it might be closer in tone to something like *The Shining* or *'Salem's Lot*. It is a book that brings you back to a certain time period ... and the sweep of it.... It's a small story but it feels grand at the same time.

Perspectives on Stephen King

I wouldn't really consider *Desperation* (1996) underrated. At the time I think *Dolores Claiborne* (1992) was underrated because he had also come up with *Gerald's Game* (1992) during that time, and everybody was all gaga over that one because it was an adult book with adult themes. Then they read *Dolores Claiborne* and said, "Oh, well, this is more of the same." Nowadays everyone goes back and reads it and sees that it's a really good book. He also uses a first-person point of view, as well as dialect. All of this to tell an unbroken monologue. You don't think about the structure of it because it's so well-written and you have this one voice that carries the whole thing and it just feels so rich. And you go back to *Gerald's Game* now, and it's a bit of a weak story and a bit of a weak character. And King, for some reason, decided to explain all of the weirdness at the very end in this long letter that Jessie Burlingame writes.

The Colorado Kid (2005) is his first Hard Case Crime book, and I think a lot of people hated it at the time. Again, this is a book without "an ending." It doesn't have firm resolution. *The Colorado Kid* was about the nature of mystery, and I thought that going into it with that knowledge in mind made the book a lot better. I always thought it didn't matter that you found out what happens to the Colorado Kid. I thought what mattered was these three characters talking about mystery and why sometimes you have to let a mystery be a mystery. I thought that was really cool.

Tell me about Wetware: On the Digital Frontline with Stephen King.

For a long time Cemetery Dance had this program where if you bought a grab bag you would get a free chapbook in it. So they wrote to me and they always wanted these chapbooks. They were like, "Can you do a chapbook?" I said, "Okay." They said, "Do you have an idea?" I said, "I kind of do," and they said, "We need it in a week-and-a-half."

That's quite a turnaround time.

So I had the idea. I wanted to write about Stephen King and technology, because the technology at the time was emerging. I thought it would be neat to go back and look at the pre-history of King and digital stuff. It was something nobody else had ever tackled before. There were a lot of talks about, "Is print publishing dead?" And it wasn't, but it was a big conversation at the time. And King, as you know, had always experimented with digital publishing.

He wrote a whole novella, *Ur* (2009), just for the Kindle. I thought, here's something that King has done—another way I can take a narrative strand of his career and go back and look at the whole thing as history. So I wrote the whole thing in about a week-and-a-half. I was very lucky. I was temping at the time and they just said, "All you need to do is sit at the front desk and do nothing. Bring a book if you want." So instead I wrote this book, working on it for like 12 hours a day, for a week-and-a-half and I turned it in.

I didn't know what to call it. I had no idea, and my husband said, "Why don't you call it *Wetware*," which was a term for the insides of people. When you work as a morgue attendant, when they open you up they call that the wetware. I thought that was a really interesting play on software and hardware.

Ink in the Veins is an interesting project, as well. How did that come about?

It's similar to what you're doing now. I thought one of the untapped veins in Stephen King study was books about Stephen King. Who are the primary writers? What are the best books? I mean, you look at something like *The Art of Darkness* (1986) by Douglas Winter. He never wrote another book on King. He had such access to King that it's still a definitive work even though it ends before *The Talisman* (1984) came out. You can still go back and read it and it's still quite good. King really opened himself up at that early crucial point in his career. I think Spignesi had similar access for a little while, but then I think King got uncomfortable with it.

The same thing happened when *Castle Rock* was out. King allowed himself some access for a while and then got nervous about it. So as you go further in books about King lose a little bit of that access, but you do gain a little more perspective, which is also interesting. The cool thing about writing about King is that there's always more. There's always something left uncovered. And there's always more in the future because he never stops writing.

I thought there deserved to be a spotlight on these writers and these books that are this cottage industry that don't really get the credit they deserve. Essentially most of these books are genuine literary criticism—stuff like Michael Collings. Then you have George Beahm's stuff, which is far more accessible to a pop audience. The same is true with Spignesi.

There are different ways of approaching King criticism and King study. All over the map. There is a book on King for kids. If I had had that when I was 12, I would have absolutely loved it. I read it and I was like, "This book doesn't talk down to kids." It's a smart, good book about King's whole career. So if you're 12 and you want to read a little more about your favorite author, you don't have to necessarily go straight to Michael Collings. This is kind of a stepping stone.

I thought all these books needed to be highlighted. At the time what I did was, I chose authors because there were certain authors that were writing a bunch of books on King. I think if I was to do it nowadays, I would focus on the most important books on Stephen King. I would like to go back and look at the criticism of the books that aren't healthy. You know, something like Harold Bloom's critical study. Harold Bloom hates Stephen King and he wrote a whole book on Stephen King.

Robert Bly wrote this unauthorized trivia companion where none of the trivia questions were correct. There was a big controversy at the time. So there is another avenue you could take with a book like that.... I'm really glad I got to interview Rocky Wood for that because it was one of his last interviews. It was very exciting to me to be able to talk to all these people and to get all these different perspectives.

Tyson Blue is a guy who is very garrulous about King and has written one major book. He then wrote a second book that hasn't been published. But he's still considered one of the top King people, which is really neat to me. Then you have somebody like Tony Magistrale, who's not Harold Bloom, and he's not Michael Collings, but he writes in a very critical way of King. He wrote this whole essay on King and sexuality and takes King to task about how he approaches that subject. I don't agree with him, but it's still a really good read. There are all these things where you talk to these different people, and there are all different interpretations, and it helps you to become a better writer and a better reader, I think. Reading books about King helps you approach his books in different ways.

Every time I reread a book I have these critical things in my head. It doesn't distract from the book, but I can put it down and say, "Okay, well, that's why Ben said this to Bev in *It* at this point rather than at a later point." When everyone talks about the group sex scene in *It*, people are like, "This is kind of gross." But I was able to say, "Well, here are the precedents for this in supernatural literature." It's interesting to be able to say, "Here's why this happened and here is why King did this. It wasn't just so he could have a bunch of preteens have sex."

STEPHEN J. SPIGNESI

Stephen J. Spignesi is a *New York Times* bestselling author who writes about historical biography, popular culture, television, film, American and world history, and contemporary fiction. He published his first book, *Mayberry, My Home Town*, in 1987. He then turned his attention to Stephen King with the critically-acclaimed tome *The Shape Under the Sheet: The Complete Stephen King Encyclopedia* (1990), which was also a Bram Stoker Award nominee. That same year he penned the wildly popular *The Stephen King Quiz Book* (1990) for Signet Books.

Through the years, Spignesi has written about a wide variety of subjects, including filmmaker Woody Allen, the Beatles, *Gone with the Wind*, crop circles, and U.S. presidents. But despite his many successes, Spignesi, the writer *Entertainment Weekly* dubbed "the world's leading authority on Stephen King," has returned to the realm of King time and time again. His subsequent volumes on the popular author include *The Second Stephen King Quiz Book* (1992), *The Lost Work of Stephen King* (1998), and *The Essential Stephen King* (2003). At the time of this writing, he was working on two more volumes on King. One is *Stephen King, American Master* (2018), and the other is a follow-up to his *Lost Work* book. In addition to these things, he has contributed to a number of other authors' books about King.

In 2005, Spignesi published his acclaimed debut novel, *Dialogues*. He has written articles and short stories for a number of publications, and has appeared as an expert on several documentaries and television shows, including the A&E episode of *Biography* focusing on Stephen King. He is a Practitioner in Residence at the University of New Haven and Adjunct Professor at Gateway Community College in Connecticut. He frequently lectures on a variety of subjects, including the work of Stephen King, and is the Editor in Chief of the small press publishing company The Stephen John Press.

What was your introduction to Stephen King's work, and what was your reaction to that?

It was 1977, and I got married that year. Either I picked up or someone gave me a paperback—it was the one with the yellow cover—of *The Shining* (1977). I read it in like three days, on the couch of our first apartment in East Haven. I was absolutely blown away. So now I'm coming in late, as I hadn't read either *Carrie* (1974) or *Salem's Lot* (1975). The first book of King's that I read was *The Shining*, and that was an awesome introduction.

So what I essentially did, was I got caught up. I said, "I want to read everything this man has written, and I want to write about him." I was finishing my *Mayberry, My Home Town* book, or at least I was working on it at the time. I hadn't sold it yet. Ultimately, when we did sell it, I said to my editor there, "I want to do a similar type of book on Stephen King." And that's how *The Shape Under the Sheet* was born. Since then he's just been my favorite writer. King speaks to me. From the very first page I ever read, the voice, the style, the story, the narrative drive—it was all what I was searching for in terms of a writer of fiction.

What do you see as being King's greatest achievement, and why?

I think without a doubt, the prolificness. I think about this all the time. I mean, I've done seventy-four or seventy-five books, okay? One novel. I find it very difficult to write fiction. I've written two or three others that haven't sold. Some of them are excellent, but they were not easy. Nonfiction comes to me. Research the facts, think about the facts, report the facts. That's how I can turn out books the way I do. But for King to be able to sit down and write fiction every day—massive books with incredible stories…. What an accomplishment that is! I'm working on three or four nonfiction books right now. When I sit down to work on them, I know exactly where I need to start; I know exactly what I have to write about; exactly where the book is going. With fiction, when I'm starting something, I can't tell you how many started and stopped novels I have on my hard drive. Short stories I can do. I can knock out a short story fairly quickly. Maybe because it's got the mojo of an article; it's short, it's got a beginning, a middle, and an end. It's got a single thesis, you know? But with novels, my mind is just all over the place. So that prolificness is what I admire most and consider his greatest achievement. He's been consistently productive and creative fiction-wise, and to be able to do it steadily and regularly.

We've all heard those stories about writers who write their first novels, and then eight years later put out their second. [Laughs.] I'm saying, "Wow, that means it took them that long to do it." My writing students always ask me, "How can I be a writer?" I say, "Sit down every day and write fifteen hundred words. Write two thousand words. At the end of the year you're gonna have two novels." How do you think King does it? He writes every day. I admire King's productivity, and the level of excellence incorporated in that productivity. One, two books a year. All of a sudden he's doing a trilogy. The *Mr. Mercedes* (2014) trilogy! Three books about the same character over a two or three year span. Okay, he had an idea and managed to get three complete, flowing books out of it. Who is this? J.R.R. Tolkien? King just turns it out. His productivity as an artist, as a writer, and as someone who is committed to telling as many stories as he can. Even during those periods in his life where he was an addict and an alcoholic and almost died—he still wrote eight hundred page novels! Amazing. Absolutely amazing. And he's so nonchalant about it. "I've got this coming out, and this…. And by the way, I've got a novel coming out with Owen [King] next year." It just blows my mind.

What are some ways that King has influenced your writing style?

He's helped my writing, and he's also helped my speaking. He's made me conversational. He's made me strive for that "Uncle Stevie's gonna tell you a story, sit down around the campfire, here's what I want you to know," even in my nonfiction. And I get reactions to my nonfiction writing all the time. From editors when I turn stuff in, from readers…. They say, "Oh, my God, I love the voice. I love your flow. I love your style." What they're telling me is that I've got the voice I wanted to communicate in. And King taught me through his writing that you can't write the way you talk. But you can write so that it *feels* like you're talking to the reader. That's not easy.

I always tell my students, nobody's first draft is acceptable. Nobody's;

not King's; not mine; not Shakespeare's. Very often writers will take that first draft and they'll tweak it and they'll polish it, but they won't look at a sentence and say, "Is this the best way to say this to a reader?" One of the exercises I used to do was to take a fourteen-word sentence and put it on the board. Then we cut it. I say, "What else can we cut?" And then basically we get down to "he drove home." You know, it's direct. It's clear. It doesn't need anything more. Of course this is a very isolated incident, but the point I would make with them is that a lot of writers try to dress up their stuff. They're like, "Look what I can do." No matter how many people hate James Patterson, one of the elements of his genius in terms of being so incredibly productive is that he writes for the mood—the zone, if you will—of our times. You know, you take a Dickens book, you open it up, and it could be six pages before he starts a new paragraph. But if you look at Patterson, he's got one or two sentence paragraphs. There's lots of white space. It's almost like watching TV. It's very quick. Your eye can scan the page and get everything in very quickly. I think he takes it to an extreme, and that's probably with it going through him after his co-writers hand him a draft, but in order to get that punchy, direct, tight tone, you end up with very short sentences. Very short paragraphs. And that is a direct result of television.

Reading has changed. Dense, thick, Faulkner-esque, Melville-esque books today—if they're even published—are referred to as "literary fiction." There's never been a bigger divide between literary fiction and genre fiction, and yet King somehow straddles that line! I've been preaching forever that King's work is literature. And now I'm seeing articles in *The New Yorker* and *Atlantic* and *Harper's* saying that Stephen King is better than people think. They're finally starting to say that Stephen King is not just a horror writer. They're finally starting to appreciate his talent and his art. We're living through his creative period. In fifty years, people are going to be looking at his stuff the way we look at Twain, Dickens, or Poe. Did you know that those three guys were perceived to be hacks when they were writing because they were so incredibly popular? Faulkner said Twain was a hack writer who wouldn't even be fourth-tier in Europe! And now we call him a classic American writer. I think we're fortunate because we're living through King's creative period. We're witnesses to this body of work he's going to leave behind. I mean, let's face it: not everything is going to be valued later. Maybe *Creepshow* (1982)...stuff like that ... the lesser-weight stuff might not. But the point is *The Stand* (1978), *It* (1986), *The Shining*, *The Dead Zone* (1979), the entire *Gunslinger* series—those are epic.

I gave a King talk a couple of weeks ago, and someone said, "Don't you think *The Dark Tower* is his magnum opus?" I said I could easily see how it could be perceived that way, because of its size and scope, but when I think in terms of writing, I still think *It* is his best work. It's just beyond anything else he's done. It's just an incredible piece of work. It's only my opinion, which is at least informed opinion, but I still believe *It* is his magnum opus—so far. But who knows? *The Dark Tower* may change in my perception. *It* may change in my perception. I haven't read either of those in a while. I have very little time to read, of course, but maybe when I get to it I'll change my thinking on *It*.

You talked a little bit about the misconception of King as a pop writer. What are some other misconceptions you see about King and his work?
Well, that "it's only horror." That he's crap. That he's a joke. That he is the Big Mac of popular literature, and that's partially his own fault, and he has since rescinded that. He's retracted that, because that kind of self-deprecation just feeds into the insanity regarding the popular perception of his work when it comes to critics. And also, and this one is *huge*—that he just makes horror movies. I frequently come across woefully ignorant, unread, uneducated people who say this.... I'm in New Haven, and we are an educated state, but it also has its roots in blue collar. A lot of these people barely made it out of high school, and they don't read. They simply do not read books. All of their perception of popular culture comes from TV and movies. So they're like, "Oh, you're a writer? What do you do?" I say I've written several books on Stephen King and the Beatles and the *Titanic*, and blah, blah, blah. And they'll say, "Oh, Stephen King? I love his movies!" And I always say, "You know he's a writer first and foremost," and they'll say, "Yeah, I don't read his books, but I like a lot of his movies." That's one of the misconceptions from the woefully uneducated—that King just makes horror movies.

There are several misconceptions. Why? How did this happen? Churning out books like crazy, people automatically think—and this is just the way our culture perceives that type of productivity—they just assume that if it's popular and if that much of it's being done, it can't be any good. King has not said he's intentionally going to churn out so much stuff that I'm not going to be taken seriously. He's writing because he's a writer. He gets ideas and he writes them.

One of the first questions I used to ask first-year writing students was, if you wake up tomorrow morning with ten million dollars in your checking account, do you show up for class? And half the class used to say no. I'd say, "But you're in a writing class.... Don't you think that even with ten million dollars in the bank you'd still have to study the craft?" And they'd say, "Maybe, but with that kind of money, I'm not going to school." And yet King has said he's never sat down to write something with the intention of making money. "I'd write them even if I didn't get paid for them." And I know exactly how he feels because what I'm doing now—teaching, writing, editorial consultation—if I was rich, I would not charge for any of that. I used to joke with the chair of the English Department and say, "You know what? If I hit the Powerball, I'd teach for free. I'll donate my salary back to the school." And I meant it. I even tell my lecture audience this: if I had a ton of money, I would do these lectures anyway, for the greater good, because they're educational, they're entertaining, and I just believe in them. And then I would hit the punchline, which is, "But I have not hit the Powerball yet, so where's my check?" And they laugh. But the underlying principle is dominant in someone like King, who writes because he's a writer. Period. That's it. It's not a job. It's an avocation. It's a commitment. It's a part of who he is. And you can always sort of sense the writers who did it to make money, because they don't turn out a lot of stuff after they hit it big.

Dean Koontz is a serious writer, and he's always writing. He's got more money than God. So I believe that he's a sincere writer, as well. And a lot of King fans love him, too. But then there are writers.... Some will say as I mentioned earlier that it's a creative lag. [Laughs.] Is it? Or is it just that you don't have to worry as much about next month's mortgage payment? You don't need an advance or to fulfill a contract to get paid after you turn in the book...

What were some of the challenges you faced in compiling The Shape Under the Sheet: The Complete Stephen King Encyclopedia?

That's a ridiculous book. It's 850 pages, and it's complete through *Four Past Midnight* (1990). It was five years of research, and I had one assistant—my mother. She was working part time and I would keep her stocked in legal pads. I had read all of King's works, but I had not taken notes on the people, places, and things within them. So I would give her *'Salem's Lot* and I would say, "Every time you come across a person, place, or thing, jot it down, give me a page number, and a brief description of who or what they are." And then I took—I still have these legal pads, and they fill two file cabinet drawers.... I would go through them page by page with the book next to me, look at her notes, and then write the entries as they appear in the encyclopedia. The encyclopedia has 18,000 entries. Add to that all the other features, including the thirty interviews, and the film stuff, and the *Castle Rock* stuff.... It kind of grew on its own. It was sort of like "It Grows On You" (1973). I'd say, "Well, I've got to include this, and I've got to include this..." And before I knew it, five years had gone by, and the manuscript—this was post-floppies, on three-and-a-half inch disks—I had like 100 of those! I wrote it in Microsoft Word 1.0, maybe 2.0. It was primitive. Today things would be different if I ever went back to it.

So the challenges were just the volume. Once again, I knew exactly what the book was gonna look like when it was done. That same thing had happened to me with the *Mayberry* book. I knew after I conceived the book exactly what it was going to look like. With the King encyclopedia, the core of the book—the entries—I knew exactly what they were going to look like. I knew that every book and every short story from each of the anthologies would be included. All the people, places, and things—they're all there. My editor was very gifted in writing and doing indexes and things like that, and he designed it. So when I turned it in, it was just this massive amount of information. Then it took another year for them to put it together.

That's when Dave Hinchberger stepped in and asked if he could do the limited edition through the Overlook Connection. I am very proud of Dave's first edition, and that was the Overlook Connection's first book! [Laughs.] So the biggest challenge was just the massive amount of work that went into it. This is why I could never go back to it. I could never, in a million years, find the time or the energy to write about everything beyond *Four Past Midnight*. A few years ago this book packager and I were talking about doing a *Dark Tower* book [laughs] and we were back and forth on formatting. I'm thinking, how comprehensive do you want it? It never happened; they just decided it was going to be too costly to do it the way they wanted. King had already approved it and we were ready to go to work on it, but I was hesitant, mainly because I'm thinking, "Oh, my God, I'm back to this?"

He's so prolific. This hearkens back to your first question about what I admire about King, and that's the output. How can someone write so well and so much so steadily? That's why he's a very unique artistic voice, and we're all blessed to be living through his creative period. Imagine being alive when Picasso was painting, and there was media coverage of his latest work. Or being alive when Dickens was writing, and there was a timely same-day review of *Tale of Two Cities* (1859) in *The New York Times*.

We take it for granted. A lot of people take it for granted—our working artists. When they're gone, we suddenly realize we are now going to miss their creative output. John Lennon died when he was only 40 years old. A lot of people took him for granted whenever he would release something new, and now we fantasize about what his later work might have looked like. Paul McCartney is the same way. People take him for granted. He's a Beatle, and he's incredibly productive. He's a genius. In 50 years people are going to look at the Beatles the way they look at Rogers and Hammerstein today—just these monstrously creative artists whom we're lucky to experience as they're producing new art.

How did your book The Lost Work of Stephen King *come about?*

It was an accidental book. After having written the encyclopedia, I was in the network. I was suddenly interacting and communicating with people who had access to things like "People, Places, and Things" and "Squad D." My book was the first that actually talked about "People, Places, and Things." Suddenly I was seeing things that were unavailable to your typical fan. After I had compiled a bunch of these things for the encyclopedia, I still had a whole load of stuff—essays, poetry, "An Evening with God." I was good friends with Charlie Fried, who had a massive collection of unpublished stuff. I also had access to several boxes containing letters and check stubs from Stephen King. I remember seeing a photocopy of a check for $1.7 million royalties for *Pet Sematary* (1983). There were manuscripts and short stories and novels and correspondence…. Long story short, between mainstream research, like finding "My Little Serrated Security Blanket"—I was the first one to write about that—or finding "What Stephen King Does for Love" in a teenage girls magazine…

Stephen J. Spignesi

I wasn't thinking, How can I exploit all these things and write a book? My immediate thought was, fans would go nuts if they knew about this stuff! I ended up writing for *Midnight Graffiti* magazine; it was an essay on the stories King had talked about writing but had never written. These were the "almost stories." Basically there ended up being enough material there for me to turn out a 75,000 word book. That went to just a mainstream publisher, Citadel, so that's how that came about. Then later they became New Page Books, who put out *The Essential Stephen King*.

So *The Lost Work of Stephen King* was kind of an accident because I had all this material and I really wanted to share what this stuff was about with serious King fans. I knew that the overwhelming majority of King readers knew him from what was on the *New York Times* bestseller list and what was in theaters. Then there was all this other stuff.... When I was doing *The Essential Stephen King* and ranking the top 100 works, I had over a thousand pieces listed. And I read pretty much everything. Fans weren't aware that King wrote book reviews and non-fiction essays and he wrote a recipe and he wrote screenplays and he wrote poetry.... He's been very prolific. In fact, I'm joking now that in this day and age, as I'm doing *Lost Work Volume Two* for Overlook Connection Press, that I should include his Twitter tweets! [Laughs.] I mean, they are his writing. That would be the kind of O.C.D. attention to detail that I would embrace the way I work. I mean, it's writing by Stephen King! I don't know if I'm really going to include the tweets. Those are all pretty mainstream. They're all over the place, so there's nothing really "lost" about them. So I'm still covering stuff that's technically lost, but not really lost—just kind of inaccessible.

What are some of your favorite obscure King pieces?
I talk about "My Little Serrated Security Blanket." I like that a lot. King was asked to review an ice ax, and King being King, his mind went down nefarious paths. It becomes a murder weapon, and he begins musing on how deep it might go—what notch it might stop at if you put it into somebody's head. [Laughs.] It's funny. It's horrific. It's short. That's a huge favorite of mine. I love "Squad D"—the story he wrote for Harlan Ellison's *Dangerous Visions*. Harland of course rejected the story unless King made some editorial changes, and King did not agree with them. That was a story that was ready to be published, and it ended up not being published. So I got the manuscript of that, and I always loved it. The idea of a person

fading from a picture.... That's spooky to me. I've always liked that kind of ghostly horror. So yeah, I'm a big fan of "Squad D."

I'm also a big fan—and King is not—of his "Garbage Truck" columns. I reviewed every one of them. He says they're not up to the standard of where he's at now. Of course they're not. But you notice that *Hearts in Suspension* (2016) is coming out, right? And there are several of those "Garbage Truck" columns included in that book. And that book is being published with King's approval. So I think he found that there are columns in that book that are very fine writing. A lot of it is fun, and film reviews, and not stuff that you would not really consider quality literature. But still, it was Stephen King's thinking back then. I believe it has great value as kind of a contribution to his ultimate literary biography. So I'm a big fan of those columns.

I like *The Plant* (1982), the first six chapters he sent out at Christmastime. I love "Before the Play," which was the beginning of *The Shining*. "Why I Wrote *The Eyes of the Dragon*" is an interesting essay. And "The Dreaded X," which was a massive essay in the *Castle Rock* newsletter. I may be wrong about this, but I don't think it's ever appeared anywhere else. It ran over the duration of two issues, and it was all about the movie-rating system. And this was sort of King's *Danse Macabre* (1981) period, when he was reviewing culture. One of the things I talk about when I do my King lecture is this letter he wrote to *TV Guide*. He was like 22 at the time, and he was talking about the criticism of a Western TV show for being overly bloody. The letter was short, but the whole point was how drama equals conflict, and if the work is going to be realistic, then there's going to be violence. It was just terrific. And in "The Dreaded X," he writes this whole big overview about how movies are rated and what counts as a negative in terms of ratings. You know, violence is okay, but sex isn't. I've always liked that essay quite a bit.

An Evening with God, the one-act play where he meets God and they watch TV. That's a lot of fun. There's a lot of unpublished stuff of his that I like. In fact, I've always dreamt of doing a massive anthology of lost works. Not write about them, but actually reprint them. Being the editor. But he'd never go for that. A lot of this stuff is unavailable because he wrote it and now he's done with it. He sometimes doesn't consider his position in popular culture and literature in American writing as heavily as someone like I do, or someone like you do—people who write about King as an artistic force. I'm guessing, and this is purely speculation, but I think he'd say, Who would want to read it? [Laughs.] And I think there would be lots of people who would want to read a big massive collection of his nonfiction and unpublished fiction, going back to 1960 up through his stuff from today. But that's just a pipe dream of mine; it'll never happen.

You once contemplated writing a biography of Stephen King. Whatever happened to that project?

George Beahm happened. He's a dear friend, and he did two or three literary biographies of King. And they're excellent. They really are. And I was thinking, you know something? I'm not going to simply reheat stuff that George has already written about. I would end up having to use him as a source because the factual research he did in those books are incredible. So I just decided, you know, I've always focused on the work. And knowing me, if I ever did decide to write a biography, it would not end up being a biography. It would be a year-by-year look at his output, and that's not a biography! [Laughs.] He doesn't think his life should be talked about or written about for fans to indulge in because he feels—he's said this many times—the work, the work, the work. "That's all I want considered." And yet he did double the size of *On Writing* (2000) to include a very-detailed autobiographical section. You know, the last autobiographical material was in *Danse Macabre* when he talked about Sputnik and growing up in Durham, Maine. But he's never written an autobiography, and yet *On Writing* is absolutely part-autobiography, part-writing tutorial. This was after the accident, when I guess he wanted to recount and recap his life and his addictions and so forth.

But again, that's him. It's *his* life. If he wants to write about it, more power to him. But in terms of actual biographies written by others.... I've never seen him talk about the biography that was written a few years back. I don't think he's ever even mentioned it or acknowledged its existence. I decided that first of all it wasn't interesting to me. In fact, George Beahm was telling me that he talked to George R.R. Martin at a convention recently about the possibility of his doing a literary biography of him. And he said do it. But George R.R. Martin said, "Who's gonna care? Who's gonna wanna read about my life? I get up and I sit in front of a computer and I write stories." George said, "Well, I think your fans would be interested," so Martin approved it. But in King's case, I think he's actually asked that question: "Who cares? Don't the stories matter the most?" I kind of ended up leaning toward that and agreeing with him. So now I'm focusing on the work, the writing.

You delved into a lot of King's work in your book The Essential Stephen King. *How did that project come about?*

I had been doing a bunch of "100" books, and the way writers think is, "Is there a book here?" And I realized there was—*The Essential Stephen King*. Usually for something like that, when I look at other ranking books, the first thing I look at is the author. I ask, is this person credible in terms of writing about what they're writing about? Is their opinion informed? Or is this a fan book, which doesn't really have a lot of lasting merit? So if I see a book ranking Dickens novels in order, the first thing I look at is the biography of the writer. If the writer is a Ph.D. in English Literature and he's been teaching courses on Charles Dickens at Oxford for the last thirty years, then I'm like, yeah, this guy knows what he's talking about! So I have respect for his opinion. So I asked myself, am I credible? Some of the others were just research-driven books about historical events and biographical people, but when it comes down to art, the writer has to be credible and has to be a student of the work. I immediately answered my own question—yeah, I think I've paid my dues in terms of studying King and writing about him whereby my opinion of his top 100 works will have merit and that it will hopefully entertain and educate readers.

So my second question was, am I going to be able to pick 100 works by Stephen King and then explain why they are superior enough to be listed here? And I still look at his work that way. Now I'm so far behind in terms of an update. I mean, look at all the books he's come out with since that book came out. I would move something out of the top 10 to put *Revival* (2014) up there. That's just Stephen King channeling Lovecraft. It's an incredible work. *11/22/63* (2011) is another one. So there you go—what do you drop? The list is 100 titles. Do I drop *Bag of Bones* (1998) to add *11/22/63*? How could I do that? So that's why I've never tackled an update of *The Essential Stephen King*; mainly because I really don't like the idea of dropping anything from the list. But it would be inevitable if I wanted to consider everything he's done since *The Essential Stephen King* came out.

You've written extensively about Stephen King. What do you think it is about his work that keeps drawing you back?

He's exciting. It's an exciting experience to read him, and that's what reading is all about. Yes, we can read to learn; we can read to become enlightened; we can read to experience the human condition in a way that is basically slice-of-life stuff. But King is a very powerful storyteller. I used to describe the experience of reading him as being pulled through the book—your eyes don't see the words. The writing process is not sublimated, but it's almost like it's superseded by this experience of being able to *see* what he's telling us. He's a very exciting writer. He engages you in ways that, for me, very few other writers do.

Paul Tremblay

Paul Tremblay was born in Colorado, and raised in Massachusetts. Tremblay had always been a smart young man, and he first started considering becoming an author just after high school. He attended Providence College. During the summers he worked at a factory job back home in Massachusetts. He received his bachelor's degree in 1993 and then a master's degree in Mathematics from the University of Vermont. He then started working on short fiction, ultimately having his work appear in a number of publications, including *Mindkites*, *Twilight Showcase*, and *Fables*.

Tremblay's first published book was a collection of short stories entitled *Compositions for the Young and Old* (2014), named after a song by Bob Mould. He then published a collection of interconnected stories titled *City Pier: Above and Below* (2007). He soon published his first novel, *The Little Sleep* (2009), which followed the story of a narcoleptic Boston detective. The book, which *Booklist* dubbed "a promising debut," established Tremblay as a talented author with a unique voice. That same year, Tremblay also published a novella entitled *The Harlequin and the Train* (2009). The following year, Tremblay published his second proper short story collection, *In the Mean Time* (2010). That same year he also published a follow-up novel to *The Little Sleep* titled *No Sleep Till Wonderland* (2010). After that, he published the novel *Swallowing a Donkey's Eye* (2012), with ChiZine Publications.

Tremblay found breakout success with the much-acclaimed horror novel *Head Full of Ghosts* (2015). The novel received lots of attention when Stephen King tweeted that it "scared the hell out of me, and I'm pretty hard to scare." *Head Full of Ghosts* would later receive the Bram Stoker Award for Best Novel. The following year, Tremblay published another novel, *Disappearance at Devil's Rock* (2016), once again to great acclaim.

At the time of this writing, Tremblay's newest novel, *The Cabin at the End of the World* (2018), described as a "home invasion horror story with an inventive twist," was nearing publication.

Do you remember your earliest interactions with Stephen King's writing, and if so, what were your thoughts on what you read?

The first time I tried to read Stephen King when I had just graduated from high school. I had just turned eighteen. I had scoliosis—curvature of the spine—so I had a spinal fusion. I was sitting in my house after a week in the hospital and I thought, I'm going to read *It* (1986). My parents owned the book, so I thought I'd give it a try. I read the first chapter and I wound up throwing the book across the room because I was so terrified by Georgie getting pulled into the sewer by Pennywise. [Laughs.] There was no way I was going to be stuck in the house all summer, just scared out of my mind. That was my first serious attempt to read Stephen King. I wasn't really someone who did a lot of reading for pleasure when I was in middle school and high school. I was a good student and I read all the books that were assigned to me, but in my free time I shot a lot of free throws in the backyard. I still thought I could become Larry Bird, which never really worked out. And I watched a lot of movies. But *It* was my first attempt, and I failed miserably.

Then, when I was in college, my girlfriend, who is now my wife, bought me a copy of *The Stand* (1978). I read the entire thing. I was just entranced by it, and I completely adored it. After I read *The Stand*, I spent the next two years up at the University of Vermont, struggling to get my Master's Degree. But while I was doing that, I read just about everything Stephen King had published up to that point. Then I moved on to Peter Straub and the like. But really, reading Stephen King when I was twenty-one, that was really when I first fell in love with reading. That was obviously the most important first step to eventually becoming a writer.

Like Stephen King, you're a voracious reader now. What do you feel that brings to a writer's work?

I can't imagine not reading. If you are going to be a writer, you have to read. You're not going to be a good writer without reading. Every once in a while you'll hear someone say, "I don't read that much." And I think, "Well, you're not going to be a very good writer." But for me personally, I like to be exposed to as many different voices as possible. And also as many different characters and stories as possible. Obviously you want to learn what works for a story and what works for a character. But even with books that aren't as successful, there's still an important lesson to be learned from them; what doesn't work, or why do you feel something doesn't work?

It's hard for me to come up with a pat answer, because for me reading is extremely important to learning the craft. I guess if I was to go back to what made me love to read, it was just the idea of losing myself in these stories. I hadn't realized that people wrote books like that—like *The Stand* or stuff I was exposed to by writers like Joyce Carol Oates. Growing up I was reading stuff for school—Shakespeare and all the other stuff you're assigned, which are all well and good. But when I stumbled across these books, I got really excited and soon realized I wanted to try to do something like that myself.

As a writer yourself, what do you see as being Stephen King's primary strengths?

I think one of his primary strengths is his characters. He seems to have a never-ending well of characters. Even with a lot of them being based on the small town Maine people, I can't think of a single King story where I felt like he just recycled his characters. That's amazing to me when you consider how much the man has written. The characters are the primary thing that continues to draw me back to his work.

What about his characterizations do you see as being something other writers can learn from?

I think there's an authenticity that's difficult to articulate. That's one of the first things I think of when I think about a Stephen King character. There's an emotional authenticity there, and for most of them there are complexities as well. I think I would certainly argue that in the larger history of modern fiction that Stephen sort of brought to the table when he arrived on the scene was that they were complex and they were authentic.

What are your favorite King works, and what are some things you admire the most about them?

I would say *The Stand*, probably because it was the first thing of his that I read. I just loved that so much. I would like to sit aside some time and go back and reread. As a reader I generally forget a lot of details about the books, but I always remember how they made me feel when I was reading them. It's unusual for me, but there are many scenes from that book that are etched in my brain. It's almost as though I just read it yesterday. I would also say *'Salem's Lot* (1975), which is a book of his that I've read multiple times. I love that, and it's one of the very best vampire tales I've ever read.

One of his newer books, which I'm actually sort of afraid to go back and read, is *Bag of Bones* (1998). That's really one of his better works. The reason why I'm afraid to go back and reread it is because there's a scene towards the end of the book that takes place in a bathroom in a bathtub.... I remember when I read it, I remember that Stephen pulled this trick where you didn't know what the character was doing, but you were in the character's head sort of realizing what was happening at the same time the character was doing it. I'm afraid to reread that, because I want to hold on to that initial memory of complete and utter shock.

I also like a lot of his short work, as well. I've reread his earlier collections, like *Night Shift* (1978) and *Skeleton Crew* (1985).

You mentioned to me previously that Stephen King's shorter work had a tremendous influence on your early short stories. What are some of King's shorter works that had an influence on you?

The Mist (1980) isn't a short story, per se, but it certainly stands out. There's one in *Nightmares & Dreamscapes* (1993) called "The End of the Whole Mess" (1986). The crux of the story is that a drug has been given to people through the water supply that causes them to slow down, like Alzheimer's. The thing that stood out to me was that the narrator sort of deteriorates as the story goes along.

"The Boogeyman" (1973) was one that absolutely terrified me. I think most people who have read that would agree that it's very effective. It's very simple, but it really packs a wallop.

Do you continue to see a King influence in your work today?

Most of my early attempts at writing were sort of like poorly veiled

Stephen King rip-offs. They'll never see the light of day, and that includes my first attempt at a novel. That was probably about 60,000 words. I have a hard time looking at my own work and saying, "This came from Stephen King..." Unless I'm sort of overtly referencing something. My novel, *Head Full of Ghosts*, did reference some of my favorite horror novels. I mentioned *The Shining* there—both the book and the film. I can't identify Stephen's influence, but it's impossible for it not to be there. I'll circle back around to when you asked me what I thought Steve really excelled at and I said, "character." To me, because of Stephen King, as a reader I tend to be a character first kind of guy. I hope that's reflected in my own writing. I'm sure that's Stephen's biggest influence on my work right there.

Are there any King works that make you say, "Man, I wish I had written that"?

For me it would be *Bag of Bones*. That really jumps out at me. I wish I could have written *The Stand*, even though I know I could never write *The Stand*. [Laughs.] It's funny that you bring that up, because I was just thinking about that randomly today. I think sometimes, "I wish I had written that book." I think maybe the highest compliment would be, "I'm glad I didn't write that book because now I get to enjoy it as a reader!" Then I can revisit it as a reader. And that's what I would say about so many of Stephen's books that I enjoy. I wish I could have written *Bag of Bones*, but in a weird way I'm very glad that I didn't, because it's there for me as a reader as a much more stress-free and enjoyable experience. It's nice when someone else writes a book you enjoy that much because then they get to do all the hard work and you can just sit there and have a good time with it.

Are there any Stephen King works that you consider extremely underrated?

I hate to keep going back to *Bag of Bones*, but I don't really think it gets as much as appreciation as it should. Most of the time when people talk about Stephen's work, that novel doesn't really come up as much as it probably should, and that's a shame. I really do believe it's one of his best novels.

And then his short stories, in general. Whenever Stephen is mentioned or discussed in articles, they tend to mostly focus on his novels. But I think he's an amazingly talented short story writer. I think the fans in general appreciate that he's an amazing short story writer, but I feel that that's sometimes left out of the general literary discussion of Stephen King. Those contributions tend to be somewhat overlooked, and I know it's because he's written so many great novels, but I still don't think it's fair.

Not to put you on the spot here, but are there any King works that don't resonate with you personally?

Yeah. I would say the one that jumps out to me is *Insomnia* (1994). I read that a long time ago, and it just didn't resonate with me. It felt a little bit slow and I had a hard time connecting with it. And maybe that's more of a reflection of my age at the time I read it; maybe I'd feel differently about it now that I'm middle-aged as opposed to my mid-twenties. Most of that novel is about an older gentleman, and I couldn't really relate to his struggles and experiences.

I haven't read it in a long time either, but I would be curious to go back and read it now, knowing that it ties in with The Dark Tower.

I'm in that same boat. I hadn't read *The Dark Tower* books yet at the time I read *Insomnia*, so maybe that would change my perception.

King has spoken very highly of your novel, Head Full of Ghosts. *I'm guessing that had to be quite a thrill for you.*

Yes! Oh, yes! You mean August 19, 2015? [Laughs.] That was one of the highlights of my writing career. It's funny. I tried to send my book to Stephen through publishers and whatnot, and I knew it was the longest of long shots. So the book had been out for a few months and I'd kind of given up on that. I figured he probably wouldn't see it, although I really hoped he would.

But it was a hot day in August, and I was moving furniture around in my house, which is never fun. I was kind of hot and cranky. And around 6:30 that night, my phone started buzzing and blinking with all sorts of messages from friends who had read his tweet before I had. So when I read his tweet, I'm not ashamed to admit that I got emotional. I mean, Stephen King not only read my book, but he really enjoyed it! And he did it without the publisher asking him for a blurb or anything. He just posted on Twitter that he really enjoyed the book. I had become a reader, and later a writer, because of Stephen King. As soon as I saw the tweet, I just stopped what I was doing, opened up my laptop, and grabbed a few adult beverages from the refrigerator. And then I just sat down and kind of basked in all the congratulations that were pouring in for the rest of the evening. It was a wonderful night that I'll never forget.

Have you had the chance to meet Stephen King?

I've never had the opportunity to meet him, but we have exchanged some e-mails over the last few years. He's very nice, very generous. He's given me a lot of book recommendations. Hopefully we get to meet in person someday. That would be a huge thrill for me.

Head Full of Ghosts *has been optioned as a movie. Does Hollywood's treatment of Stephen King's work frighten you in any way in regards to having your own work of horror adapted to film?*

There are quite a few writers who will tell you that you're better off getting the book rights purchased but then never made. [Laughs.] But I'm excited and hopeful. Even if it turns out to be a horrible movie, it makes me thrilled to have a book of mine turned into a movie. I'm sure I'll be excited if it doesn't turn out the way I want it to, but that's beyond my control. I'm not writing the screenplay, so if things go wrong I get to blame other people. [Chuckles again.] I remain optimistic. Robert Downey, Jr.'s production company and Regents Theater are the two production companies who are hard at work on it. They just renewed the option a couple of months ago. So I guess we'll just have to wait and see.

What are your favorite Stephen King film adaptations?

My favorite might be the one that Stephen hates the most. I love *The Shining* (1980). I'm able to see it as a separate entity from the book. It's just so iconic and effective. I rewatched it recently with my daughter, who was seeing it for the first time. It was a lot of fun watching that movie with someone who's never seen it before. It really holds up. Just that tight atmosphere of the movie—it's totally unrelenting for the entire two-hour running time. You can't take your eyes off it.

But, having said that, I can understand someone taking the book that you have created inside your head, and then making something that is completely different. I think you would have a difficult time being objective about that. I think that's just a part of being human.

I haven't watched it in a long time, but the original TV version of *'Salem's Lot* scared the hell out of me when I was a kid. I think *Pet Sematary*

(1989) is pretty effective. The *Different Seasons* (1982) movies—*The Shawshank Redemption* (1994) and *Stand By Me* (1986)—are some of the better ones, but I sort of prefer the horror ones myself.

Are there any elements of Stephen King's career that you particularly admire?

There are many things to admire about Stephen. He's so generous with his support of other writers. He's also very generous with his money and support of charitable causes, particularly causes that relate to literacy. I love how he uses his big platform on Twitter and is not shy at all about giving his political opinions. Those are all things I find extremely admirable.

BEV VINCENT

After earning a Ph.D. in chemistry at Dalhousie University, Texas-based Bev Vincent began writing "News from the Dead Zone" for *Cemetery Dance* magazine. The column, which he continues to write today, focuses on all aspects of Stephen King's work. His writing there has established him as an authority on King, and his essays, interviews, and book reviews have appeared in a number of publications including *Accent Literary Review*, *Hellnotes*, and the *Conroe Courier* in Conroe, Texas.

Eventually Vincent would write his first book, not surprisingly about Stephen King. The book, *The Road to the Dark Tower: Exploring Stephen King's Magnum Opus* (2004), recaps the series and "points out the most germane aspects of other King novels and stories that touch upon it, sketches its leading characters, notes influences on it, and discusses its creation and the layered, self-consciously reflexive concept that animates it" (*Booklist*). The book, authorized by King, would ultimately be nominated for the prestigious Bram Stoker Award.

That same year Vincent and co-writer Brian Freeman updated an idea that had originated with Stephen J. Spignesi's *The Stephen King Quiz Book* (1990) two decades before it, with their own up-to-date *The Illustrated Stephen King Trivia Book* (2004), featuring illustrations by Glenn Chadbourne. Vincent also saw the publication of a third work about King that year, the *Cemetery Dance* promotion chapbook *The Good, the Bad & the Ugly: Eight Secondary Characters from the Dark Tower Series* (2004).

Five years later, Vincent wrote *The Stephen King Illustrated Companion* (2009) for Fall River Press. The book, a companion to King's oeuvre, was intended to be an interactive approach to the works featuring a treasure trove of previously unseen memorabilia, letters, and documents. Vincent would receive both an Edgar Award nomination and a second Bram Stoker

Bev Vincent

Award nomination for the effort. Vincent wrote a second chapbook, titled *Twenty-First Century King*, in 2012. This was an anthology of his twenty-one reviews of King's work to date. He would then revisit Mid-World with a second book-length study, *The Dark Tower Companion: A Guide to Stephen King's Epic Fantasy* (2017), which he intended to be "one stop shopping for all information about *The Dark Tower*."

In 2018, Vincent served as co-editor with Stephen King on the anthology *Flight or Fright*, which featured stories by King, Joe Hill, and Richard Matheson, among others. Vincent is also an accomplished fiction writer. His short stories have appeared in publications such as *Ellery Queen's Mystery Magazine* and *Alfred Hitchcock's Mystery Magazine*. His short story "One of Those Weeks" appeared alongside offerings by Stephen King, Whitley Streiber, and David J. Schow in the anthology *Borderlands 5* (2003).

What was your first encounter with the work of Stephen King, and what were your thoughts on that?

It's funny. I've read a lot of authors whom I couldn't go back and remember when I actually started reading them. But I remember Stephen King very clearly. It was 1979 and I was in my first year at university. There was a used bookstore about two miles from the campus, and I used to go there every Saturday morning. At the time I was reading mostly people like Isaac Asimov, Robert Heinlein, and Piers Anthony. I'd gather up five or six books each time I went. One time when I was there I saw this black paperback on this end cap. It caught my attention. It was called *'Salem's Lot* (1975), and it had this red drop of blood on its cover. I picked it up and thought, *hmm, this rings a bell*. Someone not too long ago had suggested this book. So I just added it to the stack of things I was buying that day.

That was my introduction to King. I was hooked immediately. I was captivated by that novel, and then went about seeking out other books he had published. This was in 1979, so that was a fairly small selection. I went through them pretty quickly. That was the beginning of my addiction. I had always been that kind of guy. I didn't read just a few of an author's books. I read them all. I had read all of the Agatha Christie books.... So that kind of set me on this path. I would read everything he had out, and would then wait until his next book would come out. I was an undergrad and didn't have a whole lot of money, but the first hardcover books I ever bought were *Cujo* (1981) and *Different Seasons* (1982).

You've written about King's work many times during your career. What is it about his work that most resonates with you? What draws you back?

I'd say it's a combination of things. There's the storytelling, obviously. King writes really fascinating stories. For me, even more than that, it's been his characters. I've often said that if he started writing romance novels, I'd probably buy them and read them because I know there would be good characters that I would really latch onto and care about. That's been the main thing.

It's interesting. There have been lots of popular authors who with loyal fan bases who don't seem to acquire the same sort of fans who want to talk about the work. I first noticed that back in the '90s in the early days of the Internet. There would be forums for different authors. I would look at the ones for John Grisham, and there really weren't a lot of people there talking about his books. Then I would look at the Stephen King forum and there would be hundreds of people posting five or six times a day. It was people just wanting to talk about the books. So I'm not alone in thinking that his stuff is not only interesting to read, but that there's a lot there to discuss.

Who are some of your favorite King characters? I know you're a guy who says he doesn't really like to come up with lists or name favorites of things, but are there any who come to your mind?

I really like Stu Redmond from *The Stand*. He was a guy we spent a lot of time with, and I really grew to like him as a character. He was a gruff, sort of contemporary guy. I liked him a lot. I also like Johnny Smith from *The Dead Zone* (1979). He was a guy who was sort of put upon. It was a curse rather than a blessing, so it's fascinating to see how he handles these situations in his life and survives.

Your interactions with Stephen King started fairly early on. You wrote a fan letter to him in the early 1980s, and King wrote you back. What do you remember about that experience?

It was probably the first time I'd ever written to an author. This was somewhere around 1982 or 1983… *Different Seasons* hadn't yet come out.

I have no recollection of what I wrote. I know I talked about the various books, and I mentioned Tabby's books. *Small World* (1981) had just come out and I had read that. So he wrote back. He did that a lot at that time. There are a lot of people who have these little postcard-sized typed messages in response to fan mail.

He said, "Tabby sends her thanks." He also said, "The next book will be *Different Seasons*. I hope you pick that up." And then in a separate letter he had his office send me a bibliography of everything he'd written that was available at the time; essays, short stories that hadn't been collected. It all fit on two sheets of paper. So I carried those two pieces of paper around with me in my wallet for the next couple of years, trying to find all of these short stories that were published in *Ellery Queen's Mystery Magazine* or in the adult magazines. There was a store I used to haunt looking for old issues of magazines. So I've still got that little postcard with his signature and response on it.

You've had a few interactions with Stephen King through the years. What is Stephen King like as a person?

The main thing that stands out to me is what a regular guy he is. I think a lot of people expect him to be larger than life or creepy. He'll kind of put on that appearance and oversell that stuff because he understands that some people expect that from him. Usually when we've talked, we've discussed books we liked reading or shows and movies we liked to watch. Just the kind of things you would sit down and talk to any other person about. I think I've met him in person or six or seven times. We've always primarily corresponded by e-mail when I've had questions or have sought recommendations for TV series and books.

Very rarely have we ever talked about the business. I don't say, "What are you working on now?" or "How's the new book selling?" We just talk about normal stuff. Every now and then he'll send me a short story he's written or I'll send him one, just to entertain one another. But usually we just talk about our common interests. For instance, we both have a common interest in crime novels and television series.

You've written a lot about his work, and at times you've had to be a little bit critical of some of his stuff. Does having a relationship with King, even if it's a minor relationship, ever make it difficult for you to be objective about his work? Or, on the flip side, does it ever concern you that people might think you're not objective for that reason? Do you think about that at all?

I thought about this when I wrote my review of *The Dark Tower* (2017) movie, which I actually enjoyed quite a bit. I got some pushback on that. People were saying that I was a shill for Stephen King, because a lot of people did not like that movie. I sort of had the advantage of having interviewed Akiva Goldsman and Ron Howard years ago when I was prepping *The Dark Tower Companion*. I knew what they were planning, so I had sort of come to my own terms with it being something completely different. I was sort of onboard for what their big picture plan was, so I was able to sit back and enjoy the movie. I went back and wrote a very positive review and I got pilloried for it! [Laughs.] But point taken. It's difficult to be objective sometimes.

I remember before he and I communicated very much, I was writing my column for *Cemetery Dance* called "News from the Dead Zone." I've been doing that since 2001. And Steve had written a script for a novel called *Asylum*. He was adapting someone else's novel. The script had leaked out to a few people in the media, and someone had reviewed the script. They called it "boring." I think that's probably the highest insult you can pay to Steve about something he's written because being boring is probably as bad as it gets. So he read my column in *Cemetery Dance* and he had his assistant send me the screenplay to ask me if I thought it was boring or not. But there is a tiny bit of me thinking there's a chance that what I'm writing over here, he might read over there.... But I'm writing primarily for the fans, myself being one of them. Someone else came back at me one time and said, "I read your review of this, and I don't know if you like it or not." That wasn't my goal, saying I really liked this or I really didn't like this. It was just to give my impressions of it after I had finished reading it. And I know that sometimes the reviews I turn in to *Cemetery Dance* make me think, "I don't know what impression I'm giving here about the book." I'll write 1,500 words about it, and sometimes not be sure if it's a positive review or a negative review. But those are what my thoughts are.

A lot of King fans had problems with Gerald's Game *(1992), but you've heralded it as an achievement. What qualities about that novel personally stand out for you?*

I was young, unmarried, and a little bit naïve when that novel came out, and I don't know that I truly appreciated it when I first read it. But then I read it again a number of years later after I was married, having had a little bit more meaningful relationships with women, and when I read it that second time I found myself very, very impressed with the depth and understanding of the female character. I sort of changed my opinion of it, and it was just a matter of having been a few years older and having had more life experience. I think that's been very much underappreciated, although now that the movie is out it is being given a second consideration by a lot of people.

Are there any other King writings that stand out in your mind as being underappreciated or undervalued?

I think that whole early '90s run where he did *Gerald's Game*, *Dolores Claiborne* (1992), and *Rose Madder* (1995). I think those were critically and popularly undervalued. I think each one of those novels has its own strengths. *Dolores Claiborne* was originally intended to be part of the *Gerald's Game* novel. The long first-person point-of-view from a female narrator … to carry that on at book length was quite an accomplishment.

Steve himself has been a little bit critical of *Rose Madder*. He's called it one of his plot-driven novels. It's been a while since I've read that one, so my memory of it isn't as clear as it is with some of the other books. I remember being swept away, especially by the opening section where her whole life gets thrown upside down and she gets into this "run for your life" situation. I was quite impressed with that at the time. Especially after a couple of books in the late '80s which had left me a little bit underwhelmed, like *Needful Things* (1991) and *The Tommyknockers* (1987). Those were not my favorites of King's books.

I think Tommyknockers *is hands down my least favorite of King's novels. I don't hate it, and I think for some writers it would be seen as a pretty good novel, but I think King is a writer who is capable of much better work. But when you write sixty or seventy books, you're gonna have the occasional misstep.*

The thing that bugged me the most about *The Tommyknockers* was that I really liked Bobbi and Gard—

And then they disappear for a huge chunk of the novel.

Then they disappear. It's almost like you're just turning pages and waiting to get back to them. I don't care about the terrible, self-destructive people who do bad stuff. I want to get back to Bobbi and Gard. That was what turned me off about that novel more than anything else.

I'm assuming the Dark Tower *novels—particularly* The Gunslinger *(1982)— are the Stephen King novels you've read the most times. After those, what would you say are the King novels you've read the most frequently?*

The Stand (1978) certainly. I read the original publication several times long before the full version eventually came out. *'Salem's Lot* is definitely another. It was my first King novel, and when I'm forced to select a favorite I still pick that one, in large part because it's the one that got me hooked.

I've read the early books a lot. It's because there was a time when those were the only ones I had, so I read them numerous times. Right now I'm listening to the *It* (1986) audiobook. I'm revisiting that one for the first time in a long time. But I've read it a number of times.

I sort of went through a period where I went back and reread them all in chronological order, a little bit like what Richard Chizmar is doing now with "Stephen King Revisited." And that was an interesting experience because although I had been aware of all the interconnections, to go back to the beginning and reread them knowing what's coming in the future chronologically, you start to fit more and more pieces together. That was sort of when other people were doing that same work and annotating all these connections between these books. It was a little bit of a voyage of discovery.

*Stephen King played a significant role in your book T*he Road to the Dark Tower *by actually allowing you to read the last three* Dark Tower *books before publication. How did that come to be?*

Because I had been writing the King column for *Cemetery Dance* for so long, people would ask me, "When are you going to write a book about Stephen King and his work?" For me the model for that kind of book has always been *At the Foot of the Story Tree* (2000), which is Bill Sheehan's book about Peter Straub's work. It's a really, really deep dive into Straub's thoughts. Because Straub's oeuvre is relatively small compared to Steve's, he was able to really look at everything. I always told people it would take me the rest of my life to do justice to King's work at that same level. I didn't see myself ever doing that. But then one morning, not long after

King had announced he was working on those three books, it occurred to me that one way to look at the big picture would be to focus on this one small subset of his work, since it spans his entire writing career. He actually started working on it before he went to work on *Carrie*. It also has tentacles that sort of reach into so many of his other works. So here was something manageable that I could do.

So I bounced it off of Richard Chizmar at *Cemetery Dance* and I said, "Is this is a good idea?" And he said yes. I said, "I can get started now, but clearly this is going to be a long-term project because I can only work on the first four books." I've found that sometimes it's best to just take a leap and ask for something, because it's definitely not going to happen if you don't ask. So I put together a one-page proposal and I faxed it to King's office. I said, "This is my idea for a book and this is what my plan is. Let me know if you hate the idea and I'll go peddle paper somewhere else. I'm not totally invested in this idea yet, so if you want I can just step back. But on the other hand, it would be neat if this book could be released not long after the final book in the series. So that could happen, would it be possible for me to see the books in advance?" I just flat out asked. And I got a message back the next day that said, "Steve says yes. The manuscripts are on their way." Two days later I had twenty-five pounds of *Dark Tower* manuscripts delivered to my door. It came with a little wink and a nod from his assistant that said, "By the way, Steve knows where you live." [Laughs.] The implication being that there were lots of secrets in these boxes that I had better hold on to. "You don't want to be on Steve's bad side."

I think his publisher was a little bit on the nervous side once she found out he'd done this. So I had to talk to her and reassure her that I was going to keep the secrets. I sort of set myself a policy because I knew that once word got out people were going to ask me questions about the manuscripts. I decided the only question I would answer was how many pages were in the manuscripts. That's it. Because once you start creeping over the line and giving people information, it's a slippery slope and all hell could break loose. So I gave a vow of silence, to the extent that my editor at New American Library hadn't read the manuscripts through a long period while I was working on this. Finally, when we were getting into the advanced editing stage, we got King's permission for him to read them as well. That way he could give me some meaningful feedback on the book and we could work together on it.

It was an interesting experience. I remember sitting in my living room with these big stacks of manuscript pages. It was an interesting way to read a book for the first time.

You would later write a second book about the series titled The Dark Tower Companion. *What made you decide to revisit that world?*

The main motivation for the second book was the announcement that they were making the movie. I thought, there's a fair amount that's gone on with *The Dark Tower* since *The Road to the Dark Tower* had come out. *The Wind Through the Keyhole* (2012) had come out, and all the Marvel graphic novels. So my original idea was to update *The Road to the Dark Tower*, but my agent suggested that I come up with a different approach. The difference between the two books is significant.

The Road to the Dark Tower was written for folks who had already finished the series, so now we're going to sit back and discuss it. "We're going to talk about the ending right up front from the beginning. We won't worry about spoilers." In order to look at things in the first book that anticipate things that happen later on in the series, you have to be able to talk about those things. I wrote a warning right at the front of *The Road to the Dark Tower* saying you shouldn't read it until you'd read the entire series. You could read the first chapter safely, but after that all bets were off. "You've been warned."

With *The Dark Tower Companion* my model audience was people who maybe hadn't finished the series or hadn't read any of it yet. Maybe they were coming to *The Dark Tower* after having seen the movie or reading the Marvel graphic novels. I thought they might want to find out a little more about this stuff. You didn't have to have read all the books. This was sort of one stop shopping for all information about *The Dark Tower*, so it had listings of people and places. There were also lots of interviews because I was personally interested in how the graphic novels were put together. As someone who didn't necessarily read as much of that type of stuff as many of my contemporaries had, I was fascinated by the process. So I talked to the people who wrote the outline; I talked to the people who wrote the scripts; the guy who did the pencil drawings; the guy who did the coloring.... I looked at all the stages of development to kind of put that picture together for me as much as anyone else. Then I talked to Akiva Goldsman and Ron Howard about their plans for the movie, and they were extremely forthcoming. At a very early stage they sort of laid out the whole plan for what they wanted to do. And for the first time ever I interviewed Steve, and we talked about general *Dark Tower* stuff. I did other things, like a map of the Mid-World.

This book was completely different. There was no overlap between the two books. There's no common text at all. And the intents were different. It turned out to be quite an interesting project once it was all said and done.

As you know, there are quite a few King readers who haven't read The Dark Tower *novels. What would you tell those readers if you were trying to convince them to give those books a chance?*

I think there are a couple of things that scare people away from *The Dark Tower*. One is the conception that they aren't horror novels. A lot of people come to Steve looking for a horror novel. I'm sure there are people who are hesitant to read his *Mr. Mercedes* books because they aren't horror novels. They're crime novels. Sometimes people paint themselves into a little corner with what they're reading and they don't want to branch out much. The other thing I think scares people off is *The Gunslinger*. It's a very different kind of book. It's different from Steve's other stuff, and it's different from the rest of the series as a whole. It's very moody and it's very introspective. It's all one character, and he's not a very likable character. He does very bad things. And this is supposed to be our hero. Some people have started that book and sort of been turned away. Steve recognizes that, to the extent that he rewrote it before the final two books came out to make it a little bit less of a put-off than the original version.

When I talk to people about *The Dark Tower* series I often recommend them to not start with the first book. I recommend them to start with *Little Sisters of Eluria* (1998), which is a novella written for a collection of novellas that were set in the trademark universes of fantasy/science fiction writers. The idea was to introduce readers to these worlds through short 100 page samples so they can get a feel for the writing and decide whether they like it or not, as opposed to trying to jump into reading some 8,000 page *Game of Thrones* (1996) thing. The story takes place earlier in Roland's life, when he was not quite so broken. He was a more likable guy. I think meeting him then gives people an easier transition into the series.

Perspectives on Stephen King

The other side of things is, once you get beyond the first book, the series becomes much more Stephen King–like. There are obviously fantasy/science fiction elements to it, but it's also as much horror as it is these other things. People who are hesitant can also skip the first book altogether and go right to the second one, where they'll find more familiar territory.

Aside from writing The Stephen King Illustrated Companion *in a mind-blowing six weeks, what aspects of that book are you most proud of?*

That was a fun project. Someone approached me out of the blue because of *The Road to the Dark Tower*. Barnes & Noble had approached this book packaging company, Becker&Mayer!, about doing a reader's companion on Stephen King. So this person from Becker&Mayer! approached me about writing it. I was a little bit skeptical because I had never heard of a book packager before. So I looked into them to find out what this was all about and I found out these were the people who designed and put together books for the mainstream publishers. The book we made was sort of a lighter vision of what I had envisioned with Bill Sheehan's *At the Foot of the Story Tree*. I had to pick and choose, because obviously I couldn't cover everything. But I wanted to pick a number of books that spanned his career up to that point and had significant biographical elements to them or they were written at times when something interesting was happening in King's life. By the latter I mean books like *Lisey's Story* (2006), which was written in the aftermath of his accident. By doing this, I could tie fiction and biography together.

But for me, the most wonderful part of this was the work of these terrific document researchers who go out and find all of this material that gets packaged together in the book along with it. They don't just print it on the page; they reproduce them so they look like the original products. If you read the Barnes & Noble Edgar Allan Poe book they did, you see that the *Times* page that has his obituary on it looks and feels like an old-time newspaper page. So King gave them access to his archives at the University of Maine and to some of the photo albums. I put them in touch with one of the biggest King collectors who has a lot of really rare stuff, including old letters with his publisher and things like that. Because I turned the text around so quickly, they were able to match things to what I'd written quite well, even on this accelerated publishing schedule. From the time I wrote the first word to the time the first book was in my hands, the whole thing was just nine months. And when you look at how elaborately these books they produce are, they're just stunning. I remember when I got the first books, my wife and I sat at the kitchen table, not even looking at my words at all. We just spent the evening opening these little envelopes and pulling out all these documents. And a lot of that stuff was really, really rare. Never-before-seen early drafts of manuscripts and short stories, a copy of the telegram he received when he first sold *Carrie*.... The other mind-blowing part of it was the price on the book, which was $25. Most of the time you can go into Barnes & Noble and get it for half of that! Collectors were telling me at the time, "We would have paid $100 for this book."

Fortunately it's had a good life. It went through a second printing of the original version, and then I went back and added some new material in a second edition. It's been quite popular.

You're an accomplished fiction writer yourself, even appearing in an anthology alongside King himself. I'm assuming King has inspired and influenced your work. In what ways do you see this to be true?

When I started writing fiction back in the late '90s, I was probably more influenced by King's writing conceptually in that I ended up writing in the horror genre for quite a while. Because that was what I was reading substantially. But as my writing has progressed I find myself getting more into crime fiction. I wrote a vampire story for an anthology and it was really more of a crime story. And most of my horror that I've written in the past couple of years has really been substantially crime fiction. So I think reading Steve inspired me to write more. I really started writing short stories when I was in college, and that was when I was reading Stephen King primarily. I was writing horror short stories, and I would share them with people in the dorm. Then many, many years later I ended up publishing a few of them. So reading him made me want to write, more so than anyone else I had ever read.

I would say in terms of influences I've been influenced by a number of different people. Ray Bradbury was a huge influence. But I see that my writing is going in a different direction than someone who was primarily inspired by King would probably go. Although he, too, has done, right from the very beginning, a few crime stories. I wrote an essay for a book *Cemetery Dance* just released called *Reading Stephen King*, and the crux of my essay is "Stephen King, crime writer." If you look back over his work, even some of his really early stuff like "The Ledge" (1976) or "Quitters, Inc." (1978), you see him dabbling with straight crime fiction without supernatural elements. So when I found out he was going to be writing *Mr. Mercedes* (2014) I was quite excited. Because he's always been a really good crime writer.

That's true, and that might explain why I love King as much as I do, considering that most of what I read and write is straight crime fiction. You know what I really love? Blaze. *People don't talk a lot about that one, but I think it's magnificent.*

There's something about King's writing that makes it memorable. By comparison, there are other horror writers I've binged on and read all of their stuff, but with them some of the titles blur together. If I can even remember what a certain titled book was about, I probably wouldn't remember the names of the characters. Whereas I remember almost every character in all of King's books. I can pick up any one of them and say, "Oh yeah, I remember this character and that character…" And I can remember the plots, and we're talking sixty or seventy books now! Most other writers come and go, and their work doesn't stick with me in that way. I think that, for me, is the magic of Stephen King's writing.

Everyone seems to have differing opinions on King's more recent work. What are your thoughts on King's newer works from the past fifteen years or so?

When I did the additional work for *The Stephen King Illustrated Companion*, I wrote a new chapter about things he'd written recently that were actually ideas he'd had many years before but didn't feel ready to tackle back in those days. *Under the Dome* (2009) was something he'd taken a couple of stabs at. *11/22/63* (2011) was an idea he had when he was teaching high school in the early 1970s. And if you re-read his books, that whole concept shows up in different places. I re-read *The Langoliers* (1990) recently, and there's mention of going back in time and saving Kennedy. In *Wolves of the Calla* (2003), basically the entire plot of *11/22/63* was laid out in shorthand. So that was something that had always been with him, he just finally got to the point where he felt he was able to handle everything writing that book would require. And with *Doctor Sleep*, he's going back and revisiting characters from earlier in his career. So in those terms he's not strayed too far from classic King. From characterization and stylistic point of view they're not all that different from what he's been writing all along.

The lack of supernatural elements to most of them may disturb some people who really want that. To me, one of the most dynamic books he's written recently has been *Revival*. The thing that I noticed about that book was that it's one of the few books where he chronicles almost the entire life of his main character. He picks him up when he was just a little boy playing in the mud all the way up to advanced adulthood. That's kind of different. King often chronicles parts of people's lives, but very rarely do we see the whole thing laid out that way. Then you get to the end of that book and all of a sudden you get a punch in the gut ending that's as devastating as anything else he's written, except perhaps *Pet Sematary* (1983). That book stands out to me as a major underappreciated accomplishment.

Then there's *Sleeping Beauties* (2017), which he wrote with his son Owen. That was a fun book. It's obviously very topical dealing with women's issues and bringing all of that to the forefront. They started this project before that really broke into common dialogue. I think it's a fun, interesting book. I don't really have a feel for what the response to it is yet, but I've read it twice and enjoyed it both times.

King seems to be more open to collaboration lately, which I think is interesting and good. Do you find this to be significant in his career?

I interviewed him and Richard Chizmar about *Gwendy's Button Box* (2017). At the end of that I asked him if he planned to collaborate with anybody else. He said, "I don't have any plans to, but I don't have any plans not to." The one collaboration I think we're all waiting for is he and Peter Straub's final book in *The Talisman* (1984) series. I know that he and Peter have talked about it. It's just a matter of them both finding the time to do it and pushing everything else aside to work on it.

King is collaborating with his sons. When your sons have matured as writers, I think it's fun to do something like that. That's to be expected. The collaboration with Rich was a bit of a surprise. He started this story and couldn't figure out what to do with it. So he told Rich, "If you don't do anything with this, it's just going into one of the desk drawers." I don't think collaborating on that was something he'd really contemplated doing. It just worked out that way. But will he do more like that? Maybe not. I think he always has more on his plate than he has time to write.

He's always been innovative, and that's one thing I've written about over the years. He's always at the forefront of new ways to get things out to readers. He did an e-book way back in the 1990s. He did "Umney's Last Case" (1993) way back before the Internet stuff when you had to actually download the software onto your computer. That was before he did the online stuff like *Riding the Bullet* (2000) or *Ur* (2009). He sort of reinvented serial novels with *The Green Mile* (1996). He did this funky thing called *F13* (2000), which was a screen saver that had *Everything's Eventual* (2002) included with it, and all these funky games for your desktop. As technology has come along, he's embraced it and said, "What can I do with this?" So I think there will probably be new things coming down the pike where he thinks, "Maybe I should stick my foot into the pool and see if I can do something with this."

You recently co-edited a short story anthology with King titled Flight or Fright. *How did that come about?*

I was in Bangor having dinner at a restaurant before we saw an advanced screening of the *Dark Tower* movie. A bunch of people from King's office were there, a few people from Sony, other friends and family of Steve's, and people like Robin Furth and Rich Chizmar from *Cemetery Dance*. The restaurant was directly across the road from the airport, and a lot of us had flown in for the screening, most with tales of woe and hardship from the journey. Steve came up with the idea of an anthology of scary stories involving flying, collecting together all the great published stories in this sub-sub-sub-genre. I was sitting beside Rich when Steve came over and pitched the idea. He told Rich that *Cemetery Dance* could publish it. Then he said he needed someone to help him find more stories than the ones he already had in mind. "That'll be your job," he told me. I loved the idea, so I went to work digging up stories that fit our theme, and it all fell into place from there. Working with Steve was a terrific experience. I enjoyed every minute of it, even dealing with the contracts and paperwork end of being an editor.

STANLEY WIATER

Stanley Wiater has been called "the world's leading authority on horror filmmakers and authors" (*Radio TV Interview Report*) and "the master journalist of the dark genres" (*World of Fandom*). In 1980, Wiater won a short story competition judged by Stephen King for his story "The Toucher," which was later published in *Castle Rock: The Stephen King Newsletter*.

Wiater's first book was the acclaimed collection *Dark Dreamers: Conversations with the Masters of Horror* (1990), in which he spoke with horror's greatest authors, including Clive Barker, Peter Straub, and of course Stephen King. For his work on the book, Wiater was awarded the prestigious Bram Stoker Award for Superior Achievement by the Horror Writers Association. The following year he published a companion, *Dark Visions: Conversations with the Masters of the Horror Film* (1992), which was again a Bram Stoker Award finalist. He later published more interview collections, including *Dark Thoughts: On Writing: Advice and Commentary from Fifty Masters of Fear and Suspense* (1997) and *Dark Dreamers: Facing the Masters of Fear* (2001), on which he collaborated with noted photographer Beth Gwinn. (Both won Bram Stoker Awards.)

His memorable conversations with Stephen King would also appear in Tim Underwood and Chuck Miller's anthologies *Bare Bones: Conversations on Terror with Stephen King* (1988) and *Feast of Fear: Conversations with Stephen King* (1989). He would eventually devote an entire volume of his own to King, collaborating with Christopher Golden and Hank Wagner to write *The Complete Stephen King Universe: A Guide to the Worlds of Stephen King* (2001). This was a resource examining all of King's novels, short stories, films, miniseries, and teleplays.

Wiater also wrote about and collaborated with King's literary idol Richard Matheson. He edited three volumes of Matheson's collected short stories, as well as the anthology *Richard Matheson's The Twilight Zone Scripts* (2001). He and Mathew Bradley later co-wrote *The Richard Matheson Companion* (2008).

Wiater's other works include *The Official Teenage Mutant Ninja Turtle Treasury* (1991), *The Brian Lumley Companion* (2002), and *Comic Book Rebels: Conversations with the Creators of the New Comics* (1997), which was nominated for both an Eisner and a Harvey Award.

You were a horror aficionado from an early age, reading authors like Edgar Allan Poe, Richard Matheson, and Ray Bradbury. When you first discovered Stephen King, what stood out about his writing for you, making him a new and different voice in horror?

Going back to what you said about growing up on Edgar Allan Poe, Richard Matheson, and Ray Bradbury, the thing that struck me most about King was that he was in that group. I could tell immediately that he was another keeper. "I'm going to read everything this guy writes," and I've tried to do that over the years.

Obviously King read all of those authors, as well, and I'm sure he has a lot of the same interests in terms of the genre as you and I. Do you feel a sense of kinship with King?

Absolutely. King is only a few years older than I am. When I got to know him, got to hang out with him and become friends, it wasn't like the relationship I had with Richard Matheson and Ray Bradbury. I literally thought of myself as a son, with Bradbury and Matheson being father figures. King was basically an older brother figure for me. I felt much more at ease and much more able to let my guard down with King, whereas I always thought of those guys as being "Mr. Bradbury" and "Mr. Matheson," even though we did become friends over the years.

Your first professional sale was the short story "The Toucher" in a contest that was judged by Stephen King. That must have been amazingly validating as an author. What was that experience like for you, and did you get to meet him at that time?

No, I actually had met him before. I met him at the World Fantasy Convention in Providence, Rhode Island, in the fall of 1979. The contest was in the summer of 1980, and it was sponsored by the *Boston Phoenix* newspaper. The idea was that a group of editors would go through the submissions, selecting the ten best stories, and then he would select the final one. I had never published a story before. I had tried a few times without success, and one of the reasons I became a nonfiction writer was because I wanted to make a living at it. But I had attempted to write stories since I was a kid. Well, it turned out there were over 450 submissions in the contest. They selected the ten best, and King chose "The Toucher."

So one day, out of the blue, I get a letter from King saying, "Hello, Mr. Wiater. I'm not going to say you won because I'm a cautious bastard, but I personally chose your story to be the winner of this competition." This was a physically typed letter from a typewriter. The return address on the envelope said "King, Bangor Maine," so even before I opened it I knew who it was from. He said, "You're welcome to write back to me. Let me know about your career." I did of course write back immediately and say, "We've actually met. I interviewed you, along with Peter Straub and George Romero, at the World Fantasy Convention a year ago." But it was just one of those things. There was no connection, and he had no memory of me from 1979, nor any knowledge of me being that reporter who interviewed him when he read my blind submission.

Stephen King insists, "It is the tale, not he who tells it." Yet people like us keep producing books about the man and his work, and readers keep reading them. Do you believe King's statement is accurate, and why do you think there is an entire sub-genre of books dedicated to his work?

There are several reasons why the books keep coming. One of course is the cult of personality. King is one of the most celebrated authors in the world. He's one of the most popular authors in the world. He is the single most popular horror writer in the world. The horror community is a very close-knit community, as we all know. I've never had a horror author turn me down for an interview. I think King is the exception to the rule. He has become so important and so popular, and he is so revered and has done so much, especially today in this age of social media. And let's not forget that at one time he had no less than three books on the *New York Times* bestseller list. Who else does that? So the question I would think is, why *wouldn't* there be all these books about him? I believe there are now more than fifty books that have been written about King. Because of that, there are now books on people like Richard Matheson, Dean Koontz, and Anne Rice. The fallout from King's success has done tremendous good for the genre as a whole.

When you were working on The Complete Stephen King Universe, *were there any new things you learned or came to realize or appreciate for the first time regarding King's work?*

It's kind of a funny question to answer because the idea of the whole book was to be maybe the first ones to connect the dots. Myself, Christopher Golden, and Hank Wagner were all Constant Readers of Stephen King, and we noticed the similarities, recurring characters, and recurring places. So it was a voyage of discovery. It took us three years to reread all the books up to that time, and then do the writing of the book. It was a labor of love. Although we made a fair amount of money from that project, when you split the advance and the royalties between three writers, and this is for three years' worth of work, you're talking pennies on the dollar. [Laughs.]

What we learned as we went along was that, whether consciously or not, King has laid out what we could call a multiverse, not just a universe. It was fun to do it, and I would like to go back to it one day. We did go back and revise it from *The Stephen King Universe* to *The Complete Stephen King Universe* a decade after it was first published. But our publisher said, "A third time back to the well? We don't think that's necessary. How much more can Stephen King write?" [Laughs again.] And of course, a dozen or so books later, we could easily get a third updated edition. It was already 500 pages long. We could easily add another 100 pages to it.

His output is crazy. He's 70 now, and he's still churning out novels, novellas, short stories, poems. There were four movies made from his work this year alone, and two new television series. It's incredible.

It really is crazy. Years ago when he was almost killed by that van when he was walking along the road in Maine, he told me in an interview that he was seriously considering giving up publishing. He was in so much pain and was still taking so many painkillers that he was just going to write for himself. That was such a startling statement, and it actually got picked up by ABC News. They quoted him from my interview, saying, "What a revelation this would be if there were no more Stephen King books coming out." And the question back then was, how much more can Stephen King write? Maybe this is the end of the Stephen King universe as we know it. But the fact that he's done it all and seen it all, is probably the most popular writer in the world, is the most successful writer in the world.... He's 70 and he's always going to have a certain amount of pain from that injury. It just staggers the imagination. It's not like the average writer who, when they turn 60 or 70, write the occasional short story. No, he's still churning out 800 page novels. Again, that's why there are more than 50 books written about him. Because you look out your window and you see Stephen King, there ain't nobody else standing so tall in that field as him, in any genre.

I remember back when the miniseries Rose Red *(2002) came out, King publicly recognized that it was derivative of his previous work and he was sort of questioning whether he had anything new to say. That's funny now, considering how many new and original things he's written since.*

I'm amazed by the critical acclaim he continues to have. There are so many bestselling writers who have had long careers—Jacqueline Susann and Irving Wallace—who had close to no critical acceptance largely because of their popularity and the genres they were writing in. And yet here Stephen King continues to win award after award. His books come out and the critics are still praising King to the heavens. The guy has written over fifty books! There's got to be a point where the critics say, "Oh my God, do we have to see another Stephen King book?" And he's still pumping them out at the rate of about one book a year. You can go to his website and there's always an ad for his next book, and we don't know if his next book is going to be twenty short stories, four novellas, or a thousand page novel. People still can't get enough of Stephen King.

I'm a little bit excited about this new phase of his career where he's collaborating more. He has always been able to deliver the goods without any assistance, but I think maybe him writing with other people will help keep him fresh and rejuvenated, while maybe keeping him from repeating himself.

I think it's always great to collaborate and open up new horizons. Harlan Ellison over the years collaborated on short stories and novellas with other writers to great success. I'm personally ready for a third collaboration between King and Peter Straub. I think in many ways on a sheer technical level that Peter Straub is a better writer than Stephen King. And I'm sure Stephen King would agree with me on this. He just has such gravitas that when you read a Peter Straub novel, you say, "This is not just a horror novel. This is literature." So when they do get together, it's always something wonderful. Both of them have promised the public that someday there's going to be a third collaboration between them. To me, that's two masters combining forces.

It's also great to see King collaborating with his sons. What are the chances of any writer of any stature having two sons who also have published to great critical and popular acclaim? I can't think of anyone else who's done that.

You refer to your Dark Dreamers *interviews as conversations, and that's an apt description. As you and I both know from experience, there are different types of subjects in terms of their attitudes towards being interviewed and the way they respond to your questions and observations. Having interviewed many, many horror greats, how does King personally rate for you as an interview subject?*

I have to say this with some hesitation. I started interviewing King in the fall of 1979, and I've interviewed him about a dozen times throughout his career. But there was a time when he was addicted to cocaine and alcohol. That never hurt his interviews any, but he was so free with his time. You could just sit down with him at a convention before he became too popular to even go to a horror convention. He became a major pop culture sensation. But back then you could just talk to him for hours and if you bought him a beer, you'd get another half hour. It was always informal conversation, and he was open to any subject. He would answer you on any topic. The thing that has kind of dried up the interviews is that he did so many interviews and basically never said no to a legitimate media outlet. He told me years later that he'd become "interviewed out." He just couldn't do anymore interviews, because he had done so damned many of them.

As you know, there are at least two complete books on Stephen King that are just collections of interviews, and they include my interviews with him early in his career. How many authors do you know who have given so many interviews, and this was twenty years ago, that they could fill entire books?

What do you see as being King's biggest contribution to the genre?

In terms of public consumption, his being a bestselling author, and also having had so many of his books translated into films and television, he gave horror a brand-name legitimacy. Before Stephen King, if you went up to someone at the bookstore or someone on the street and said, "Name your favorite horror writer," a lot of people would have said Edgar Allan Poe. Before Stephen King ushered in modern horror, there really was no modern horror. Richard Matheson was packaged as a science fiction writer for most of his career, as was Bradbury. But then Stephen King came out, and all of a sudden, horror went from all small letters to being in all caps with an exclamation point. Horror is now something that everybody is now aware of. If you ask somebody "what is horror?" now, they'll turn around and say, "That's Stephen King." Or they might say, "The next Stephen King novel, and it's going to scare the hell out of me!"

I think that was the largest contribution at the time—that Stephen King gave horror a legitimacy and brand-name recognition.

Inadvertently, have there been any negative effects to the horror genre as a result of King's unprecedented success?

Yes. Again, this is something we can blame the publishers for. You had people like Dean Koontz, Anne Rice, Clive Barker, and one or two others that were promoted by the publishers, and nobody else was. It was the idea that, would the publishers go out and promote and publish an additional 50,000 copies of a Jack Ketchum novel, or would they publish 50,000 additional copies of a Stephen King novel? The same thing with advertising. They could put more money into advertising Jack Ketchum, or they could put more money into advertising the next Peter Straub novel. Of course publishers wanted to make money, so they're going to put that money behind the most already commercially successful authors. So that did hurt a lot of authors who didn't have the power of the publisher behind them. A lot of people say, "I'm a big fan of horror." Then you say, "Okay, name me your five favorite horror writers." And then they'll answer, "Stephen King, Stephen King, Stephen King..." And they couldn't get beyond that.

One impact of King's success that I saw was that in the 1980s there were so many paperback originals coming out, a lot of which were terrible, but they were packaged as being like King. After The Shining *(1977) came out, there were suddenly a million books with titles ending in "ing."*

The Dripping, The Howling, The Scratching, The Melting. Anything they could stick an "ing" on. They also packaged novels to look like Stephen King novels. There was that whole boom in the 1980s, which was the golden age of paperback horror, where publishers would imitate Stephen King as much as possible in terms of book packaging. There was a book that came out last year called *Paperbacks from Hell* (2017) that I highly recommend. It's a nonfiction book about all the horror paperback originals, and in looking at that you see how better or worse—usually worse—good, bad, or indifferent novels all looked alike. The publishers didn't care anything about the books themselves so long as they could say "in the style of Stephen King."

What is your personal favorite of King's works, and what is it about it that resonates with you?

I've followed King in chronological order since 1975. When *The Dead Zone* (1979) came out, that one really hit me. As you know, it's a tragic love story. King was trying to scare you, but at the same time it was really about the idea of how fate affects our lives and how we really have no control over them. Even more frightening when you think about it today is the fact that there is the evil politician character; when Johnny Smith, the protagonist, shakes hands with him, he realizes that he's going to be elected President one day. He will have his finger on the nuclear button, and that he's totally insane. Considering our political situation now, that novel is as timely today as it was in 1979. This was one of the few novels in my life that have moved me to tears when I ended them, because you knew from page one that this wasn't going to end well for anybody.

You've worked on books dedicated to both King and his literary idol Richard Matheson. Do you see King as sort of an heir to the throne, and in comparing their work, what do you see as being the primary factors for King ultimately being more successful than Matheson?

Publisher promotion. He was packaged as the king of modern horror. It was a perfect storm. As I've said, Matheson considered himself basically a horror writer. In fact, he didn't even like that term; he considered himself a "terror" writer. He always said he felt that horror was something that's revolting, whereas terror is something that is scary but not necessarily in a physical sense. But King has his own legacy, as does Matheson. It's generational. King has stated, as everyone knows, "the writer that had the biggest influence on me was Richard Matheson." He's also stated that "without Ray Bradbury there would have been no Stephen King." Both of these men are giants in the field. It's not that one is inheriting from the other, but in terms of popularity King is so gigantic that there's really no comparison. Every Stephen King book, to my knowledge, is still in print. Here's a man who's produced over fifty books, beginning back in 1974, and they're all still in print in some form. I may be wrong, but I don't think that even Ray Bradbury or Richard Matheson can make that claim.

Are there any aspects to strengths of King's that stand out to you that you feel aren't discussed as frequently as others?

His conversational tone. If you're ever blessed to do an interview with Stephen King, he speaks in conversation to you exactly the same way he does in his books. When you listen to his books on tape, you really get the sensation that it's Stephen King talking directly to you. That's a strong aspect of his writing. He doesn't try to set up any artifice between the reader and the narrator. He really just tries to be a storyteller having a one-on-one conversation. King himself recognized that early on when he popularized the term "Constant Reader." As long as he keeps telling good stories, he knows he's going to have loyal readers.

This is probably a controversial question, but is Stephen King as good at what he does today as he was thirty or forty years ago?

He is, but I will say this with a caveat; he's always had a "problem" in that once he became a massive-selling behemoth, there was no longer an editor who could come in and say, "Stephen, that's a great thousand page novel, but it really could be a TWENTY page short story. You're telling a great story, but you came up with an idea where the people in a small town in Maine woke up one day to find out their town had been cut in half by an invisible dome. Do you really need a thousand pages to tell that story, or could you do it in twenty?" He's admitted this himself. He calls it "elephantitis." He's always, because of his love of words, found it difficult to rein it in. So it's been difficult for me, even as a Constant Reader, to look at his books over the years and say, "I want to read this book, but do I literally have the time to read a thousand page novel?" Look at the novel *Cell* (2006). It's a very short, effective novel. He's capable of that when he wants to do it. But there's no one to tell him, "Steve, you're a brilliant writer, but I really don't think you need a thousand pages to tell this story." At the end of the day, he's the god of his domain.

Perspectives on Stephen King

Over the years there has been a lot of talk about the number of King film adaptations that don't work. Do you feel there is something specific about his work that might not work in translation, or do you feel King has had about the same ratio of cinematic hits and misses as everyone else?

The way I look at it is, name me any other writer besides King who has had more adaptations of their novels and short stories. To the best of my knowledge, King is the most adapted writer of all time. So there's got to be a ratio to good, bad, indifferent. I think King's doing as well as anyone. Some of his work, such as *Stand By Me* (1986) and *The Shawshank Redemption* (1994) are all time classics. Somehow *It* (2017) just became the most successful horror film in history. So I think he's had a pretty good batting average, but it is odd that at the same time he'll have something like *It* come out and be a raging success, *The Dark Tower* (2017) will come out and be a raging failure.

So it still happens to him, and I think it's always going to happen with his books. But it's like the old story where someone tells the author that Hollywood has ruined his book, and the author then takes a copy of the book down off the shelf and says, "They didn't ruin it. It's right here, complete on the pages between the two covers." King's attitude has always been that the book is the book, and the movie is the movie.

The problem that I've always seen with some of those movies like, say, Graveyard Shift *(1990), is that some of his lesser ideas that aren't as strong as others still work as books or stories because of King's writing ability. I think there are also some things in some of his works that are difficult to translate visually. King has the ability to describe things and make them work on the page. But when it comes to conveying that visually, I think some of it gets lost in translation.*

I remember Roger Ebert joking that next King would make a movie about a refrigerator that comes to life and kills people. That sounds ridiculous, but that's kind of what The Mangler *(1995) was. That works as a short story, but maybe it shouldn't be a movie.*

I was reading a review last week of the Netflix film *1922* (2017), which was adapted from King's novella. The reviewer said it was a good effort, but he said out of all the Stephen King novels and novellas that are still available, why did they choose this one? It's basically a three character story out on a farm, and the reviewer found it boring. Not scary, but boring.

And even King himself, as good as he is as a novelist and short story writer, he's not the best screenwriter in the world. If you look at the original screenplays he's written, none of the films that have come from those have been what you would call classics.

So it is a tough nut to crack when you're adapting a book into a screenplay and then a film. It's an equally tough nut to crack to write an original screenplay, like *Sleepwalkers* (1992), and have that be a successful film.

INDEX

The A-Team 102
The ABC News 184
The Academy Awards 9
Accent Literary Review 166
Agent Cody Banks 10
The Alamo Drafthouse 81
Aleas, Richard 22
Alexander, Scott 9–21
Alfred Hitchcock's Mystery Magazine 22, 167
All the President's Men 87
Allen, Woody 145
American Broadcasting Company (ABC) 29
The Andromeda Strain 126
Anthony, Piers 167
Apt Pupil (film) 84, 86–87, 127
Apt Pupil (novella) 116
Arbogast, Roy 71
Arcel, Nikolaj 63
Ardai, Charles 22–32
Asimov, Isaac 167
Asylum 170
At the Foot of the Story Tree 172, 176
Atlantic 148

Bachman, Richard (pseudonym for King) 10, 23, 97, 141
The Bachman Books 134
Bag of Bones 156, 161, 162
Baker, Ginger 109
Band, Charles 82
The Barbarous Coast 83
Bare Bones 181
Barker, Clive 37, 181, 187
Barnes & Noble 14, 176, 177
Barry, Dave 109
The Base: Guilty as Charged 82
Bates, Kathy 127, 138
Batman: The Animated Series 90
"Battleground" 102, 105
Beahm, George 133, 134, 135, 141, 143, 155

Beal, Jeff 107
The Beatles 136, 145, 149, 152
Beaumont, Charles 97, 125
Becker&Mayer! 176
"Before the Play" 154
Bergman, Ingmar 12, 15
"Best New Horror" 122
Big Driver (film) 102, 103, 107–108, 110
Big Driver (novella) 102
Big Eyes 9
Biography 145
Bird, Larry 159
Bissette, Steve 33, 38
B.J. and the Bear 102
Black House 46, 60, 121
Blaze 23–24, 97, 141, 178
Bloch, Robert 83
Block, Lawrence 22, 25
Blockade Billy 51
Blockbuster 19
Blood in Your Ears 133
Bloom, Harold 144
Blue, Tyson 33–45, 141, 144
Bly, Robert 144
Boam, Jeffrey 87
Bonaventura, Lorenzo 12, 13, 16
"The Boogeyman" 161
Booklist 158, 166
Borderlands 167
Borgo Press 38
The Boston Phoenix 183
"The Boxer" 40
Boyce, Brandon 86
Boyle, Peter 20
Bradbury, Ray 97, 98, 99, 177, 182, 187, 189
Bradley, Mathew 182
Brak the Barbarian 85
Bram Stoker Awards 145, 158, 166, 181
The Brian Lumley Companion 182
"Bridge Over Troubled Water" 39
"Brooklyn August" 37

193

Index

Bubba Ho-Tep 90
Buckner, Bill 125
Burroughs, Edgar Rice 83

Cabin at the End of the World 159
Cain, James M. 27, 100
Candles Burning 123
Carpenter, John 65, 71
Carrie (film) 35, 43, 66, 69, 84, 87, 127, 139
Carrie (novel) 1, 10, 49, 57, 66, 67, 83, 92, 99, 104, 132, 146, 173, 177
Carrie (play) 104
Castle Rock (newsletter) 33, 35, 37, 40, 143, 151, 154, 181
Castle Rock (television series) 1
Cell 60, 120, 141, 189
Cemetery Dance (magazine) 33, 46, 47–48, 135, 166, 170, 172, 177
Cemetery Dance (publisher) 133, 173, 180
Chabon, Michael 114
Chadbourne Glenn 166
Chappelle, Dave 10
Charnel House 133, 134
Chart of Darkness 133
"The Chattery Teeth" 49
The Children of the Corn (film) 18, 73, 137
ChiZine Publications 158
Chizmar, Billy 46
Chizmar, Richard 46–55, 121, 172, 173, 180
Christie, Agatha 167
Christine (film) 65, 71–72, 84, 138
Christine (novel) 10, 67, 132
The Chronicles of Amber 107
Cinema Retro 82
Cinemax 123
The Cinematheque 18
Citadel Press 153
City Pier: Above and Below 158
Clancy, Tom 45
Clark, Kathie 70
Clark, Robert 70
Clarkson, Patricia 43
Class of 1999 82
Clavell, James 85
CNN 105, 110
Cocoa Puffs 16
Cohen, Lawrence 87
Cold in July 96
Collings, Michael 134, 137, 143, 144
The Colorado Kid 22, 24, 26–28, 29, 32, 119, 142
Comic Book Rebels 182
The Complete Stephen King Universe 181, 184
Compositions for the Young and Old 158
Conan the Barbarian 83
The Conroe Courier 166

Cooper, Al 109
Cornell University 124
Coscarelli, Don 90, 96
Coulter, Jean 70
The Courier-Herald 33
Created By 103, 109
Creepshow (film) 84, 85, 148
Creepshow (graphic novel) 134, 148
Creepy 83
Crichton, Michael 30–32
Cronenberg, David 87, 127
The Cubs 130
Cujo (film) 65, 67, 68–69, 73, 139
Cujo (novel) 66, 168
Curry, Tim 78
Cusack, John 13, 15, 16, 17, 18, 19, 20, 21
Cycle of the Werewolf 133, 134

The Daily Orange 33
Dalhousie University 166
Dangerous Visions 153
Danse Macabre 89, 125, 154, 155
Dante, Joe 66
Darabont, Frank 33, 39, 40, 42, 44, 76, 79, 127, 139
Dark Dreamers: Conversations with the Masters of Horror 181, 186
Dark Dreamers: Facing the Masters of Fear 181, 186
The Dark Half (film) 85
The Dark Half (novel) 38, 108
Dark Thoughts 181
The Dark Tower (book series) 49, 56, 58, 61, 114, 117, 118, 119, 129, 163, 167, 172, 173, 174, 175
The Dark Tower (film) 56, 63, 170, 180, 190
The Dark Tower (graphic novel) 62
The Dark Tower: A Complete Concordance 56, 61
The Dark Tower Companion 167, 170, 174–175
Dark Visions 181
Dawn of the Dead 82
The Dead Zone (film) 42, 84, 85, 87, 100, 127, 139
The Dead Zone (novel) 66, 71, 97, 199, 125, 126, 132, 149, 168, 188
The Dead Zone (series) 30
"The Death of Jack Hamilton" 60
DeFilippo, Marsha 58
DeLaurentiis, Dino 85, 88
DePalma, Brian 87, 127
Desperation 142
DeVito, Danny 10
Diabolique 65
Dialogues 145
Dickens, Charles 148, 152, 156

Index

Different Seasons 116, 126, 132, 165, 168, 169
Dikty, Ted 37
Dillinger, John 60
Doc Savage 83
Doctor Mordrid 82
Doctor Sleep 178
Dolores Claiborne (film) 138
Dolores Claiborne (novel) 42, 142, 171
Dorchester Publishing 25
Downey, Robert, Jr. 164
Dracula 125
"The Dreaded X" 154
Dreamcatcher (film) 139
Dreamcatcher (novel) 74
Drug of Choice 31
Duck Soup 13
Duel 106
Duma Key 140
Dunaway, Don Carlos 69
Dystopia: Collected Stories 103

Ebert, Roger 190
E.C. Comics 71, 126
Ed Wood (film) 9
Edgar Allan Poe Award 22
Edgar Awards 166
Elba, Idris 63
11/22/63 140, 156, 178
Ellery Queen's Mystery Magazine 22, 46, 167, 169
Ellison, Harlan 22, 33, 37, 38, 153, 185
"The End of the Whole Mess" 161
End of Watch 119
Entertainment Weekly 1, 145
The Essential Stephen King 145, 153, 156
"An Evening with God" 152
Everyday People 124
Everything's Eventual 180
Eye of the Needle 88
Eyes of the Dragon 37

F-13 180
Fables 158
The Face in the Crowd 124, 131
Faithful 124, 129–130, 131
Fall River Press 166
Famous Monsters of Filmland 82
Fangoria 65, 82
Fantastic Fest 81
Faulkner, William 96, 148
Fear Itself 46
FEARnet 133
Feast of Fear 181
Fenway Park 131
Fever Pitch 129
Fifty-to-One 23
Finders Keepers 119, 140

Firestarter (film) 82, 88, 139
Firestarter (novel) 67, 135, 140
Fish, Albert 60
Fitzgerald, F. Scott 35, 124
Flanagan, Mike 81
Flight or Fright 1, 167, 180
Flynt, Larry 10
Footsteps 33
Four Past Midnight 150, 151
Four Three Film 65
1408 (film) 10–21, 84, 85
Fox News 118
Frazetta, Frank 83
Freeman, Brian 133, 137, 166
Fried, Charlie 152
The Friends of Eddie Coyle 87
Frogs 68
From a Buick 8 46, 141
From a Whisper to a Scream 82
Full Dark, No Stars 74, 75
Full Moon Fright Night 82
Furth, Robin 56–64, 117, 180

Gambin, Lee 65–73
Game of Thrones 175
"The Garbage Truck" 154
Garciaparra, Nomar 130
Gardner, Earl Stanley 25
Garris, Mick 44, 72, 109
Gates, Bill 120
Gateway Community College 145
Gauntlet Press 34
Gerald's Game (film) 80, 81
Gerald's Game (novel) 142, 170–171
Ghosts 33
The Ghouls 83
Golden, Christopher 181, 184
Goldman, William 85, 87, 133
Goldsman, Akiva 170, 174
Gone with the Wind 145
The Good Earth 83
The Good, the Bad & the Ugly 166
Goosebumps 10
Gordon, Keith 71
Grave Descend 31
Graveyard Shift 137, 139, 190
Grease 70
Green, Arthur 25
Green, David Gordon 124, 127
The Green Mile (movie) 40, 42
The Green Mile (novel) 39, 84, 180
Greenberg, Matt 12
Grisham, John 168
The Gunslinger 64, 114, 132, 149, 172
The Gunslinger Born 62
Gwendy's Button Box 1, 46, 50–54, 120, 121

195

Index

Gwinn, Beth 181
Gwynne, Fred 71

Hafstrom, Mikael 10, 12, 15, 18, 20
Hammer Studios 132
Hanks, Tom 41
Hap and Leonard 90, 96
Hard Case Crime 22–32, 84, 142
Hardcastle and McCormick 102
Harlan, Renny 82
The Harlequin and the Train 158
Harper 87
Harper's Bazaar 148
Harvard Medical School 30
Hatlen, Burt 56, 58
Haven 22, 29–30
HBO 130
Head Full of Ghosts 158, 162
Hearts in Atlantis 48–49
Hearts in Suspension 154
Heinlein, Robert 167
Hellnotes 166
Hemingway, Ernest 93
Henson, Brian 107
Higgins, George V. 87
Hilditch, Zak 74–81
Hill, Joe 23, 101, 114, 120, 121, 122, 167
Hinchberger, Steve 38, 151
Hitchcock, Alfred 83
Hogan, Hulk 1
Hooper, Tobe 84, 87, 127
Hope and Miracles 34
Hopkins, Lightning 98
Hornby, Nick 129
The Horror Writers Association 82, 181
Hour of the Wolf 12
Howard, Robert E. 83
Howard, Ron 170, 174
The Howling 66
Huckleberry Finn 95
Hunt, Bonnie 41
Hunt Through the Cradle of Fear 23
Hurt, William 106, 107

I Am Legend 102
The Illustrated Stephen King Movie Trivia Book 133, 137, 166
I'm on Fire 133
In the Mean Time 158
In the Walled City 124
The Incredible Hulk 102
Ink in the Veins 133, 143–144
Inside the Dark Tower 116
Insomnia 49, 117, 163
The International House of Pancakes 119
The International Thriller Writers 82
The Internet Movie Database (Imdb) 19

Irving, John 135
It (film) 80, 190
It (miniseries) 42, 72
It (novel) 23, 39, 47, 75, 78, 134, 136, 144, 148, 149, 159, 172
"It Grows On You" 151
It Takes Two 102

Jackson, Michael 1
Jackson, Samuel 16
Jackson, Shirley 64, 125
Jakes, John 85
Jane, Thomas 74, 77–78, 79
Jaws 65
Johnson, Dave 40
Johnson, Diane 87
Johnson, Robert 98
Joyland 22, 24, 26, 28, 32, 140
Joyner, C. Courtney 82–89
Juno 22, 24
Jurassic Park 30–31

Karaszewski, Larry 9–21
Keene, Day 25
Kennedy, John F. 90
Ketchum, Jack 187
King, Owen 101, 114, 120, 121, 122, 123, 147
King, Tabitha 61, 114, 121, 127, 169
Knight Rider 102
Kobritz, Richard 71
Koontz, Dean 44, 102, 104, 110, 150, 184, 187
Kubrick, Stanley 35, 43, 87, 100–101, 127

Lambert, Mary 72
L'amour, Louis 1
Landau, Martin 9
Lange, John (pseudonym for Michael Crichton) 30–32
The Langoliers 178
Lansdale, Joe R. 46, 90–101
"The Ledge" 178
Lehane, Dennis 133
Lennon, John 1, 152
Leonard, Elmore 83, 85
Leonard, Stephanie 35
Lester, Mark L. 82, 88
Lethem, Jonathan 125
Levin, Ira 125
Lewis, C.S. 56
Lilja, Hans 135, 137
Lippert Pictures 85
Lisey's Story 119, 176
Little Girl Lost 22
Little Sisters of Eluria 175
The Little Sleep 158
Locke and Key 122

Index

A Long December 46, 52, 53
Loose Cannons 102
The Los Angeles Review of Books 119
The Lost Work of Stephen King 141, 145, 152, 153
Lovecraft, H.P. 64, 82, 83, 156
Lurking Fear 82

MacConaughey, Matthew 63
Macdonald, Norm 10
The Macon Telegraph 33, 35
Mad Max 106
Madonna 1
Magistrale, Tony 119, 144
Man on the Moon 9
Manches, Greg 31
The Mangler 190
Mann, Stanley 88
The Mark 88
Mars Attacks! 9
Martin, George R.R. 155
Marvel Comics 62, 174
Massacred by Mother Nature 65, 67–68
Masters of Horror 46, 102
Matheson, Richard 46, 51, 97, 102, 109, 121, 167, 182, 184, 187, 188–189
Matheson, Richard Christian 102–110
Maximum Overdrive 33, 35, 36, 88, 100
Mayberry, My Home Town 145, 146, 151
McBain, Ed 25
McCammon, Robert 99
McCartney, Paul 152
McCormack, Mary 16
McDonald, John D. 95
McDonald, Ross 83
McDowell, Michael 123
McFarland & Company 117
Medak, Peter 69
Mediascene 33
Melville, Herman 148
Meteor 88
Metro Silicon Valley 46
Midnight Grafitti 33, 153
Midnight Marquee 56
Midnight Promises 46
Mike Shayne Mystery Magazine 92
Miller, Carl Lewis 70
Miller, Chuck 181
Miller, Henry 93
The Millerrese Ann 70
Mindkites 158
Miracles Ain't What They Used to Be 90
Misery (film) 42, 67, 79, 84, 85, 87, 127, 139
Misery (novel) 103, 108, 132, 136
The Mist (film) 74, 79, 86, 114, 138
The Mist (novella) 161

Mr. Mercedes 147, 175, 178
Monash, Paul 87
"The Monkey" 47
"The Monkey's Paw" 51, 127
Monsters and Other Stories 46
Morgan, Donald 71
Morgan, Gary 70
"Mostly Old Men" 121
Mould, Bob 158
Murphy's Law 82
"My Little Serrated Security Blanket" 152, 153

The Names of the Dead 124
The Nebraska Review 124
Needful Things (film) 43
Needful Things (novel) 171
Nemo Rising 83
Netflix 81, 190
New American Library 173
New Page Books 153
The New York Times 145, 152, 153, 176, 183
The New Yorker 129, 148
"News from the Dead Zone" 166, 170
The Nice Guys 23
Nicholson, Jack 43, 44, 101, 127
The Night Country 131
Night of the Living Dead 126
Night Shift 92, 125, 161
A Nightmare on Elm Street 16, 139
Nightmares & Dreamscapes (miniseries) 102, 105–107
Nightmares & Dreamscapes (short story collection) 37, 161
Nightshift 134
Nightwing 68
1922 (film) 74, 75–81, 190
1922 (novella) 74, 75, 190
No Sleep Till Wonderland 158
Nope, Nothing Wrong Here 65, 69–70

O. Henry Award 113
Oates, Joyce Carol 160
Obama, Barack 39
Observations from the Terminator 33, 37, 38
O'Connor, Flannery 96, 98
The Official Teenage Mutant Ninja Turtles Treasury 182
O'Hara, John 99
On Writing 13, 39, 58, 84, 155
O'Nan, Stewart 121, 124–132
"One of Those Weeks" 167
One on One 123
Orca 68
The Overlook Connection 151, 153
Oxford University 156

197

Index

Paperbacks from Hell 188
Parker, Molly 76–78
Parker, Robert 133
Patterson, James 148
Patton, Mike 80
Paul, Alexandra 71
Paxton, Bill 98
The Peacemaker Award 82
Pearl, Barry 70
Pearson, Ridley 109
"People, Places, and Things" 152
The People vs. Larry Flynt 9
The People v. O.J. Simpson: An American Crime Story 9
Pet Sematary (film) 67, 72, 93, 134, 164
Pet Sematary (novel) 126, 127, 132, 134, 141, 152, 179
Pete's Dragon 70
Peyton Place 99, 125
Phantasm 90
Phantasmagoria 133
Phantom of the Paradise 65
Phillips, Max 22, 24, 28
Philtrum Press 37
Picasso, Pablo 152
Pintauro, Danny 65, 70
The Pirates 125
The Pirate's Alley Faulkner Award 124
The Plant 35, 37, 154
"The Plant: The Unseen King" 37
Poe, Edgar Allan 64, 83, 126, 148, 176, 182, 187
Polanski, Roman 12
The Postman Always Rings Twice 27
A Prayer for the Dying 131
Presley, Elvis 90
"Prey" 106
Price, Vincent 82
Prison 82
Problem Child 9, 11
Providence College 158
Public Enemies 82
Purefoy, James 90

Quigley, Kevin 133–144
Quincy, M.E. 102
"Quitters, Inc." 178

Radio TV Interview Report 181
Rage 134
Rat Patrol 83
Reading Stephen King 133, 177
Reagan, Ronald 69
The Red Sox 125, 129
Regents Theater 164
Reiner, Rob 127, 139
Repulsion 12

Revival 156, 179
Rice, Anne 184, 187
The Richard Matheson Companion 182
Richard Matheson's The Twilight Zone Scripts 182
Riding the Bullet 180
The Right Stuff 87
Riley, R.D. 1
Rise of the Dead 33, 39
Rita Hayworth and the Shawshank Redemption 116, 119
Road House 2 46
The Road to the Dark Tower 166, 172, 176
The Rock Bottom Remainders 108–109, 134
Rockwell, Sam 127
The Rocky Horror Picture Show 65
Romero, George 43, 183
Rose Madder 171
Rose Red 185
Rotten Tomatoes 80
Rowling, J.K. 133

The Saga of Billy the Kid 82
'Salem's Lot (miniseries) 71, 84, 87, 127, 164
'Salem's Lot (novel) 34, 47, 55, 57, 95, 99, 119, 125, 126, 132, 141, 141, 146, 151, 161, 167, 172
Salomon, Mikael 102
Saturday Night Fever 65
Saw 113
Scars and Other Distinguishing Marks 103
Schaech, Jonathan 46
Schow, David J. 96, 167
Scream 65
Screwed 9
Scribner 32, 56, 59
The Second Stephen King Quiz Book 145
A Separate Peace 83
Serling, Rod 1
Shakespeare, William 114, 160
The Shamus Award 22
The Shape Under the Sheet 38, 145, 146, 150
Shatner, William 82
The Shawshank Redemption 42, 69, 80, 84, 138, 165, 190
Sheehan, Bill 172, 176
Sheen, Martin 42
The Shining (film) 10, 33, 35, 43, 69, 79, 87, 100, 127, 164
The Shining (novel) 95, 119, 126, 134, 140, 141, 146, 148, 154, 187
Shogun 85, 88
Shotgun 83
Silver Bullet 72
Simon, Paul 39

Index

Simon & Garfunkel 40
Simon & Schuster 53
Simpson, O.J. 10
Singer, Bryan 127
Skarsgaard, Bill 78
Skeleton Crew 92, 161
Sleeping Beauties 1, 120, 179
Sleepwalkers 72, 139, 191
Small World 169
Snelgrove, Victoria 129
Snow Angels 124, 127
Sole Survivor 102, 104, 107
Song of Susannah 61
Songs of Innocence 22
The South Dakota Review 124
Spacek, Sissy 66, 127
Spare Parts 133
The Speed Queen 132
Spignesi, Stephen 1, 33, 38, 133, 141, 143, 145–157, 166
Springsteen, Bruce 136
Sputnik 155
"Squad D" 152, 153
Stallone, Sylvester 1
The Stand (film) 80
The Stand (novel) 10, 33, 55, 78, 85, 119, 120, 126, 132, 148, 159, 160, 161, 162, 168, 172
Stand by Me 42, 84, 127, 138, 165, 190
Star Wars 119
Starmont House 33, 37, 38
Stealing Candy 82
The Stephen John Press 146
Stephen King, American Master 133, 145
The Stephen King Companion 134
The Stephen King Illustrated Companion 166, 176–177, 178
The Stephen King Movie Quiz Book 1
The Stephen King Quiz Book 145, 166
"Stephen King Revisited" 172
Stephen King: The Art of Darkness 37, 143
Stephen King's Battleground 102
Stephen King's The Bill Hodges Trilogy Concordance 56, 64
Storm of the Century 40
Straub, Peter 34, 60, 121, 141, 159, 172, 181, 183, 185, 187
Streiber, Whitley 167
The Sum of All Fears 45
The Sun Dog 103, 104, 110
Susann, Jacqueline 185
Swallowing a Donkey's Eye 158
SyFy Channel 22, 29
Syracuse University 33

A Tale of Two Cities 152
The Talisman 121, 143, 179

Taylor, Tom 63
Teague, Lewis 65, 69, 70
The Tenant 12
Theater of Blood 88
There Will Be Blood 79
These Final Hours 74, 75, 76
Thompson, Hunter S. 94
Three O' Clock High 102
Three Penny Review 124
Three's Company 102
Thriller 92
Throttle 121
Tin House 121
Titanic, RMS 149
TNT 107
Tolkien, J.R.R. 147
Tomb of Terror 82
The Tommyknockers (novel) 1, 84, 116, 120, 136, 171
"The Toucher" 181, 182–183
Trancers III 82
The Trap 123
Tremblay, Paul 158–165
Trinity College 124
Truck Stop Women 88
Turner, Barbara 69
TV Guide 154
Twain, Mark 91, 148
20th Century Ghosts 122
Twentieth-Century King 167
20,000 Leagues Under the Sea 83
Twilight Showcase 158
The Twilight Zone (magazine) 33, 36
The Twilight Zone (series) 1, 54, 106, 125
2 AM 33
2001: A Space Odyssey 44

"Umney's Last Case" 180
Under the Dome 120, 125, 178
Underwood, Tim 181
University of Maine 56, 58, 141, 176
University of New Haven 145
University of Southern California School of Cinematic Arts 9
University of Vermont 158, 159
The Unseen King 33, 36, 38, 40
Ur 142, 180

Valdez Is Coming 83
Vampirella 83
Verill, Chuck 25, 32, 49
Verne, Jules 1
Vietnam, Texas 82
Vincent, Bev 117, 166–180
Voices from the Night 34
Vonnegut, Kurt 91, 94

Index

Wagner, Hank 181, 184
Walken, Christopher 42, 127
Walking the Mile: The Making of the Green Mile 34, 40, 41
The Wall Street Journal 31
Wallace, Dee 70
Wallace, Irving 185
Warner Bros. 40
Warner Bros. Fantastic 83
We Can Be Who We Are 65
Weinstein, Bob 12, 13, 14, 16, 19, 20
Weinstein, Harvey 12, 19
The Weinstein Company 18
West of Sunset 124
The Western Writers of America 82
The Westerners 83
Westlake, Donald 22, 25
Westworld 31
Wetware 133, 142–143
"What Stephen King Does for Love" 152
"Why I Wrote *Eyes of the Dragon*" 154

Wiater, Stanley 181
Widow's Point 46
Wild Strawberries 12
Williams, Michael K. 90
The Wind Through the Keyhole 174
Winter, Douglas 37, 143
Winters, Shelley 70
The Wit and Wisdom of Stephen King 1
Wizards and Glass 62
Wolves of the Calla 61, 178
The Woman in the Room 40
Wood, Edward D., Jr. 9
Wood, Rocky 144
World Fantasy Convention 182, 183
World of Fandom 181
The Writers Guild 9, 10
The Writing Family of Stephen King 121

The X-Men 119

Zero Cool 31

www.ingramcontent.com/pod-product-compliance
Ingram Content Group UK Ltd.
Pitfield, Milton Keynes, MK11 3LW, UK
UKHW042006140426
5217IPUK00015B/1004